T0162261

ARE YOU TRYING TO SEDUCE ME,

MISS TURNER?

ARE YOU TRYING TO SEDUCE ME,
MISS TURNER?

RICHARD OUZOUNIAN
TALKING TO THE STARS

McArthur & Company
Toronto

First Canadian edition published by McArthur & Company 2003

McArthur & Company
322 King St. West, Suite 402
Toronto, Ontario
M5V 1J2

National Library of Canada Cataloguing in Publication Data

> Ouzounian, Richard, 1950-
> Are you trying to seduce me, Miss Turner? : talking to the stars
> / Richard Ouzounian.

> ISBN 1-55278-360-X

> 1. Celebrities—Interviews. 2. Entertainers—Interviews. I. Title.

> PN1583.O99 2003   791'.092'2   C2003-900138-5

Design/Composition & Cover: *Mad Dog Design*
Cover Image: *Len Prince*
Printed in Canada by *Transcontinental Printing Inc*.

An honest attempt has been made to secure permission for all photographs, and if there are errors or omissions, these are wholly unintentional and the publisher will be grateful to learn of them.

The publisher would like to acknowledge the financial support of the Government of Canada through the Book Publishing Industry Development Program, the Canada Council, and the Ontario Arts Council for our publishing activities. We also acknowledge the Government of Ontario through the Ontario Media Development Corporation's Ontario Book Initiative.

10 9 8 7 6 5 4 3 2 1

To my parents, who first took me to see the stars.

CONTENTS

INTRODUCTION

Getting To Know You

I t all began with Nanette Fabray. As I write this, the 82-year-old comedienne is still making appearances on stage and TV, but her biggest successes occurred many years ago. In the 1940s, she dazzled Broadway with Tony Award-winning performances in musicals like *Love Life*, *High Button Shoes*, and *Make a Wish*.

Fans of *The Band Wagon* recall her singing "That's Entertainment" with Fred Astaire and Oscar Levant, while vintage comedy buffs will recall her work with Sid Caesar, for which she took home three Emmys in the 1950s.

Fast forward to 1962.

Fabray was attempting a Broadway comeback in the most highly awaited show of the season: *Mr. President*. With a score by Irving Berlin and direction by Joshua Logan, it looked like a sure thing and had an unheard-of (for that time) US$2 million advance sale. Unfortunately, the show was a disappointment — even to a 12-year-old musical theatre fan in his first year of high school.

(That would be me.)

But though I found the proceedings drab and old-fashioned, Fabray still shimmered, and as I sat there watching her making the audience smile, a thought slipped into my head: "I'd like to know her better."

The high school I went to — named Regis — had a student newspaper which that was called *The Owl*, in honour of the school mascot.

1

Most of the time, it printed the usual articles about how our basketball team had done (badly), or what the next dance was going to pick as its theme ("Camelot"). I asked if I could submit an interview with Nanette Fabray, and Mr. Stanley, our faculty advisor, laughingly said, "Go ahead," confident it would never happen.

What I'm going to reproduce below is the piece they eventually printed, in its entirety. I don't do it out of any vainglory over the achievements of my youth, but more as an amusing curiosity.

And if you feel that my writing style hasn't changed in the intervening four decades . . . well, maybe you're right!

No, No, Nanette

I decided to make *Owl* history on January 5, 1963, by interviewing someone *not* connected with Regis H.S. or its environs. This startling innovation was prompted by my witnessing Irving Berlin's new musical, *Mr. President*. Its star, Nanette Fabray, truly one of today's most vivacious theatre ladies, seemed to be the perfect choice for an interview.

Last Saturday, I bravely entered the St. James Theatre, 45 minutes before curtain time, notebook in hand. The stage manager, after viewing my credentials, gave me the A-OK sign to enter Miss Fabray's dressing room.

I was almost alarmed at the cordiality with which this award-winning actress greeted me and began the conversation.

"You know, I've been turning all other reporters down," she told me, "but you're lucky we both got here early today."

Considering the title of her latest venture, I asked her opinion of the "First Family" album and other political satires.

"I think they're sensational!" was her emphatic reply. "I have it (First Family) and my four- year-old son knows it by heart."

The question if she thought these records were insulting to the President and his family brought a vehement denial.

"Maybe you're too young to remember this, but Will Rogers always poked fun at government officials, and people thought it was funny to criticize each other's accents, nationalities, and even physical defects. People seldom do that any more, and when they do, we think it's terrible. But when we can't laugh at ourselves, then we're in serious trouble!"

She had other opinions on:

Irving Berlin: "One of the few musical geniuses left."

Robert Ryan (her leading man): "Very, very nice — a pleasure to work with."

Theatrical Work: "It separates the men from the boys. Many people from Hollywood come out here and can't 'cut the mustard.' We started work in July, worked seven days a week, fourteen hours a day, and only had one holiday. We're always terribly rushed."

I thanked Miss Fabray for the interview, and realized that not only does she portray the First Lady on stage, but in my opinion, she is the current "First Lady of the Musical Stage."

I sent her a copy of the interview, thinking that would be the end of it, but a week later, a letter arrived at the school, thanking me for what I had written — signed Nanette Fabray.

If this were a Hollywood saga, I would tell you how my first effort immediately launched me into a world of tell-all celebrity pieces, but that's never how it works out.

Over the next 35 years, my life took many turns — into theatre, television, radio — but I kept doing the occasional interview with people who intrigued me. Cleo Laine, Jerry Herman, Peter Brook. Every now and then, unique figures like these would cross my path and I would get to write about them, but such encounters were few and far between.

When I began working for the *Toronto Star* in June 2000, I became aware that I was finally in a position to revitalize my never-really-dormant interest in celebrity profiles. Although my title officially was (and is) Theatre Critic, my editors were always generous about allowing me leeway to explore other avenues of expression.

The profile of Barry Manilow I did in July of that year proved to be the first of 80 such pieces I've written. Fifty-six of them are included here, an eclectic selection that pretty well covers the waterfront.

There are a few things worth noting about why and how I conduct my interviews. The initial impulse that makes me decide someone is worth talking to remains the same as it did with Ms. Fabray, 40 years ago: a feeling that whoever this person is, I'd like to know them better.

That's the major reason you'll find no character assassinations in this collection. The *Star* wisely doesn't assign me to specific people; it lets me select them myself, and I don't want to spend a lot of time and effort on someone who I think I'm going to dislike.

But not every one of the pieces that follows is a valentine. Sometimes the most fascinating individuals have an edge to them, and if it reveals itself in our conversation, then I report it.

The location of these interviews ranged from Toronto and New York through Los Angeles and London, with side trips to places like Minneapolis, Princeton, and Shanghai.

Sometimes artists welcomed me into their homes, but on other occasions we talked in the back seat of limousines, or met at the theatres where they were working.

There were breakfasts, lunches, and dinners, as well as some *very* extended cocktail hours. Some of these encounters took place in hotel rooms, in that horribly artificial situation where you shake hands, come out fighting, and have 20 minutes to get to know each other. But luckily, I've been able to spend a couple of hours with most of the people in these pages, and that's plenty of time to have a significant dialogue, if you know what you're doing.

Technically speaking, I tape every interview. It leaves me free to make eye contact, which is all-important. It also means you have a record if anyone ever denies having said something. (Although, touch wood, that hasn't occurred to date.)

These pieces all were published initially in the *Toronto Star*, but in many cases, what you'll read here is very different from what appeared in the paper. The two reasons for that? Time and space.

Sometimes (especially during the Toronto International Film Festival), I rushed from an interview right back to the paper and had an hour or two to file before deadline. That put the brakes on exploring every last nuance of a personal encounter.

Space also dictates a lot of what winds up in print. It doesn't matter how wonderful I may have thought my 2000-word session with Star X turned out to be, if there was only room for 1000 words, I had to cut it down to size.

So this book is a chance to take a second look at "the ones that got away," and the final result can be varied and enlightening.

One final note. These pieces were never meant to be read all at once, so take them a few at a time. Look on this as a box of celebrity candy and consume in moderation.

I'd like to thank the many publicists who helped arrange these encounters, among them: John Karastamatis, Sue Toth, Carrie Sager, Grant Ramsay, Deborah Knight, Dianne Weinrib, Beth Sulman, Kelley Teahen, Bill Bobek, Laura Quinn, Janice Luke, Bill Coyle, Adrian Bryan-Brown, Chris Boneau, Matt Polk, Juliana Hannett, Marc Thibodeau, Kendra Reid, and anyone else I may have inadvertently forgotten!

At the *Toronto Star*, my gratitude to John Ferri and Peter Scowen for being the kind of bosses who always encouraged me in this work; to Mo Gannon, Joe Fox, Janet Hurley, John Terauds, Ariel Teplitsky, and the other editors who brought these pieces to the page with style; to Bob Crew, who shares the theatre beat with me and keeps the home fires burning in my absence; and to publisher John Honderich, managing editor Mary Deanne Shears, and assistant managing editor Phil Bingley for graciously allowing my newspaper writing to find another life in these pages.

A cheer to the gang at McArthur and Company, for sticking with me once again: Kim McArthur, Ruth Shanahan, Janet Harron, Ann Ledden . . . as well as for the impeccable editing of Pamela Erlichman, and the creativity of those designers at Mad Dog.

Last, but not least, at home base, I couldn't do any of this without the love and support of my wife, Pamela, and my kids, Katherine and Michael — who try their very best not to sigh "Where are you going this time?" when they see me pack my suit-case yet again.

Toronto, Ontario
April 2003

I

THE SINGERS

Barry Manilow
AP/World Wide Photos

BARRY MANILOW

Tryin' to Get the Feeling Again

This was the first interview I did for the *Toronto Star*, after I'd been on the job only a few weeks. The news that Barry Manilow was in town and available for publicity washed over the entire Entertainment section with a wave of apathy — except for me.

As the story below reveals, I had been a long-time fan, and although that can sometimes be dangerous when it comes to finally meeting your idols in the flesh, it proved beneficial in this case.

Manilow was a nice guy, if a bit wary at first after years of condescending press treatment. But once he realized I genuinely liked his work, he opened up and we got along just fine.

Mo Gannon, who was in charge of our Sunday edition, decided to put the piece on the front page, and searched far and wide to find a picture of Manilow at the Uris Theatre in 1976. She found one, and it looked great. The public response was immediate and tremendous. When I came into work the next morning, John Ferri, the entertainment editor, was waiting for me.

"We discussed your piece at this morning's editorial meeting," he began with great severity, "and some people wondered if we should continue to employ anyone who liked Barry Manilow so much."

Then he broke into a huge grin. "We loved it. Do more of these. A lot more."

And that's how it all started.

He's sitting at a grand piano, dressed in white, blazing in a spot-light. It's Christmas night 1976 at the Uris Theatre in New York and Barry Manilow is midway through a record-breaking sellout engagement.

I'm ten rows back, on the aisle, in killer seats. With me is the lady I'll marry the following May, but neither of us knows that's going to happen yet. Right now we're simply blissed out, listening to one of our favourite performers.

"I've been up, down, tryin' to get the feeling again;
All around, tryin' to get the feeling again."

Twenty-four years later, Manilow and I are backstage at the Hummingbird Centre, where his musical *Copacabana* is about to begin its Toronto run.

A lot has happened to his career since that night in New York. Just like the lyric says, he's been "up, down . . . all around," going from triple platinum to double bankruptcy and becoming the butt of hundreds of jokes while hanging on to thousands of fans.

He was born Barry Alan Pincus in Brooklyn, N.Y., on June 17, 1946, and music was going to be his life from the very start. He wrote his first song at 12, had his own band at 15, and was performing as an opening act for Joan Rivers by the time he was 22. After that, it was a short hop to becoming Bette Midler's musical director and a heady three years that included her star-making turn at the Continental Baths.

By 1974, Barry had struck out on his own and made it big, really big, with a song called "Mandy." It hit Number 1 and spent 12 weeks on the Top 40.

Then came "It's a Miracle," "Could It Be Magic?" and the monster hit "I Write the Songs," which spent almost five months near the top of the charts.

"That's when it all changed for me, and there was no looking back. I was a star." He winces at the word, and then owns up to it. "Yeah, I was a star."

Manilow remained one of the pop world's hottest performers for a decade. He had 25 consecutive Top 40 hits, a record that remains unbeaten to this day. He won an Emmy (for "The Barry Manilow Special"), a Grammy (for "Copacabana"), a Tony (for that show I saw in 1976), and was even nominated for an Oscar (for *Foul Play*'s "Ready to Take a Chance Again"). His concert tours consistently broke records around North America.

And then, in 1983, it all changed. "I walked away from it. I actually walked away from it." From a distance of nearly 20 years, he still is amazed at how he just "stepped off of that Top 40 treadmill. I looked up one day and said, 'I really don't know what else to do.' And so I stopped."

He didn't stop performing. Manilow will do that shortly after he stops breathing. But since that day, he hasn't written, recorded, or sung any new pop songs. It's been nothing but "greatest hits" and tribute albums for nearly 20 years.

The Manilow who made white spandex a way of life in the '70s is dressed today as if he's asking for a bank loan: sober suit, monochrome shirt and tie. The Regis Philbin Look. I half expect him to ask me if that's my final answer.

Instead I wonder aloud if those 25 consecutive hits were too much of a good thing. He stares at me for a while before answering. I study his face. Much the same as in the superstar days, but thinner now at 54, with deeper lines.

He decides to take the bullet, not dodge it. "Yeah, I think it suddenly turned on me. It's overkill after a while. All those records bombarding the public. A backlash. It happens. It happened to Michael Jackson, it happened to Michael Bolton, it happened to me. A lot of people just didn't want to hear any more from Barry Manilow."

"And I've looked high, low, everywhere I possibly can;
But there's no tryin' to get the feeling again.
It seemed to disappear as fast as it came."

He's right. From being the hottest thing in pop music, he turned into a joke almost overnight. People mocked his clothes (the bouffant hair, the glitter jumpsuits), his enthusiasm ("Hey, I'm the guy who put the 'p' in promotion," he still admits), and his heart-on-the-sleeve emotion (22 of his 25 hits were ballads).

It seems like millions of people went into Manilow Denial. They had never liked him, never listened to him, never bought his albums. The garage sales of the early '90s always had lots of Manilow vinyl for sale, but it was usually buried in the back, way behind *Hotel California* and *Rumors*.

If you got caught admitting you listened to songs like "Weekend in New England," your friends practically staged an intervention to get you into a 12-step group for hopeless senti-mentalists. ("Hi everybody, my name is Richard, and I'm a Barryholic.")

The younger generation could be particularly devastating in its scorn. "Barry Manilow? You're interviewing Barry MANilow???" snorted my teenage daughter. "That's really lame."

She had a point, especially when you consider the phenome-nal ABBA revival that's all around us. Because if you look at the simple statistics, ABBA was never as big as Manilow in North America. ABBA's first hit, "Waterloo," broke six months before "Mandy" did for Manilow. And for the next decade, they frequently shared places in the Top 40. But during that time, ABBA had only 14 hits to Manilow's 25 and was on the charts for a total of 135 weeks, compared with Manilow's 220.

So how come it's awesome to like ABBA and bush league to dig Barry? How come *Mamma Mia!* based on ABBA's music is sold out months in advance around the world, while *Copacabana* is slinking around playing one-week gigs? I ask Manilow if he has any theories why. He looks away before answering, going some-place else.

He starts slowly, warming to the topic as he thinks it through. "ABBA didn't want to continue performing. They stopped touring, writing, recording. They just stopped. I never did. You see, walking away from the Top 40 isn't the same as walking away from the whole business. I've been on the road having a great time, singing my songs for the past twenty years."

That consistency has paid off. Manilow may no longer be a superstar, but there are still hundreds of thousands of followers, an International Fan Club, and numerous Web sites like www.barrynet.com and www.manilow.com.

He has been recording during all these years as well: compilations of past hits as well as jazz, show tunes, '70s hits, Sinatra favourites, Christmas songs. All excellent albums, but none of them sold like his old ones.

Does he ever think about where he'd be now if he had taken the route ABBA did? The question surprises him.

"You mean, would I be a bigger Barry Manilow today if I had just quit in '83? Maybe." He plays the scenario through in his mind. "Yeah, maybe. The big hits would be even dearer if you hadn't heard me singing them all the time. I mean how can you miss me if I never went away?"

I offer another reason for the ABBA revival. Most of its songs are kitschy novelty numbers, easy to shoehorn into a show like *Mamma Mia!* where each song cue generates a burst of appreciative laughter from the audience. But Manilow's songs are quite different.

"That's right!" He leaps on the suggestion. "You wouldn't laugh at 'Looks Like We Made It' — you couldn't. I have to believe the songs I do. I have to crawl inside them. If I couldn't get into them, I'd be phoning them in, and I don't."

But there's another reason I don't mention. Think back to the ABBA-Manilow demographics. Most of the people who loved their songs are in their forties and fifties now, working on second mortgages, second families . . . or both. They want to remember when they could boogie all night with their fantasy date to "Dancin' Queen," not how they lost their heart to the wrong person during "Can't Smile Without You."

Only one Manilow song fits into the fun, fun, fun mode. And that's really why I'm sitting in a claustrophobic room filled with fruit trays far too early on a sunny July morning. The song is "Copacabana."

Let's try a test. I say "Her name was Lola," and I bet you respond, "she was a showgirl." It's embedded in our genes, that Frankie and Johnny story set to a percolating Latin beat with just enough disco underneath to make it stick in your mind forever.

How do you write a song like that? Blame Bette Davis. In 1974, Manilow had just finished accompanying her on *The Dick Cavett Show* when he dashed off to Rio de Janeiro for a vacation with his long-time lyricist, Bruce Sussman.

With Bette Davis on their minds, Sussman quoted Paul Henried's line to her from *Now, Voyager* as they sailed into the harbour at Rio and spotted the Copacabana Palace hotel: "Copacabana: there's music in that word."

Good idea, but it took a few years for Sussman to act on it. He finally did, writing the now-classic lyric that tells of Lola, Tony, Rico, and their doomed romantic triangle.

Manilow sat down at the piano and wrote the tune in 20 minutes, "maybe less.' The song was released as part of Manilow's *Even Now* album in 1978, went gold, and won Manilow his first Grammy Award. It became a TV special, then a nightclub show, and finally a musical comedy.

Manilow is quick to point out that *Copacabana* is not like *Mamma Mia!* Aside from the title song, it's not a potpourri of his hits. Every song is new, written specifically for the needs of this affectionately splashy tribute to the movie musicals of the 1940s.

When asked to pick his favourite songs from the score he wrote with Sussman, he unhesitatingly selects the romantic numbers "Who Needs to Dream?" and "This Can't Be Real." I wonder what's in his psyche that makes him love ballads so much.

"I go for the melody every time. It's something deep inside me. Me." And then, with a self-deprecating chuckle, he brings up another piece of his past: "I learned it when I wrote commercials — had to come up with the catchiest melody possible in thirty seconds."

The list of famous clients from those glory days in the early seventies included Band-Aids, KFC, State Farm Insurance, and most infamously, it was Manilow who wrote "You deserve a break today" for McDonald's.

Yet that's not what's on my mind as our allotted time draws to a close. I'm thinking of that Christmas night concert at the Uris. He was singing "Weekend in New England" in front of a black scrim with a simple four-piece band.

But when he got to that patented Barry Manilow key change, the lights came up behind him to reveal a 40-piece orchestra against an electric blue sky. The moment was thrilling, and I believed he could do anything he wanted.

> "I want to get that feeling;
> I've got to get that feeling;
> I've got to get that feeling again and again.
> I've been tryin' to get the feeling again."

And maybe, just maybe, he can.

It would be nice to report that *Copacabana* launched a Manilow renaissance, but that wasn't how it worked out.

A few nights after my interview appeared, I had to review the show. It was a real stinker, and my notice began: "They don't make shows like *Copacabana* any more. They also don't make eight-track tapes or leisure suits for the same reason."

The tour soon died and plans to bring the show to Broadway evaporated, but another original musical called *Harmony* begins Broadway tryouts in 2003.

Queen Latifah
AP/World Wide Photos

QUEEN LATIFAH

Memories of Timbuktu

Some people lost sleep over the idea of casting rapper Queen Latifah as Mama Morton in the movie version of *Chicago*.

I didn't.

Having followed her career for years, I believed this woman could do just about anything she wanted to.

When I finally got to interview her during a New York press weekend for *Chicago* in December 2002, I was pleased to discover that with at least one star, the image and the actuality proved to be the same.

It's good to be the Queen. Just ask Dana Owens.

Don't recognize that name? Then try referring to her by her chosen title, Queen Latifah.

The presence of royalty makes itself felt as soon as she sashays into the room where I've been waiting to discuss her current appearance as Mama Morton — the prison matron with Enron morals — in the film *Chicago*.

Check her out. Gold eye-shadow in abundance, rings for days, and a giant pendant with the initials "QL" suspended from her neck, in case anyone needed reminding.

She regards me warily and then sits down.

Assuming it would be wise to start with a nice, neutral question, I ask her how she got involved with the project.

"How do you think? I put a gun to the guy's head and said, 'Give me the frigging role.'"

I laugh — but not too much, recalling her 1996 arrest for driving with a loaded .38 in her car. This is a woman who knows her way around firearms.

Her Majesty is in an upbeat mood today, even if the early morning hour doesn't agree with her. ("Can't we do this at seven tonight?" she asks conspiratorially. "I tell you, I'd be good and warmed up by then.")

The reason for her positive vibe has to do with her obvious enthusiasm for *Chicago*.

"They showed me a lot of love in this project. It was nice to be part of something where nobody was trying to be the big honcho."

She didn't even mind having to convince director Rob Marshall that she was right for the role. He had his cap set for Kathy Bates, but Miramax boss Harvey Weinstein wanted the Queen, and what Harvey wants, Harvey gets.

Even if it takes a while.

"Man, I auditioned three times!" she recalls. "Singing, acting, and dancing. After the dancing one," she grins, "they told me I had the job."

It seems bizarre for a Grammy Award-winning rapper to be so pumped about the world of Broadway show tunes, but the Queen is full of surprises.

"I knew musicals, sure I did. When I was a kid, every now and then my momma would take me to Broadway. I saw *The Wiz* with the original cast, and they even took me to something called *Timbuktu*." She's talking about a flop 1979 version of *Kismet*, set in Africa.

"Man, all I remember about that one is Eartha Kitt being carried in by a bunch of big black men. I tell you, she was one scary lady!" The memory makes her laugh nearly 25 years later.

"Yeah, musicals meant a lot to me as a kid. Growing up in the projects, this is the escapism that you love. All those singin' and dancin' movies were fantasy time for me.

It's understandable that she needed a place to hide from the real world. She was born in 1970 in Newark, N.J., Her father, Lance, was a policeman. He split before she was even a teen "but he taught me two things: how to hold my ground and how to hold a gun."

Her mother Rita moved the kids to the housing projects in East Orange, N.J., and started to rebuild her life. She worked two jobs while attending community college and wound up as a high school art teacher.

Latifah began acting early on (her first role was Dorothy in *The Wiz*), and played power forward on her high school basket-ball team. She also got into rapping with an all-female group, Ladies Fresh, and acquired her current title.

"Latifah" means "delicate and sensitive" in Arabic and was a nickname given her as a child by a Muslim cousin. And as for "Queen," this is a woman with regal assurance to spare.

She was working at a Burger King and attending Manhattan Community College when Tommy Boy Records heard her rap "Princess of the Posse" and offered her a contract in 1988. Her first album, *All Hail the Queen* went platinum and she was on her way.

In 1991 she made her film debut in Spike Lee's *Jungle Fever* and she was riding high.

"But that's when you gotta watch out," she says with a faraway look. The following year, she became embroiled in a bitter contract dispute with her label over royalties, and her beloved brother, Lance Jr., died. He had become a policeman and was riding off-duty on a motorcycle Latifah had bought him when he crashed.

"I still think of him," she says quietly. "I think of him every damn day."

After a while, she went back to work, and her star kept rising. She landed a regular role on the WB comedy series, *Living Single*, which ran for five seasons.

But once again, bad times followed on the good. Two hoodlums carjacked Latifah and her bodyguard in Harlem. He was shot and seriously injured. She escaped unharmed but was severely shaken. Six months later, she was arrested for driving under the influence of marijuana, and a loaded gun was found in her car. She was fined and put on probation for two years.

Since then, life has been reasonably calm, except for an arrest last fall for a liquor-related driving infraction. She doesn't deny the things she has done but puts them in perspective.

"Shit goes down, baby," she says, "you just gotta make sure you don't go down with it."

In the past few years, acting has dominated her career to the exclusion of music, but now the Queen seems ready to correct the balance.

Motown recently put out a Greatest Hits collection of her work called *She's a Queen*. She'll appear on the *Chicago* soundtrack, not just with her signature tune "When You're Good to Mama," but with a special version of "Cell Block Tango" with L'il Kim and Macy Gray.

After that, "I'm gonna drop two singles on the market before we release my next CD. Gotta season the audience. Get them used to hearing the La again."

"Although I gotta tell you something. I like these show tunes. They're clever and funny, and they sure stick with you."

She isn't kidding. During our time together, she's been constantly humming one of the songs from *Chicago*, a number she doesn't even sing in the film.

"Yeah," she admits, getting up to go, "ain't it strange? I just can't get that tune out of my head."

Maybe not so strange. After she leaves, I suddenly remember its name: "They Both Reached for the Gun."

Queen Latifah continued to amaze people when she earned a Best Supporting Actress Oscar nomination for *Chicago*, even though she lost to her co-star, Catherine Zeta-Jones.

She didn't have any time to be gloomy, because that was when her comedy *Bringing Down the House* (co-starring Steve Martin) opened, and stayed number one for three weeks in a row, bringing in well over US$100 million at the box office.

Denny Doherty
Jim Ross/Toronto Star

DENNY DOHERTY

A Case of Crown Royal

Denny Doherty crossed my path twice before we finally did this interview.

In 1966, when I was a college freshman at New York's Fordham University, The Mamas and the Papas played a concert for our Homecoming Weekend. I stood near the front, clapping and singing along with "California Dreamin'," but that's as close as I got.

Thirteen years later, in 1979, I was a young freelance director, working in every theatre that asked me, and I found myself in Halifax, Nova Scotia, staging a musical called *Eighteen Wheels* with a local lad made good who had come back home — Denny Doherty.

We had an amiable enough time together, but Doherty was still too close then to the vanished fame of his rock 'n' roll days to want to discuss it. There weren't a lot of stories about John and Cass and Michelle going down back then.

That took another 22 years, until the summer of 2001, when Doherty had finally decided to tell all about his glory days, and we met for lunch to make up for lost time.

Blame it on the Crown Royal.

The way Denny Doherty tells it, if he hadn't introduced John and Michelle Phillips and Cass Elliott to that classic Canuck tipple, The Mamas and the Papas might have had a different name.

"We all loved the stuff, and we drank so much of it that there were little purple bags everywhere. The girls even started using them as purses."

It's just one of the many stories the 60-year-old Doherty has on his mind as he prepares for the Toronto premiere of his autobiographical musical, *Dream a Little Dream*.

"We were all blitzed on rye whisky," he remembers, "lying around the Landmark Hotel in L.A. on a Monday night. We'd just signed the recording contract with Lou Adler that would make us famous, and here we were, all four of us, feet up, watching TV."

Doherty's smile twinkles, making him look like the world's biggest leprechaun, as he recalls that night 36 years ago.

"A guy named Les Crane was on the tube, interviewing the head of the Hells Angels, who was defending the honour of biker women. 'They're not sluts,' he insisted, 'they're our mamas.'

"Well, that tickled Cass and she said, 'I wanna be a mama, too.' Of course, Michelle squealed, 'So do I,' and then John decided the men were papas, and finally Cass raised her glass of Crown Royal: 'That's it, we're The Mamas and the Papas.'"

Nice story. Fade out, happy ending.

Except for a little thing that happened later that evening. "After John and Cass passed out," Doherty admits, shame still clouding his eyes, "Michelle and I tiptoed down the hall and went to bed."

The only trouble was that Michelle was married to John, while Cass was unrequitedly in love with Denny.

"We wrecked it all that night we signed the contract, and it was over before it began. No one got what they wanted. Cass wanted me, John and I wanted Michelle, and Michelle, well, she wanted everything."

Discoveries, recriminations, and quarrels followed (Fleetwood Mac, does this sound familiar?), and the group only lasted until 1968 when the personal soap opera swallowed up the professional success.

"It all happened too quickly," admits Doherty.

"A few months before, we were so broke we didn't have the money to fly home from the Virgin Islands." They had gone down there to find a new sound for their folk group, The Journeymen, but they got the governor's nephew stoned on acid, and were ordered back home.

"We got as far as San Juan. There were nine of us, and we had fifty dollars between us." Doherty still can't believe the story he's telling. "But John grabbed a taxi and we hit the casino at the Caribe Hilton. Michelle had never gambled in her life, but he handed the dice to her, and she made eighteen consecutive passes."

"John swaggered back to the Pan Am ticket counter, put his winnings down and said, 'First Class to New York, one way, nine tickets. Tell me when to stop counting.'"

Doherty roars with laughter, but then it fades as he thinks about how the whole thing ended. "We grabbed the brass ring on the merry-go-round before we even knew how we got on the ride."

Dream a Little Dream is his attempt to understand that crazy carousel, while offering up a tribute to the person he feels never got sufficient credit for her contribution — Mama Cass.

"She was the sound of the group," insists Doherty, "she made us what we were, but nobody knew it.

"John wrote his book, Michelle wrote hers, but Cass died in '74 of a heart attack, and not from a heroin overdose, or choking on a ham sandwich or any other shit like that.

"She never got a chance to tell her side, and I never got a chance to tell her I was sorry."

Doherty is still living with the guilt of having rejected the overweight Elliott time and time again, while he launched an adulterous affair with the slim blonde Phillips.

"Let me tell you the kind of thing Cass did." Doherty leans forward now, pushing aside the eggs Benedict and coffee he's lunching on. No Crown Royal, not for many years now. ("I like living too much.")

"John, Michelle, and me were crashing at Cass's pad in L.A. We were working on a new tune, but singing it in our old style." He launches into a legato Kingston Trio sound "All the leaves are brown, and the sky is grey..."

Doherty's eyes light up. "Cass was standing there, ironing some shirts, when suddenly she started slamming her iron down in rhythm on the board. 'It's 1965, you assholes, haven't you heard of a backbeat?' And she rocked the tempo, 'I've been for a walk on a winter's day.'"

You hear the difference instantly.

"Well, that's what we did on the demo for Lou Adler. Paul Horn was playing on another session down the hall, so he wandered in and did the flute riff.

"Yeah, that's how we made 'California Dreamin'. And you know the rest."

It's been a long journey for Doherty, both to and from that time.

He was born to a working-class Halifax, Nova Scotia, family on November 24, 1941, and formed his first folk trio, The Colonials, by the time he was 18.

After touring across Canada, they changed their name to The Halifax Three, only to break up soon after.

Young Doherty loved New York in the sixties. "You got to understand, for a kid from Canada, it was like I'd fallen into Sodom and Gomorrah, but I loved it! The women, the booze, the good times . . . oh, brother." He chortles ruefully at the memories.

"Then I met Cass," he says quietly. "When I thought back on those days years later, after my mind was clear, I realize that she fell in love with me right away, but I was too blind, or selfish or stupid to see it. All I saw was this big fat girl, and I was off chasing the beauties. Oh, Doherty, what a fool you were."

Romantic reservations notwithstanding, Doherty joined Elliot and they soon paired up with Zal Yanovsky and John Sebastian, calling themselves The Mugwumps. Their lightly rocking folk sound never quite came together, and before too long. Sebastian and Yanovsky left to form The Lovin' Spoonful.

Elliott and Doherty joined with fellow folkies John and Michelle Phillips to become The Mamas and the Papas.

The money they made in those chart-topping days was enormous, but it all vanished in high living, bad management, and a hazy cloud of Crown Royal.

The years that followed were tough ones for Doherty, "when I spent too much and lived too hard." What he now feels saved him was the fact that he never got lost in hard drugs the way many others did. "My dad always said 'It's okay to scratch your ass, just don't tear it apart.'"

But now, life is tranquil, and Doherty has the perspective to look back on the moment that changed it all in every sense of the word for The Mamas and the Papas: that rye-soaked Monday night at the Landmark Hotel.

Or as they once sang:

"Monday, Monday, can't trust that day,
Monday, Monday, sometimes it just turns out that way."

Dream a Little Dream was enough of a success in Toronto that Doherty was able to start it on the long and weary road to New York, where it finally opened off-Broadway in April 2003.

Rosemary Clooney
AP/World Wide Photos

ROSEMARY CLOONEY

One Note at a Time

I t was a holiday weekend in the summer of 2002 when the word came down the wire that Rosemary Clooney had died on June 29.

I thought about the one time we met, nearly 30 years before, and knew I had to write about her.

F. Scott Fitzgerald wrote, "There are no second acts in American lives," but then he never met Rosemary Clooney, who died at the age of 74 because of complications from her six-month battle with lung cancer.

Singers who hit the skids are a dime a dozen, but ones who come back the way that she did are rare indeed.

Universally regarded as one of the great song stylists of the past century, Clooney enjoyed two distinct and successful careers, divided by a decade of personal tragedy.

She was born in Maysville, Kentucky, on May 23, 1928, the granddaughter of the mayor. But her childhood life wasn't a picture-postcard dream of Americana. Her father was an alcoholic, and her mother used to go off on unexplained "journeys," leaving Rosemary and her younger sister Betty with relatives, saying, "You can do it, Rosie, you're the strong one. You can fix things for yourself."

Her mother finally remarried when Rosemary was 13, putting the girls in the care of their father. Three years later, he abandoned them at a bus station in Cincinnati, with 20 cents between them.

Rosemary took Betty down to radio station WLW, where they auditioned for a local music program and were hired as The Clooney Sisters. The salary was $20 a week and the station manager gave them a dollar in advance so they could eat.

They were soon heard by bandleader Tony Pastor, who took them on the road. For two years they toured North America. By 1949, Betty wanted to quit, so the act split up and Rosemary headed to New York.

She soon landed a recording contract with Columbia, and broke through with a 1951 novelty number called "Come On-A My House." The song became such a big hit that her first cheque was for $130,000. Other humorous dialect numbers such as "Mambo Italiano" followed, and then in 1952 Paramount Pictures brought her to Hollywood.

She appeared in five films, most notably the 1954 classic *White Christmas*. But by then movie musicals were on the way out and Clooney had decided to settle down after marrying José Ferrer.

Ferrer has nearly been forgotten since his death in 1992, but in the early 1950s he was one of America's major stars, a theatre actor and director who made the move to Hollywood with ease, winning the 1951 Best Actor Oscar for his performance in the title role of *Cyrano de Bergerac*, and later receiving a nomination for his performance in *Moulin Rouge*.

To the outside world, their marriage looked perfect. They had five children in five years (Bob Hope once accused them of playing "Vatican roulette"). But the truth behind the scene was very different. Ferrer was a womanizer who began cheating on Clooney during their honeymoon and convinced her that his infidelities were because of her inadequacy.

She put her still-sizzling record career on the backburner and devoted herself to Ferrer and the kids, reaching for tranquillizers to numb the pain. They divorced, remarried, and finally split up for good in 1966. Clooney had a heartbreaking affair with arranger Nelson Riddle, kept popping pills, and resumed her performing career with manic intensity.

"Manic" was the operative word, however, and she gradually began to spin out of control. Matters came to a head in the summer of 1968. Fanatically devoted to Robert Kennedy, she began to follow him around on his campaign for the presidency and was present at the Ambassador Hotel when he was assassinated on June 5.

Clooney refused to believe it, and finally broke down in the middle of a performance in Reno a few weeks later. She was forcibly institutionalized, suffering from "psychotic reaction with severe depression and paranoid features."

A long, slow, and painful process of recovery began, weaning her off the prescription drugs that she had been living on for the past decade and tracing the root of her mental problems.

Four years later, she tentatively started her comeback, 80 pounds heavier but clean and sober, with a concert at Copenhagen's Tivoli Gardens. Her voice was still recovering from the abuse of the past years, and so she kept away from the major performing centres.

I met her in 1973 when she was doing a guest shot on a television show in Edmonton. I was working there at the time, and got myself invited to the taping as well as to the wrap party after. I remembered she had been a star when I was a kid and, like everyone, I knew all about her troubles.

At one point in the evening, I found myself alone with her for few minutes. I voiced some pleasantries about her performance, and then, with the brutal honesty of youth, asked her simply, "How do you do it?"

She appreciated my candour and offered hers in return. "One day a time. One song at a time. One note at a time. And I make all of them as honest as I can."

Sipping at her ginger ale, she offered me this: "God gives some of us second chances, and when He does, you have to use it as well as you can. I'm gonna try."

And she did. I recall that night as her career kept sailing on for the next three decades. Bing Crosby brought her back to the big time in 1974 with an appearance at the gala to celebrate his 50th anniversary in show business. Concord Jazz began an amazing series of albums with her in 1977, and from then on she was back, some say better than ever.

It's true her voice lacked the supple brightness of her early years, that open, unguarded quality that made a song like "Tenderly" grab you where you lived when she remembered how "Your arms opened wide and closed me inside."

But instead, she offered wisdom, warmth, and the honesty that she had said she would try to give. As time took away the notes, it taught her more to put behind the words and the end result was still sublime.

Lyricist Alan Bergman summed her up best a decade ago when he said, "Singers should have it in three places — the heart, the head, and the pipes. Rosemary does."

I remember her singing Bergman's "The Promise":

> *"I am not afraid to say I love you,*
> *And I promise you I'll never say goodbye."*

A few months after this piece appeared, I spent some time with George Clooney, and we swapped stories about his wonderful aunt.

"Once when I was just out of my teens, I was goofing off, partying too much, and she sat me down to read me the riot act," Clooney recalled. "'Just because I got a second chance,' she said, 'doesn't mean you're gonna get one, too.'"

He smiled, remembering the moment. "Just after that, I packed myself out to California and got into acting. She's the one who lit the fire under me, and I don't know if I ever got to thank her enough."

Ute Lemper
Diane Bondareff

UTE LEMPER

The Queen of Cabaret Confrontation

"What you see is what you get" definitely doesn't apply to Ute Lemper.

The dynamic diva known for her SM getups and torrid sexuality as much as for her singing is something totally different offstage.

As her voice throbbed into my ear during a late-night phone call to set up the time and place for our interview, I had visions of her in a leather bustier, dimly lit, with smoke in the air.

But when I showed up at her West Side Manhattan apartment on a snowy Monday afternoon in February 2003, I couldn't have been more surprised with what I found.

A bunch of crayon pictures are taped to the front door. A stack of PlayStation games rests on the chair and there's a pile of Lego under the coffee table.

This is Ute Lemper's apartment?

Where's the leather-clad song stylist who loves to make her audiences squirm?

The wholesome, attractive blonde who stretches out on the sofa looks like someone you'd love to sit next to at the PTA, but hardly the Queen of Cabaret Confrontation.

"I haven't changed at all," she laughs — part Little Red Riding Hood, part Big Bad Wolf — "you're just getting a peek behind the curtain. I have children. They live here. Max is eight, Stella is six, and they make my life very rich."

"When you have kids, they bring a whole different side to your life. You have less time for yourself, and self-indulgence becomes a rare luxury."

That hardly seems like the kind of talk you expect from a diva whose stage persona radiates sheer unbridled love of self, but Lemper insists, "It's ultimately annoying to have yourself in the centre of your life at all times. I did that between the ages of twenty and thirty, and then I was sick of myself. All that egocentric torture ..." She dismisses it with a wave of her hand, "At the end of the day, it can be destructive."

But Lemper is also quick to maintain that her onstage character is more than just a creation of sheer artifice.

"It comes from me as a person. The edge, the confrontationality. I like provocation. I like the game of yourself against the other. Taking people with you into a journey of danger and seduction. I go deeply into pain and loss onstage."

Then her smile brings a Chinook that takes the chill off her words.

"I've learned that if you do it onstage, you can avoid it in life. I'm much more romantic in life than I am onstage. Much."

What she's offering this time is a show based on her most recent CD, *But One Day*. After the intensely contemporary repertoire she favoured in her last album, *Punishing Kiss*, "I wanted to take a step back into more truly theatrical music" and this new collection is "more eclectic. It's a summing up of me, it shows the whole rainbow of me."

Songs from the Argentinean Astor Piazzolla co-exist with material from Jacques Brel, original compositions from Lemper herself, and — as expected — Kurt Weill.

She speaks of Weill with the affectionate respect some women reserve for their fathers. "He's a classic, a genius, he created a genre of pop music that educated people to look at their lives, their society. I always carry him with me in the pocket of my coat, through the years, although the keys I sing him in get a little lower as I get older."

Proof that she hasn't lost her edge (if you ever doubted it) resides in a pair of collaborations between Bertolt Brecht and Hanss Eisler, featuring lines like:

"I came to live with people in a time of uproar,
And I began rebelling with them."

"My mission is to bring everything into today's time and make it urgent and important. Most of the songs I sing were created in times of chaos or instability."

Lemper herself was born in 1963 into relative tranquillity in a comfortably bourgeois family in Munster, Germany. Her banker father and opera singer mother indulged their talented daughter, offering her all the music, dance, and drama that was available.

"That little city of Munster," muses Lemper, not all that affectionately. "I got out of there once I had sucked all the information out of it that I could. I was thirsty for life, for learning."

She was singing with a jazz combo by the time she was 15, and a year later joined a punk group called "The Panama Drive Band."

Then she broke into acting at the age of 18, and spent two years with the Stattstheatre Stuttgart, and on her 20th birthday, she was playing Grizabella in the Viennese production of *Cats*.

More stage successes followed, including an acclaimed Parisian production of *Cabaret*, and her award-winning London turn as Velma in *Chicago*, later repeated in New York and Toronto.

But along with her stage work, Lemper was carving a name out for herself as one of the most original and popular modern entertainers to carry on the true European tradition of cabaret — singing work that was intimate, personal, and frequently edgy.

Her 1987 album of Kurt Weill songs served as her introduction to the world, and she's since followed it up with a series of albums (and concurrent live performances) that run the gamut from "contemporary to classical to rock — but always in my own style."

Even though she moved permanently to New York in 1998, Lemper says, "I still definitely feel very German. The way I think and even how I speak. No matter where I travel, there is a piece of Berlin in me."

She suddenly leans forward to make a point. "But not the Berlin of today. I'm talking of those years between the wars when laws were being broken in every way: art, music, literature, architecture. Everyone felt the need to describe things as cruelly and directly as possible. At the same time, there was a lot of eroticism and passion. The tension between good and evil was being explored in those years."

A puzzled look crosses her face. "If the Nazis hadn't interrupted it, I wonder what would have happened to this great cultural world that was asking so many searching questions? I guess that's why I keep exploring it myself."

Exploration is also the theme of Lemper's next project, tentatively entitled *Nomad*, in which she plans to sing songs in Russian, Hungarian, Yiddish, Arabic, and Hebrew.

Lemper the *provocateur* is at it again. "This is music that transports very well into today's world. And I love the political aspect of it as well: the Arab song after the Israeli one, the Hungarian after the Russian."

Canadian opera director Robert Carson is in charge of the staging, and Lemper promises it will be "unlike anything you have ever seen before."

But as for a return to conventional musical theatre, she is resolutely negative.

"It doesn't make me happy to do the same show eight times a week. It's an overdose of something you like to do, which makes you hate it after a while. It's Sisyphus work, conveyor belt work. I love to improvise. I love to improvise. I love to have a moment on stage when I don't know what's going to happen and I leave it open to the collective creative impulse."

She continues to warm to her theme. "I don't like the whole Broadway performance style, the way they yell out all the songs with that vibrato thing going on. I love the intimacy, the transparency, the brokenness in the voice, the pianissimo note. I don't like fortissimo all the time. I like letting people into the inside and taking a close-up of me."

Lemper turns 40 on July 3 and she laughs with a kind of bravado as the event is mentioned.

"Oh, I've thought about it a lot. It's a real issue for women. Less so for men. I think it all *begins* for men at forty. That's when they *start* to look interesting. It's only then that they begin to have a face that tells a story. They finally forget about their mothers and get on with their lives."

"But me? I have a super life. I'm very fulfilled with everything. Okay, a couple of wrinkles here and there, but what can you do? If my face reflects the years of my life, that's all good. After all, I'm not sixty yet, only forty."

Recent years have seen the departure of her husband (and father of her children) actor David Tabatsky, "after several separations." The new man in her life is her former drummer, Todd Turkisher, now the co-producer of *But One Day*.

And, as expected, Lemper has one final thought to impart: "The message of my music is: today is what you have, so go for it."

Lemper was true to her word, and she kept away from the musical stage, while continuing to stretch the envelope of cabaret entertainment with her new and provocative works.

It's nice to know that some artists are as good as their word.

Mandy Patinkin
Lana Slezic/Toronto Star

MANDY PATINKIN

Take the Moment

Mandy Patinkin's singing arouses the same feelings as anchovies on pizza: people either love it or hate it.

The fans praise his incredible openness; his detractors call it overemotionalism.

I come down on the positive side, which is why I was glad to get a chance to spend some time with him.

The interview occurred in Manhattan, several weeks after 9/11, and although that topic was to haunt many of the people I spoke to in the fall of 2001, the immediacy of this particular conversation made it all very important to Patinkin.

Originally, he had no time to see me, but I pressed the issue, and he finally invited me up to his apartment on my way to the airport at the end of my trip. I arrived laden with suitcases, and received an instant welcome.

It wound up being one of the most intense hours I've ever spent . . . but, knowing Patinkin, that's hardly surprising.

Mandy Patinkin has always worn his heart on his sleeve, and lately that's been a very good thing.

The 48-year-old star of television (*Chicago Hope*), film (*The Princess Bride*), and stage (*Evita*) is going to appear at the Hummingbird Centre on October 15 as part of a concert tour he began in New York City the night before the attack on the World Trade Center.

Even now, weeks later, the memory of that evening is enough to bring a haunted look to his eyes. "I guess you could say the way I ended that first concert was ironic. I had two tiny toy flags — one from Palestine, one from Israel — and I put them on the stage."

Patinkin's hands gently hold the imaginary banners. "First I sang 'HaTikvah' (the Israeli national anthem) sweetly, as if to a child. Then I went into my version of 'You've Got To Be Carefully Taught.' I knocked the flags over, the stage turned blood red, and I screamed out the lyrics like Hitler on the podium."

The passion in his eyes is truly frightening, but just as suddenly, it vanishes. "Then it calmed down, I put the flags upright, the lights went back to normal, and I finished by singing 'Children Will Listen' like a prayer."

He pauses, swallowing hard. "The next morning I turned on my television and ..." He leaves the sentence unfinished, but you can see the images flickering behind his eyes. He reaches for a drink of water, waits a few moments, and then continues. "Well, after the events of that day, nobody needs any explosions or loud noises. They're not necessary in the world ever again.

"But I wanted the prayer to be heard more than ever, and so now instead of shouting and screaming it, I sang it almost like to an infant sleeping. Yes, I still want there to be peace in the Middle East, but more importantly I want there to be peace all over the world, and I don't want anybody to shut the door on that prayer."

Some people are quick to mock Patinkin for his passionate openness, but sitting right across from him in the eclectic catch-all he calls an office, it's hard not to be moved by his sincerity. His apartment in the West 90s of Manhattan is only 10 kilometres from Ground Zero, but it seems far removed.

The sunlight pours into the high-ceilinged rooms, and wherever you look there are mementos of his amazing career. Here's a farewell present from the cast of *Chicago Hope*, there's a collection of photos from his extensive national tours, artwork from his latest CD, and everywhere, everywhere, proud signs of his Jewish heritage.

But perhaps most important, on the front door, next to the mezuzah, there's a hand-lettered sign: "Imagine all the people living life in peace," and the barefoot guy wearing jeans could just as easily be at a demonstration in the late 1960s.

The only difference is that this guy has one of the most malleable voices of our time, capable of ear-melting sweetness and heart-rending savagery with only a breath between.

"God almighty," he says, standing up suddenly, "I am so lucky to have this right now. It's a great gift that I have the chance to perform for other people at this moment. I feel very blessed. It's the most extraordinary experience to sing words written by genius lyricists who put down on paper what they wished for the world. Well, now those prayers are wished for more than ever. And I'm just the mailman. I'm the messenger boy."

Except for a few minor changes, the material in Patinkin's concert hasn't been altered, but as he admits: "Every word you sing somehow reflects on September 11. Every word has an image, and my task is not to deny the echo and the reverberations of the moment, but not to get so mired down in it that we can't celebrate our lives at the same time."

The energy in the room grows more intense. "We all put on our game faces. You put your reporter's face on; I have my actor-being-interviewed face on. We have our mom and dad face on to our kids, we put on our performing face when we're in front of people, but the minute we let them down, when we're by ourselves, we're weeping again."

"The task for all of us is to allow that mourning to take place whenever it needs to take place. Whether it's at my concert or when you're alone doesn't matter. The important thing is to deal with the task at hand, which is to live, to celebrate our lives. We have to fight for that celebration. And then, we have to move on, as Steve Sondheim wrote."

Sondheim is never far from Patinkin's thoughts: "He's the Shakespeare of our time." Patinkin's preparing a new Sondheim album, working on an all-Sondheim show, and even seeing to it that this concert has a sufficient amount of songs by his favourite composer.

"He speaks to me on a profound level." Patinkin slips into a hushed sound, free of his usual manic energy. "He is my teacher; he is my voice. If I could write, I would write every word he said."

I quote my favourite Sondheim lyric (from an obscure show called *Anyone Can Whistle*) to him:

> *"Crazy business this, this life we live in.*
> *Can't complain about the time we're given.*
> *With so little to be sure of in this world, we had a moment..."*

He looks at me differently. "You *really* love his work, don't you? Then I think you have to see this."

And, like a kid revealing his stash of Pokemon cards, Patinkin brings out a trunk of memorabilia he has saved from the original 1984 production of Sondheim's *Sunday in the Park with George*, where he played the leading role of pointillist artist, Georges Seurat. Props, costume pieces, souvenirs — and a pile of drawing paper.

"Here's the sketches I made on stage every night," he enthuses, revealing a stack of papers that were pretty good portraits of Bernadette Peters, his leading lady. "I really tried to learn how to draw the best I could. I tried to do everything the best I could for Steve. That was such a magical show. ..."

Is there one memory he cherishes most clearly from the experience? He thinks for a second and nods fiercely.

"It was during the first workshop. I knew I was going to have a song in Act I about what the act of creation meant to Georges, and we all felt it had to be important. Maybe because of that, Steve felt blocked and couldn't write it.

"We actually went into previews without it, and then one morning, we got the word: Steve had the song. A few of us crowded into this tiny studio to hear it. The room was hot and I could see the sweat pouring down Steve's face, and then I realized it wasn't just sweat, but tears. This song meant so much to him. He finally finished it:

> *"Look, I made a hat,*
> *Where there never was a hat."*

And we were all crying. That's what the artist does. Makes us look at a hat, a song, the world in a different way. And that's why I love Steve's work so much."

In fact, he admits, "I use his lyrics and music to take you on a journey through my life and my experience. Steve has had a difficult troubled life, and I've had to struggle with my existence as well."

There's a bit of a pause, and then Patinkin whispers, almost as though betraying a confidence. "Once, we were discussing how fate really treats you horribly sometimes. Steve looked at me and said, 'You know how I feel about bad luck? Thanks, but no thanks, but thanks.'"

After decades of being considered an "elitist" taste, Sondheim is suddenly riding a wave of popular acceptance with numerous high-profile productions of his shows, and I ask Patinkin why he thinks the pendulum has swung regarding his hero.

"The public is starved for quality entertainment for their soul. All they seem to find is fast food and they want something more. Well, Steve has always served a dinner that nourishes you and has a taste that is indescribable."

He starts to sing a lesser-known song Sondheim wrote for *Do I Hear a Waltz?* with Richard Rodgers, infusing it with extraordinary feeling:

> *"Take the moment, let it happen.*
> *Hug the moment, make it last ..."*

The emotion fills the space between us. There's a long pause before Patinkin continues. "We're here, we're alive, we're survivors, and we're living in a very changed world."

What's the most important thing to him right now? "To say words that have to do with my beliefs and with my wishes for myself and for the world at that given moment in time. It doesn't matter if those words are in a song or in a play or on a TV show."

He talks briefly about his last, unsuccessful Broadway show, *The Wild Party*, insisting: "It was too dark, too dark for me in a way that didn't show the light. I don't mind showing darkness if the outcome is something that is illuminating, as long as it isn't too dark for my taste."

And since September 11, has the whole world grown too dark for Mandy Patinkin?

"No. It's a place that demands light more than ever now. The darker the world is, the more reason and need I have to fight that darkness, to fill it with light, and the stage is my battlefield."

Patinkin continues his amazing career. The summer of 2002 saw him unveil his one-man tribute to Stephen Sondheim at the Kennedy Center, where it received rave reviews.

He later brought it to Broadway where I was privileged to see it in December 2002. It was a performance like nothing I have ever witnessed: a seamless 90-minute simultaneous exploration of Stephen Sondheim's songs and Mandy Patinkin's soul.

We can only wait and see what he brings us next.

Sarah Brightman
Ron Bull/Toronto Star

SARAH BRIGHTMAN

Cleopatra Does the Classics

I had actually met Sarah Brightman once before when we sat down for this interview in November 2001, but I didn't think it wise to remind her of the circumstances.

It was the summer of 1989, and I was working as Hal Prince's assistant on the Toronto production of *The Phantom of the Opera*.

Shortly before rehearsals started, Brightman came to town with her then husband, Andrew Lloyd Webber, in a concert tour of his music.

I sat at the back of the theatre during an afternoon rehearsal, where Lloyd Webber was not pleased with what he heard and went ballistic, snatching music from the orchestra and vowing the show would never go on that night.

It did, and everything was fine. Brightman was shy, but gracious when I met her afterward, and seemed profoundly embarrassed by what had happened that afternoon.

I was reminded of the whole event 12 years later, when Brightman discussed how and why her marriage fell apart.

Sarah Brightman is to crossover classical music what Diana Krall is to jazz: a talented musician whose album art seems designed to sell sex along with singing.

Everyone had a field day discussing Krall's high heels and cleavage. Well, now it's time to turn to Brightman's electrified white hair and golden jewelled thong. The artwork that adorns the back of her CD, *Classics*, is sensational in every sense of the word, and that's just what the honey-voiced soprano intended: "As I listened to the music that makes up this collection again and again to try and capture the feeling I wanted to convey, I found it extremely sensual. So what came to mind actually was Botticelli's Venus. It's almost like she could have been in an opera when you look at her. She's ancient but there's something very contemporary about her, there's a vulnerability, she's incredibly female."

It almost sounds like Brightman is describing herself. She is perched on a sofa in her hotel suite, lithe and lovely, her cascading curls and black leather skirt making her resemble a stylish ebony exclamation point. Maturity has mercifully removed the over-abundant cheeks that led more than one critic to describe her as a chipmunk in her early days.

She's quite elegant now, with tanned skin and feline blue-green eyes, a combination that makes you wonder if that's what Cleopatra might have looked like.

One sure thing: the Queen of the Nile never sang like Brightman. Her current collection consists of selections from the classical repertoire she's embraced in recent years and the cool crystal of her voice runs like a mountain stream through selections that vary from "Ave Maria" to a new setting of Albinoni's "Adagio" called "Anytime, Anywhere."

"This is what I've always wanted to sing," she insists, sipping at room service tea and gingerly nibbling at a cookie as she sniffles her way through a cold, "even if it's taken me a long time to get here."

The 40-year-old Brightman has been a professional since she was 13, when she made her West End debut in a musical called *I and Albert*. Extensive dance and voice training followed, but by the time she turned 17, "I wanted to get out of school, and so I joined a kind of disco pop group."

It was called Hot Gossip and had one big hit: "I Lost My Heart to a Starship Trooper." Brightman laughs at the memory. "Oh, it was *very* fashionable, and we got on all the Top of the Pops kind of shows. The only trouble was none of the group could sing except me so they renamed us Sarah Brightman and Hot Gossip. It made me see how wonderful and horrible it could be at the same time."

The wonderful part "was the great fun we had, because, let's face it, there's a real immediate kick to being in a successful pop group. The acceptance, the buzz, all the trappings of celebrity that you dream of materialize in a flash, just like Cinderella's Fairy Godmother had waved her wand."

But the more enduring "horrible" side was "realizing how much you depended on having a hit single. I didn't feel safe with it." And when the group virtually proved to be a one-hit wonder, Brightman went into premature celebrity withdrawal. " It caught me off guard. It all happened so suddenly, the ups and the down. I didn't know where I was going to go or what I was going to do."

And so for nearly two years, she literally did nothing. "It was my desperate stage," she confides, lowering her eyes and looking like a high-fashion version of The Little Match Girl.

Finally, she answered an open call for auditions for a new musical called *Cats.* "When I walked in, they looked at me and said, 'Why are you here? You're a pop star.' I didn't have an agent or a manager or anything. I certainly didn't feel like a pop star. I felt like a total failure and I was only twenty."

But after six callbacks, she got the job, catching the eye (and ear) of composer Andrew Lloyd Webber. They were married in 1984 and divorced in 1990, but Brightman calls those six years "an amazing time. I know some people say I was his muse. I don't know if that was necessarily true, but I did get his mind into writing for a soprano."

The result, of course, was the role of Christine in *The Phantom of the Opera,* which she performed in London and New York, even though Lloyd Webber had to threaten to cancel the Broadway production when American Actors' Equity didn't deem Brightman a big enough star to be allowed to perform.

They capitulated and she opened the show, but "I always felt there was an enormous amount of resentment toward me. People thought I was only in the show because I was Andrew's wife, and that hurt me a great deal. I've only started to re-examine that period in my life recently, but I'm sure all that negativity helped to destroy our marriage."

She's reluctant to speak ill of her ex, but she will say that "Andrew is very controlling, of his work and of the people who perform it. When you're singing his music, it doesn't matter if you're his wife or not, you'd better hit the bloody notes to his satisfaction . . . or else."

Brightman left her marriage in 1990, and the musical theatre about three years later, finding them both a bit too confining.

"I started to realize I was just an instrument within a production, without being allowed to give much creative interpretation to the parts I was playing. I was working with tremendously talented people, but it began to feel like just a job."

And so she broke away from her security, went to Italy, and spent a year studying opera. "It was very difficult. People didn't want to accept me at first. They wanted me to stay a musical theatre star and that would have been the easy way out. It took a lot of courage and a lot of time and it was very scary."

The ramrod-straight back slumps a bit. "A lot of people laughed at me, and I'm not very good at responding to that kind of assault. So I just vanished inside my cocoon for a while, hoping I'd emerge as a stronger sort of butterfly."

The last laugh was Brightman's. Her albums have sold more than eight million copies, her concerts consistently draw huge crowds, and her TV specials are fundraising magnets on PBS.

"People like my music because it's peaceful. You don't exactly listen to it when you're running," she smiles. "Music is my strength, my centre. I'm proud of what I've accomplished, but I know I've got a long way to go. That's the beauty of music. With luck, I'll still be singing when I'm eighty."

One thing remains unanswered. Why the wild cascades of electrified white hair that adorn her head on the cover of *Classics*?

"This is my memory of things I've done and I thought about those collections of Jimi Hendrix songs they used to put together. They looked like that. It seemed the right thing to do."

Botticelli's Venus combined with Jimi Hendrix. Whoever said that Sarah Brightman wasn't full of surprises?

Brightman continues to record and tour to a large and devoted public.

To date, Lloyd Webber has never equalled the incredible success he knew with *Phantom* and *Cats*, while his most recent musicals — *Whistle Down the Wind* and *The Beautiful Game* — haven't even made the journey across the Atlantic.

His current marriage, however, seems to be a success. His wife's not a singer.

Nancy LaMott
Stephen Mosher

NANCY LaMOTT

The Girl with the Smile Like Bottled Sunshine

N ot everyone that I wrote about for the *Star* was famous —
but here's someone whom I wish had been given that gift.

When you read her story, it might remind you of Eva Cassidy
— a great song stylist dying in her prime before she reached the
mass audience she deserved.

The difference is that — because of legal wrangling after her
death between her manager and her family — LaMott's recordings were taken off the market and are now collectors' items.

That makes the following piece written in December 2000
even sadder.

> *"What's good about goodbye?*
> *What's fair about farewell?"*

Those lyrics by Leo Robin haunt me every December when I start
to think about the artists and friends who have left us over the
past 12 months. And when the calendar moves inexorably
toward the shortest day of the year — that time when it almost
looks as though the darkness might swallow up the sun — I find
myself dwelling on the memory of one absent friend in particular,
a great artist I felt very close to, although I only met her once.

Her name was Nancy LaMott, and December 13 marks the
fifth anniversary of her death.

Unless you're an aficionado of the New York cabaret scene, you've probably never heard of Nancy. She recorded five albums in her lifetime, plus one released after her death, and they were all on a small independent label called Midder Music.

How did I encounter her? By sheer chance. In December 1992, I was wandering through Tower Records near Lincoln Center in New York. Suddenly I heard a voice of unearthly purity and warmth singing "Moon River." I thought that no one could have made that song seem fresh again, but I stopped dead in my tracks at the depth and beauty of what I heard.

I asked a clerk who was singing; he told me and handed me a copy of her latest CD, a Johnny Mercer collection called *Come Rain or Come Shine*. Sensing a fan in the making, he told me it was her second CD, and also offered me a copy of her first, *Beautiful Baby*.

I didn't listen to either until I got home to Toronto. But once I began, I wanted to share her gift with the world.

Here was an artist who could fill a song to the brim with emotion and never spill a drop. No wanton excess for her, no shameless theatricality. Just what Jonathan Schwartz, one of North America's great connoisseurs of popular music, would call "a specific kind of generosity that only an honest woman can offer."

Soon after, I began playing Nancy LaMott on my CBC Radio program, and every time I did, the response was the same. People wanted to know who this lady was, and how they could hear more of her.

It was hard doing research on a woman who seemed to have spent most of her professional life within one square mile of Manhattan, but I persisted, and found out that her personal story added even more resonance to her work.

The child of a broken home in the American Midwest, Nancy's father ran a dance band on the weekends, and by the time she was 15, she was his singer.

Shortly after, she was diagnosed with the debilitating bowel disorder called Crohn's disease, and her adult life was spent struggling against pain and embarrassment. "It's hard to think of yourself as a sophisticated seductress," she told me on the one occasion we met, "when you have to perform sitting down."

But Nancy persevered, moving first to San Francisco, and then finally to New York, where she slowly but steadily made a name for herself in a series of cabarets no bigger than most people's living rooms.

Nancy's fans were growing. In Canada, she could number Brent Carver and Albert Schultz among her admirers, and in the States, the television types were starting to sit up and pay notice.

Then, in the spring of 1995, I picked up the *New York Times* one Sunday to notice that Nancy was performing at Tavern on the Green. I made a split second decision: I had to be there. Something was driving me to see her in person this time.

The next Saturday night found me sitting near ringside, gazing at this small blonde girl with a smile like bottled sunshine.

She had a wonderful way with patter, describing the combination of fairy lights and stuffed moose heads that adorned the room as "a gay hunting lodge."

But most importantly, she sang some songs she said she'd be recording in September, including one I'll never forget about the kind of love affair that was "Kisses and linguine, set to Mercer and Mancini."

And the older numbers in her repertoire seemed special too, as bright and newly minted as they had been on her recordings. She was the kind of gifted vocalist who realized that every time you sing a song has to be the first time.

After the show, I quietly slid forward and introduced myself to Nancy. Her eyes lit up: "You're the guy in Canada who keeps playing me on the radio! My relatives in Michigan told me all about you." We spent a few minutes in pleasant talk, she gave me a copy of her Christmas CD as a gift, and then I floated off into the soft Manhattan night.

What I didn't know then was that Nancy had just been diagnosed a month before with uterine cancer. She would delay the necessary operation until after she had recorded her last album, *Listen to My Heart*.

That delay proved fatal. At just the moment when her career was about to take off — with television deals, command performances at the White House and a quarter of a million dollars worth of contracts all waiting — it ended. Nancy died on December 13, 1995 at the age of 43.

But I still cherish her memory as well as that of all the other artists who depart this world too soon but leave behind the legacy of their work to console us and inspire us.

I'd like to think their message is the same one that ends the final song Nancy LaMott ever recorded: "Goodnight . . . don't be afraid."

A few weeks after this story appeared — on New Year's Eve, to be precise — the phone rang at my home.

"Is this Richard Ouzounian from the *Toronto Star?*" asked an elderly female voice. After admitting I was, she introduced herself as Nancy LaMott's stepmother. It seems that a friend of their family had been in Toronto on business the day my article appeared. He clipped it out and saved it until he saw the LaMotts again. Once they read it, they were moved to track me down.

"Nancy's father and I just wanted to thank you, because you brought our girl back to us again. Even though you only met her once, you knew just what she was like. 'The girl with the smile like bottled sunshine.' That was her."

II

THE COMEDIANS

Barry Humphries
David Cheskin/PA Photos

BARRY HUMPHRIES

Nothing Like the Dame

W as it two interviews for the price of one, or the other way around? In the fall of 2000, Barry Humphries and his alter ego, Dame Edna Everage, were about to start an extended North American tour with stops in Minneapolis and Toronto.

The gladioli-grasping Dame had never been shy of publicity, but her quieter half was quite another story.

I was offered an interview with Edna, and I agreed, but only on the condition that it be preceded by one with Humphries. After a great deal of bargaining, the parties agreed — if I would fly to Minneapolis.

And so, I found myself in Mary Tyler Moore's old sitcom home (yes, there's now a statue immortalizing her famous role as Mary Richards perched downtown). I was to meet Barry for morning tea, Edna just before her evening show.

It made for quite a day.

Barry Humphries has just about had it with Dame Edna Everage.

"That woman," he sighs to me, "with her tremendous arrogance and enormous vanity assumes of course that everyone is only too delighted to look at the world through her rhinestone-encrusted spectacles."

Well, it was bound to happen after 45 years.

They've been joined at the hip since that day in 1955 when

Humphries brought her on to the stage as part of a touring Australian revue called *Return Fare*.

Looking for something to amuse his fellow actors (who included Zoe Caldwell) while on tour, Humphries had developed a cloying Melbourne matron, "rather dowdy, mincing and coy, almost apologetic. Her preoccupations were those of the average Australian woman: family and home."

In that very first sketch, she discussed the billeting of athletes in her home for the upcoming 1956 Olympics, and simperingly vetoed all "Zulus, Serbs, Portuguese and Alsatians," concluding that "Aussies will do me fine."

Audiences embraced this strange woman instantly. "She was a *cri du coeur* of protest against the suffocation of suburban life. It was an overeducated priggish undergraduate having a go at his parents and their generation."

The 66-year-old Humphries smiles indulgently at the memory of the young man who invented Edna.

He sits on a grey Saturday morning looking out over the city of Minneapolis at the end of the first week of an eight-month North American tour. The Hilton Hotel's idea of tea (bags of Lipton and a carafe of tepid water) has been sent packing in favour of specially brewed coffee that Humphries' fourth wife Lizzie (daughter of British poet Stephen Spender) makes in the room.

As he offers me a cup, I study his face: ruddy, smooth, a few age spots, a bit of silver in the auburn hair that flops over his forehead as it has in every picture of him taken since the age of 16.

He could be a vigorous country squire, ten years younger, or at least that's how he's dressed: checkered tan sports coat, green corduroy trousers, pale silk tie.

The only nod (more of a wink) to who he really is rests in his lapel: a gold and rhinestone arrangement of gladioli, Dame Edna's trademark flower.

He's pleased at how things are going in Minneapolis — good reviews, packed houses, enthusiastic crowds — but he's anxious to move on to Toronto, where "I haven't been since 1962, when my beard fell off as Fagin during a performance of *Oliver!* at the O'Keefe."

Humphries had created the part of Sowerberry the Undertaker in the original London production, and also understudied Fagin for 18 months without ever going on. When the show moved to America, he wasn't invited to go along with it. But at the last minute, producer David Merrick (think Captain Kidd meets Garth Drabinsky) whisked Humphries secretly to Toronto. On arrival, Humphries was told that Clive Revill, who was playing Fagin, had developed laryngitis and Barry would have to go on in a part he'd never actually played.

"I walked on to that enormous stage as in a dream. I somehow pulled it off. I also, in a frenzy of compensatory overacting, pulled off my false beard, although it's unlikely the audience noticed this, since they seemed miles away."

Although he's spent very little time here, Humphries has had eclectic links to Canada over the years. Toronto actor Louis Negin played opposite him as the villainous Hugo Cretin in the 1974 film *Barry McKenzie Holds His Own*. Bruce Beresford, who was later to direct *Driving Miss Daisy*, could have called this film *Elevating Mrs. Everage*, because during one scene, Gough Whitlam (then Prime Minister of Australia) ad libbed the line "Arise, Dame Edna."

Humphries shakes his head at the memory of her cheekiness. "Edna appropriated the title and has ever since, although there have been many disputes as to its legality." He gets a bit of a faraway look in his eye. "That was when she began to get *folie de grandeur*, as you say in Canada."

Another Canadian from Humphries' past was author Elizabeth Smart. When I ask him about their friendship in the London of the Swinging Sixties, he repeats her name with a long slow exhalation. "Elizabeth . . . I haven't thought of her in years."

"She wrote that one wonderful book about her affair with George Barker."

Humphries is referring to *By Grand Central Station I Sat Down and Wept*. "He was a snake in the grass, a frightful, horrid fellow.

"When I met Elizabeth, she was still extremely attractive and very bright, but every evening she was drunk, very drunk. She lived in that alcoholic milieu in Soho, and her friends were all these people who could have gone on to much better things.

"She was working for *Queen Magazine* and she was one of the pioneer editors there. Her work was highly regarded. She would pull herself together every morning, and it was only in the evening that she went to pieces . . . "

Humphries glances down at his coffee cup. I remind him of another absent friend: Peter Cook, with whom he appeared as Envy in the original film of *Bedazzled*.

"Peter would sit watching television, smoking and drinking vodka all night. He wasn't self-destructive, but he had a kind of bemused contempt for life. It wasn't cynicism, it was a kind of jaunty despair. I don't know how else to describe it. It terrified me to witness his decline."

Humphries looks at me with moist eyes. "They're all dead now, except for little Dudley Moore, and he's so infirm." (Moore was to die in 2002.)

Barry Humphries survived, although at his worst, he outdrank all of them.

He still carries with him the memory of one night when he awoke in an unfamiliar hotel room next to a girl he didn't remember, looked at his watch and realized his show was supposed to have started 15 minutes earlier. He found his way to the theatre, "stumbled into the gaudy costume, burst on to the stage, and for the next two hours struggled for the forgiveness of laughter."

Thinking about it 30 years later, "it makes my flesh crawl."

He finally wound up in "a hospital for thirsty people" just before Christmas 1970. He took one last goblet of brandy and quoted Kafka: "Dear parents, I have always loved you all the same."

Humphries has been candid with other journalists up to this point, but he has never discussed his actual recovery, and I ask him what that period of his life was like.

"My recovery was a slow process, rather like my decline. Recovery is sort of decline in reverse. You know I hate the way showbiz people go on about how they've beaten this demon and conquered that one, because I never really think that one can conquer your demons. They're simply playing cards, quietly, waiting for you to beckon them again. They don't go away. They're always there. You just have to decide that life is much better lived without their assistance . . . or interference."

With sobriety came increased creativity, energy, and international stardom. There have been six wildly successful Dame Edna shows in London, two television series, and a sellout season on Broadway that was capped with a special Tony Award in 2000.

But, insidiously, Dame Edna has taken over. She used to be one of Humphries' many creations, now it's like a cable network: "All Edna, All The Time."

"She's appropriated the entire show," snaps an exasperated Humphries, "she's annexed the evening. There's no room for me or for anybody else."

More and more, in fact, she starts to sound like Humphries' mother, a woman who never missed a chance to twist the knife.

On his last trip home to Australia to see her, she was listening to a radio show as he walked in the door. "They were talking about what a bad picture of Australia I gave the world, and my mother looked up and said, 'You see, Barry, that's what they think of you.'"

"I felt helpless. Then I went into the other room. Dame Edna was there and she called the radio station. She said that they were right. Barry Humphries was a disgrace and she knew his mother agreed with her."

He looks up sadly, "That's the closest I ever came to telling her how I felt, and I had to go into another room and let Edna do it."

I ask him point-blank if Dame Edna is his mother. "In the old days I would strenuously deny it, but yes, of course there are parallels. The things I say, the things I do, that benediction of embarrassment that Edna bestows on the people. My mother's there. Yes, she's there."

I quote to him from Congreve:

> "She likes herself, yet others hates
> For that which in herself she prizes.
> And while she laughs at them, forgets
> She is the thing that she despises."

Humphries' hand flies up to the cluster of gladioli on his lapel. "Oh my God," he says, "that's her. You'll see when you meet her."

I didn't have to wait for long because a few hours later, I found myself hurrying through the Minnesota twilight for a date with the grandest Dame of all.

Dame Edna Everage
Vince Talotta/Toronto Star

DAME EDNA EVERAGE

Hunting for Possums

After spending a revealing day with Barry Humphries, I was eager to welcome in the night with Dame Edna.

For just over an hour, she ushered me around her backstage domain, dropping pearls of wit and wisdom — some of them unprintable. But never once did she drop out of character, or speak about Barry Humphries in any other way than the third person.

Some performances are so good that they're actually kind of frightening.

Like this one.

Dame Edna Everage has just about had it with Barry Humphries.

"The man's a total parasite. He's been taking credit for me and living off me for forty-five years, and I won't take it any more."

I vow not to mention Mr. Humphries again, because up to this point, Dame Edna has been charm itself.

She greeted me at the stage door of the State Theatre in Minneapolis, 90 minutes before a soldout Saturday evening performance. Presidential candidate Al Gore and rocker Marilyn Manson were both in town, but only Edna was packing the house.

I didn't know what to expect, but I was charmed by this willowy woman with lilac hair and matching rhinestone glasses. The purple day dress she was wearing revealed shapely calves, no bosom to speak of, and surprisingly broad shoulders. A kinder, gentler Mike Tyson.

She handed me a strange-looking flower, clucking her tongue. "As you can see," she murmured sadly, "it's mildly mutated. Very sad cases around Minneapolis of six-legged frogs and double-pronged gladioli."

Gladioli are very important to Dame Edna. At the end of every performance, she pelts the audience with dozens of them, and then exhorts them to wave them proudly in the air.

"People try to say the mimosa is the Australian national flower, but I hold out for gladioli. They've got a kind of optimism, an upright thrusting sensation." I look at Edna's face as she makes unmistakably phallic gestures with the gladioli. ("Flesh-coloured, my favourite.")

Her expression is totally innocent, and I begin to see how she gets away with saying some of the outrageous things she does onstage. ("You know why so few people take taxis here in the evening? It's hard to say, 'Get me to the State Theatre' in Somali.")

She weaves her arm through mine as we amble backstage to meet the technical crew, lined up docilely like schoolboys. "I want you to say hello to my wonderful team. Good evening, lads, are we looking forward to tonight?"

"Yes, Dame Edna," they respond in unison, and I wonder how many other stars could get hard-bitten union stagehands to stand at attention while she does her nightly rounds.

She leads me proudly onto the stage. "I want to show you something, Richard." I've learned another secret. She uses people's first names incessantly, almost like an incantation. It makes you feel special, included, loved by Edna.

"Look at this lovely theatre. Did you know that in 1989 the city council decided by only one vote to restore this theatre and not demolish it?"

Playing straight man, I ask her if she found that one voter and thanked him.

"No," she growls in her lower register, "but I'd like to find the others and thrash them."

The voice is a kind of harsh falsetto — but it has an intimate whispery quality that is irresistible. She confides in me: "A lot of people I could name but won't — and you can guess who they are, Richard — would tour North America with just a curtain and a spotlight. Not I."

"Look at this beautiful set." She points proudly to a painted assortment of lavender swirls that approximate a suburban Melbourne housewife's idea of heaven. "Oh, the money I pour into this!" Her voice goes up a notch. "My money, you hear, nothing from that cheapskate Barry Humphries."

Then without a beat, she changes back to Sweet Edna. "Look at this gilding, and these beautiful murals. Why is there an unhealthy eagerness to destroy buildings of this kind? Is it because they shame the more recent structures and make them look wretchedly imaginatively impoverished?"

I suggest that she's starting to sound a bit like Prince Charles. She giggles: "A close personal friend, bless his little heart."

I ask her about another personal friend, and the rumour that he might name her Saint Edna. She looks around suspiciously and then confides, "I can only tell you three things about him: he's single, he's Polish, he lives in Rome."

This gets Edna musing on bigger issues. "There have actually been a lot of approaches, Richard, for me to start my own religion. The Church of Edna. Everyone wearing diamanté eyeglasses and purple hair, coming to me for help, for healing. The cleaners tell me they find things abandoned on the floor after my show, a few neck-braces, the odd prosthetic device. I do what I can."

I ask her what the tenets of such a religion would be. "Caring, sharing, the sort of things I spread now. Not too much sweetness, not overly sentimental, and my ultimate code: putting oneself first. My wants. My needs."

I wonder what those needs are. "I think I'd like to be remarried." Her husband Norm passed away from "a prostate murmur" in the late '80s. "Oh, Richard, the offers I've received! Well, if I had to pick one of the men I've met, it would probably be Charlton Heston. He could part my Red Sea anytime he liked. But that gun fetish of his, well, that would probably ruin it."

She sweeps into the box office, instantly going up to a young couple who are having trouble finding seats. Edna takes a liking to them and gets them in.

"You're an attractive young woman. You remind me of Meryl Streep. A bit more personality than little Meryl, though. You know what I mean, she sits so quietly in her films, just twitching away."

Another box office employee hopes Edna will keep her health up. "I'm doing fine, dear, I've found a lovely masseur here named Earl. He's blind and black. It's kind of like having Ray Charles work on you."

She pauses at the door asking the staff if they've noticed that "the audience are happy when they leave my show." They all agree and she sighs. "Isn't it amazing the ability I have to bring this joy to people?"

As she sweeps back toward the stage, I ask her how she feels about having aced her competition. "Marilyn Manson, hah! So much for your shock rockers! Only here for one pathetic night, while Dame Edna fills two whole weeks, possum."

And what about Al Gore, then in the final days of his doomed campaign against George W. Bush? She lowers her voice. "On the whole, I think he's the preferable person. People who know him say when he's not making a political speech, he's actually quite bright."

But then she shakes her head. "Oh Richard, America has this enormously cumbersome elephantine system to find the best person to rule the most powerful country the world has ever known, and then they produce these two non-events."

It's time for her moments of solitude before the show. "A vocal warmup, a physical warmup, just a little nip of coffee. Don't want the central nervous system going berserk."

Then she's gone, and I find my seat in the theatre. That night's show is truly hot. Edna is on with a vengeance, and the Minneapolis audience laps up every insult about their weight, their clothing, their houses, their local personalities. She even "outs" a local TV weatherman, to the delight of the crowd.

Edna can do no wrong tonight, and she knows it. At one point the hilarity gets so out of hand that even her piano player and chorus girls lose control, slipping into helpless laughter.

While she waits for it to subside, Edna turns it to her advantage. "You see, possums? I wouldn't insult you with a rehearsed show."

As we crested from one wave of manic hilarity to another, I thought of a memory Barry Humphries had shared with me that morning.

"The first comic I ever remember was an old chap by the name of Tommy Trinder. I'd never seen anyone hold a crowd like that, make them laugh as one. And when he had them in the palm of his hand and you thought they couldn't laugh any more, he'd shout out his catchphrase, 'You lucky people!' and off they'd go again. That's what I want to do, give them a good time."

He certainly did. But one thing I won't forget from that night is the opening number, where Edna dispenses gobs of her own mother's advice to the crowd.

The only thing is, I couldn't tell whose mother was being evoked — Dame Edna's or Barry Humphries' — when the song got to the lines:

> *"That low self-esteem*
> *And now I'm gonna call the shots, it's true.*
> *So look at me, possums,*
> *When I'm talking to you ..."*

During Edna's subsequent sellout run in Toronto, I became quite friendly with her (and with Humphries, of course) and neither one of them ever admitted they might possibly be the same person, even off the record.

Going out to dinner with Humphries after his final Toronto performance, he spoke of how "I shall miss this city, and I believe Edna will too." At one point, when another guest crossed the line by asking him, "How do you throw those gladioli so far out into the audience?" Humphries regarded him frostily and said, "That is something you'll have to ask Edna."

Nia Vardalos
AP/World Wide Photos

NIA VARDALOS

Miracles Happen

Don't you love happy endings? The come-from-apparently-nowhere success of Nia Vardalos was one of the most joyous show business stories of recent years.

But, in the spirit of full disclosure, I have to confess a certain vested interest in her career.

Back in the 1980s, I was the artistic director of the Manitoba Theatre Centre in Winnipeg, and every season I gave a scholarship to someone from the city who wanted to pursue a career in the theatre.

One year it went to Nia Vardalos, and she used it to go to Ryerson Theatre School in Toronto.

I have to confess that I forgot that fact totally until nearly 20 years later, when Nia came up to me at the L.A. opening of *Mamma Mia!* By that time, *My Big Fat Greek Wedding* had been picked up by Tom Hanks and Rita Wilson, but they hadn't even set a filming date.

When we met, I certainly knew who Nia was, and offered my congratulations on how well her project had gone so far.

"I've been meaning to catch up with you for years," she said, and instantly I wondered what I had done. "You gave me that scholarship back in Winnipeg, and that's how my career got started. I would never have done it without you."

Is it any wonder I wanted to spend some time with her in New York in December 2002 to report on the story of a person who deserved every bit of the success that the showbiz gods had seen fit to shower on her?

It's been a big fat wonderful year for Nia Vardalos.

People magazine named her one of the "25 Most Intriguing People of 2002." *Entertainment Weekly* placed her No. 4 on its "Entertainers of the Year" list. She has just snagged two Golden Globe nominations and Oscar buzz is in the air.

All of this thanks to *My Big Fat Greek Wedding*. Vardalos starred in the movie (as well as adapting it from her original stage play), which has currently grossed more than US$215 million, making it the most successful independent film of all time, with a spin-off CBS television series called *My Big Fat Greek Life* going into production next month.

The runaway triumph of this film has alerted the studios to the fact that they better keep their eyes and ears open, because nobody can predict where the next big fat thing may come from. It's the kind of Cinderella story everybody loves, especially when the gal in question is a 40 year old from Winnipeg who wouldn't be caught dead in a glass slipper.

Gucci boots are another thing, however, and she peels off a pair of them in the back seat of the limo that's racing her to the airport. "I'm not wearing these on a flight to the coast," she announces, slipping into a pair of running shoes. "My feet would never forgive me."

Vardalos may be the Girl of the Hour, but there are only 24 hours in the day, and she's having "an incredibly crazy time" trying to crowd everything in.

I ask her to catalogue what she has on her plate for the day surrounding our conversation, and the answer is mind-boggling.

"Okay, I flew into New York yesterday, had four interviews with the foreign press, got my hair done, taped *The David Letterman Show*, had dinner, came back to my hotel, wrote a scene for my new TV series, watched myself on Letterman, and slept.

"Then I got up at seven, more interviews, taped an episode of

The View, hopped into this car, and started talking to you. After this, a conference call with Universal about my next movie, fly to L.A., go home, change, and show up at the premiere of *About Schmidt* tonight. Don't you love Jack Nicholson?"

All of this bubbles forth with the joy of a kid describing her plans for a day at Disney World, but that has been the glorious part about Vardalos' success. It hasn't changed her — except to make her even happier.

It has been such a head-spinner of a year that I nudge her back to last January 1 to recall how it began.

"Oh God, let me think!" she sighs, going back to a time when "I didn't have to sign autographs every time I went to the mall to buy underwear.

"Okay, I remember. I woke up and made my resolution that I was going to take singing lessons. Then Ian and I ate some left-overs and hung out around the house."

Ian is her husband, actor Ian Gomez, and it's the saga of their courtship and marriage that drives *My Big Fat Greek Wedding*.

"Of course, it's all true," insists Vardalos, "except the stuff I left out because it's so outrageous no one would have believed it."

Actually, the whole arc of her life story has such a storybook feel to it that it's hard to imagine it really happened.

She was born in Winnipeg on September 24, 1962, one of four children, and named after her grandmothers, Antonia and Eugenia. A scholarship from the Manitoba Theatre Centre gave her the opportunity to study at Ryerson in Toronto, after which she fell into the assortment of odd jobs and soul-shrivelling gigs that are the fate of most young performers.

"Dinner theatre," she says with a shudder. "I did enough bad dinner theatre for several lifetimes . . . several very scary lifetimes."

But then, here's the key to the Vardalos mindset: she even finds something worthwhile in that experience. "Hey, but I'm finally getting to use all that in my next movie, and this time, it's going to be fun."

She's talking about the recently announced movie *Connie and Carla*, which she will write, star in, and executive produce for Universal.

The story of two girls in dinner theatre who have to go undercover as drag queens, Vardalos describes it as "*Some Like It Hot* meets *Tootsie*. It's a buddy movie, but not a chick flick. I like to make films that guys don't have to squirm through."

After those dinner-theatre days, she found herself trying to break into the dream home of all young comics, Second City.

There were no vacancies on stage, but the resourceful Vardalos took a job at the box office, making sure that "I watched the show every night and knew every minute of it." When a cast member was rushed to the hospital just before curtain time one evening, she jumped in and scored such a success that she stayed with the company for two years.

After that, she moved to the Chicago home of the comedy troupe, where she stayed until 1994. During that time, she met Gomez, who was also a member of Second City.

"I got very lucky," confides Vardalos, still very much in love. "I married the one ego-less actor in the world. He's the only child of only-child parents. He hates any publicity. When people run after me for my autograph, he says, 'Hey, I'll be at Starbucks.'"

The crazy courtship documented in the movie ensued and they wound up getting married on September 5, 1993, at St. Demetrios Greek Orthodox Church in Winnipeg "before several thousand of my most intimate family and friends," she quips.

Shortly after that, they left the security of Second City and moved to Los Angeles to better their careers.

Gomez did well almost immediately, landing the recurring part of Larry Almada on *The Drew Carey Show* for five seasons (1995–2000), overlapping with the featured part of Javier Clemente Quintata in *Felicity* from 1998 to 2002.

But Vardalos had a tougher time. Her unquenchable optimism sags a bit as she remembers those days.

"I felt so incredibly invisible in Los Angeles because I wasn't twenty-two and skinny. Casting agents were always telling me I was too old, not old enough, too ethnic, not ethnic enough. I was everything except what they wanted."

She has no trouble recalling one of the worst moments. "One woman said to me, 'Look, honey, you've got a greater chance of getting hit by lightning or breaking the bank in Vegas than making it in Hollywood.'"

How did she take that advice? "I told her that the first two things hadn't happened to me, so maybe the third one would."

And then she set about making it happen. "Everybody told me my stories about my family were funny, and so I started with them. I borrowed a computer from a friend and began writing them down."

She tried out bits and pieces at the HBO Workspace, and put together a screenplay and a sitcom pilot about her experiences, but no one was interested. (Remember this later . . .)

So, desperate to get her material seen, she turned into a one-woman stage show, which opened in 1998 at the Hudson Theatre in L.A. and was so successful it moved to the Globe Theatre for a four-month run.

"Lots of producers came to see it and wanted to turn it into a movie, but not with me. 'This would be great if we changed it to a Hispanic family and cast Jennifer Lopez.' I just kept saying no. I knew I had something special here."

Fortunately, Rita Wilson felt the same way.

The Greek-American wife of Tom Hanks saw the show and fell in love with it, persuading her husband to check it out. He agreed with his wife and called Vardalos a few days later to say he wanted to turn it into a movie — with her starring in it.

"He phoned while I was on the treadmill. Between the exertion and the excitement, I nearly fainted." They signed a deal soon after.

The movie was shot in 2001 in Toronto, and "we all had a

great time doing it." Her parents, Gus and Doreen, even wound up (along with many other friends and relatives) as extras in the wedding scene.

But nobody really knew what they had.

For Vardalos, she thought the high point was going to be "the Los Angeles premiere on April 19. I had forty-nine of my relatives there, and I deliberately sat behind them so I could see their reaction. I watched their heads bobbing up and down with happiness. That was the most satisfying thing. I thought, 'I don't care what else happens. My family loves the movie.'"

Fortunately, a lot of other people loved it as well. "Around May, people started asking me for my autograph. I thought for sure my parents had sent them over. 'Here's ten bucks, go ask my kid for her autograph.'

"But then we got to June . . . I had strangers from every possible type of mixed marriage coming up to tell me their story and I knew we had crossed a line."

By the July 4 weekend, the film had grossed $20 million (all figures US), and Hanks said to her, "Enjoy this — it doesn't happen very often."

Then it went through the roof. By October 4, it had grossed $148 million, passing the record set by *The Blair Witch Project* and earning it the top-grossing spot in independent-film history.

And the very next week, she had dinner with Queen Elizabeth in Winnipeg, who said she could relate to Vardalos' story, because "Well, you know, Philip *is* Greek . . . "

When the movie passed the $200-million mark, Hollywood started wondering if "the little film that could" might be an Oscar contender.

"Sure I'm being buzzed about it," admits Vardalos. "In fact, my friends keep sending me e-mails that just say 'Buzzzzzzzzzz.' Look, lots of people live their whole lives and never even get this close. I am so lucky."

She willingly admits that she enjoys what sudden celebrity has done to her life. "I talk to lovely people who start sentences with 'I love you.' Anybody who thinks that's not great, well then, it isn't for them."

One wistful note hints at how tough the tough years were for her, when she says, "Now it's parties and fun and people are nice to me for a change."

The limousine is pulling into the airport, so I ask her how she plans to end this incredible year.

"I'll be in Toronto. My sister Marianne, who's a professor at Humber, has had a big fat Greek baby, and I've got to check it out. And on New Year's Eve, Ian and I are going to hang out with our two best friends in the world, Kathryn Greenwood and her husband, John Dolan. We'll drink a bottle of wine in their back-yard and be grateful."

I end with the question that has been on everyone's mind since the film has made such an enormous success. Why does she think so many people have adopted her story?

"Because I'm out here pulling for everybody. I'm just a normal person, but if I can make it, then why not you? Things happen. Miracles happen."

The miracles continued to happen — for a while.

Vardalos got her Oscar nomination (for Best Screenplay), even if she didn't win, and *My Big Fat Greek Life* went on the air for CBS in March 2003.

Then her former agent filed a lawsuit and her series was abruptly cancelled in May 2003 amidst rumours of Vardalos having grown increasingly difficult to work with.

Only time will be able to write the ending to this story.

Andrea Martin
AP/World Wide Photos

ANDREA MARTIN

Edith Prickley Gets Real

When I first met Andrea Martin in 1973, she was very disappointed.

She was acting at the Charlottetown Festival and heard that I was coming to pay some friends a visit, so she told them to make sure we were introduced to each other.

At a post-show party, she seemed distracted during a conversation I kept trying to engage her in, and she finally said, "Excuse me, but I'm waiting for Richard Ouzounian."

I told her that I *was* Richard Ouzounian, and her jaw fell. The Armenian Martin was hoping I was another *haygagan* (fellow countryman).

Despite my ethnic name, my blond hair and blue eyes indicated that I wasn't exactly a purebred Armenian. (In fact, I was a Scotch-Irish kid adopted by an Armenian-Italian-Finnish family.)

Martin got over her initial disappointment, and we met many times over the next three decades, but it wasn't until May 2002 that we actually got a chance to sit down and have a real conversation.

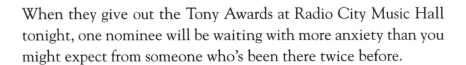

When they give out the Tony Awards at Radio City Music Hall tonight, one nominee will be waiting with more anxiety than you might expect from someone who's been there twice before.

Andrea Martin is best known as one of the stars of *SCTV*, and, in fact, she won a star on the Walk of Fame along with the rest of the cast last week for her involvement in that beloved comedy series.

That would make an exciting enough week for most performers, but Martin is also nominated for a Tony Award for Best Supporting Actress in a Musical for her role as Aunt Eller in the Broadway revival of *Oklahoma!* It's a category she's familiar with, having won it in 1993 for *My Favorite Year* and having been nominated again in 1997 for *Candide*.

But this time it's not quite the same. Her life and her acting have both changed in the past few years, and now the stakes are considerably higher. After 25 years of being everybody's favourite featured funny lady on stage, screen, and television, Martin has broken new and serious ground with her performance in *Oklahoma!*, and it makes this Tony nomination more important to her.

"It's a different emphasis, I think," says Martin, feeling her way with a bit of caution around the issue as she picks at a plate of arugula and sliced rare steak. "I'm doing something I've never really done before. I'm not just trying to be funny. I'm trying to be real."

We're sitting in Orso, a popular celebrity dining spot in the heart of the theatre district. Elaine Stritch is a regular here (she always asks for a doggy bag), as are the likes of Vanessa Williams and Bernadette Peters.

Yet the chorus of admiring waiters treat Martin like the superstar, smiling as they offer her mineral water, balsamic vinegar, and ground pepper.

There's something about this diminutive woman that attracts people. She doesn't look anywhere near her 55 years, with a cascade of auburn curls and those molasses-drop eyes that light up at the slightest hint of fun.

She'd prefer to be chuckling at some Toronto show-business gossip or swapping stories about her alumni buddies from the

SCTV days, but she knows that she has to talk about the Tonys, and so she sighs, nibbles at a piece of bread and continues.

"The first time I was nominated I was such a novice that I had no expectations at all. The show (*My Favorite Year*) had been closed for six months, and I was back living in L.A., so I wasn't part of the craziness. I just flew in for the awards, and when I won, it was like — 'Wow, what hit me?'"

"The second time (*Candide*), I didn't really believe I was going to win, because it wasn't a good enough performance in a good enough show." Martin is nothing if not candid. She giggles slightly, remembering her reverse arrogance. "I didn't even write an acceptance speech."

"But this time," she says, putting down her fork, "it's a bit more weighted. I'd love to be validated for doing a part that's different from all the other things I've ever done."

That's what's changed this time around. For the first time in a 30-year career that has had its share of awards (two Emmys for *SCTV* writing to put next to that Tony), Martin is playing a role that's more serious than comic. Sure, her Aunt Eller can still provoke the theatre-filling belly laughs when necessary, but the core of the character is in earnest, and that's something new for Martin.

"All the comedy I've done until now has been in a performance mode, which is exterior rather than interior. That doesn't mean my heart hasn't been in it, but it's been rooted in the externals. I'd like to integrate every part of me."

Martin reached this decision two years ago after taking a long, hard look at her career. On the surface, it was a career that many people would envy.

The Portland, Maine, native followed a boyfriend to Canada in 1972 and soon found herself starring in the Toronto production of *Godspell* along with the likes of Victor Garber, Gilda Radner, and Paul Shaffer.

Two more of her fellow cast members, Martin Short and Eugene Levy, would later join her when she became part of the wildly popular comedy series *SCTV*, which kept reinventing itself in various forms from 1976 to 1984.

Martin's characterizations from those years remain memorable: the snorting, leopard-clad Edith Prickley, the adenoidal Edna Boil, the unctuous Libby Wolfson are all part and parcel of modern comedy.

But after *SCTV*, Martin kept being the gal you brought in for quick comedy zaps. Whether she was hawking paper towels on TV or adding some zing to a long-run comedy series like *Kate & Allie*, she was always, somehow, on the edge of it all, never really hitting it big.

"My career wasn't going where I'd hoped it would have gone," Martin's eyes grow even wider as she opens up with the truth. "I kept busy all the time, but it was a lot of funny voice work, or those comedy cameos where you make everyone laugh for a few minutes in a movie and then you're gone. Nothing of any substance."

The plate of steak and salad is only half finished, and that's how it's going to remain as she gets down to serious business.

"It's so easy to blame other people for not seeing you the way you believe you should be seen. I have so many fans — in and out of the industry — everybody says they love my work. Then what was the problem? I didn't believe I could do it. I didn't believe I'd be interesting if I really came from my heart."

So she turned to someone for help — one of Hollywood's best-known acting coaches named Larry Moss. This was the man who coached both Hilary Swank and Helen Hunt on their Oscar-winning performances, so he obviously knows what he's talking about.

Still, Martin was scared. "I'd never taken an acting lesson in my life, but I went to him and said, 'I want to turn my career around.'"

The advice Moss offered was drastic and direct: "Get into therapy to discover who you are, stop performing for a year, turn down every role, and come to my acting class."

Martin followed his advice, and the first big hurdle that came her way when the year was up was *Oklahoma!* "I had to audition for it three times," she admits with a bit of a blush. "(Choreographer) Susan Stroman and (producer) Cameron Mackintosh wanted me right away, but (director) Trevor Nunn wasn't sure. He didn't know anything about me."

Her jaw sets in that prairie-gal way that makes her Aunt Eller so endearing. "I worked so hard on it. I was so determined. I went in with my tail between my legs, with humility, determined to get to the truth of the role."

And it worked, although Martin concedes that Nunn "wasn't really sure when he gave me the part. Only in previews did I convince him. It was a challenge, but in the end, he was happy."

So were the New York critics, who hailed the warmth of her performance. And certainly the woman who sits on a bench sharing life truths with her orphaned niece, Laurey, is light years removed from the world of Edith Prickley.

"When Laurey says, 'I wish I could be like you,' I answer, 'Fiddlesticks! Scrawny and old, you couldn't hire me to be the way I am.' I think about how much of her life she has ahead of her, and I think of how much of my own life has gone by. Oh, I certainly know what it's like to be getting old and afraid of dying."

The other thing Martin understands is the character's struggle to keep going against all odds, which is rooted in her Armenian heritage. Her grandfather's last name was Papazian, and he fled Turkish oppression in the early 1900s to settle in America.

"I had nine Armenian friends who came to see the show last week," Martin reveals, "and when they were there, I found myself near tears for most of the performance, thinking about the survival mode that everybody has to be in who calls themselves Armenian."

Right now, she is content with her life and work. "It all feels integrated. That's the great thing."

She's even come to terms with the lasting success of *SCTV*, which actually bothered her for many years. "For a long time I fought it, because I thought, 'Is that all I could do? Don't you think I'm more than Edith Prickley?' But now, because I've proven to myself I can do other things, I'm delighted that it still makes people so happy."

Why does she feel the series is still so popular after 25 years? "The simplest answer is that it was funny then, and it's still funny now because it's timeless. And we had fun doing it. There was no pretension about it, and people like that."

She asks the waiter to pack up her remaining steak ("If it's good enough for Elaine Stritch, it's good enough for me") and talks about the future.

She's got a nice featured role in an independent comedy made by Canadian Nia Vardalos called *My Big Fat Greek Wedding*, which has just opened to encouraging response.

"It's a sweet little film," enthuses Martin. "Warm, funny, nice. I hope lots of people go to see it."

And the Stratford Festival has tried to lure her back (she hasn't been there since *Private Lives* and *Candide* in 1978) to play the lead in *Hello, Dolly!*, but so far, the timing just hasn't been right.

"I'd love to do it, though, so I hope they ask me again."

But for now, she's a Broadway Baby, with her eyes on the prize.

It's strange how show business fate works.

Martin didn't win the Tony Award, but that "sweet little film" she was in, *My Big Fat Greek Wedding*, proved to be the monster hit of the year, grossing over $250 million and breaking all box office records for an independent movie.

Of course it led to a television series, *My Big Fat Greek Life*, and since Nia Vardalos took as many people from the film as she could with her, that's where Martin is currently (and happily) employed.

Mark McKinney
Diane Bondareff

MARK McKINNEY

The Kid Is All Right

B ack in the 1990s, a certifiable group of lunatics called *The Kids in the Hall* went a long way to changing the face of comedy in Canada, with their outrageous characters and non-linear sketches.

They finally exploded, like the atom, sending particles into the comedy world all around North America.

Mark McKinney was probably the sanest of the bunch, and (while never totally abandoning the world of sketch comedy) he carved out a career for himself in the theatre.

I caught up with him in New York, a week after 9/11: an event that we both agreed not to discuss in the interview.

But that's about the only thing we didn't talk about.

People have been saying for years that Mark McKinney should be committed.

Well, it's finally going to happen.

Best known for being one of the kids in *The Kids in the Hall*, McKinney is about to make his Toronto legit debut in *Fully Committed* — an off-the-wall comedy that has already proved a smash hit in New York, San Francisco, and Los Angeles.

He plays Sam, a phone reservations clerk in one of New York's hottest four-star restaurants. He also brings to life 40 other characters in that restaurant's world, from the psychotic maître d' to Naomi Campbell's stressed personal secretary.

It's a comic tour de force, and McKinney certainly has all the right stuff to pull it off, because playing an assortment of nutbars is right up his street. "The thing you've got to remember," he assures me, "is that comedians are shape-shifters."

Well, McKinney certainly knows what he's talking about, because in the course of a 90-minute chat over a couple of cranberry-and-sodas at Joe Allen's (the theatre district's hangout of choice), McKinney must have easily morphed into two dozen distinct personalities.

That's only to be expected from this 42-year-old sketch-comedy veteran of five seasons with *The Kids in the Hall* and two and a half years on *Saturday Night Live*.

But doing it "live from New York" onstage, eight times a week, is something he's only gotten into during the past four years. When he decided to leave SNL in 1997, he could have headed out to La La Land like so many of the show's alumni, but he chose to remain in Manhattan.

And before you could blink, he was headlining classy comedies by Georges Feydeau and Richard Brinsley Sheridan in organizations as reputable as the Roundabout Theatre and the Williamstown Festival. Last year, the *New York Times* profiled him as "one of the top-flight comic actors on the New York stage."

Pretty good for a guy who flunked out of Memorial University in Newfoundland at 19 and thought his life was just about over.

"I'll tell you something," says McKinney after a robust swig of his drink, "if you make two smart decisions in your life, then you're ahead of the game. After I left SNL, I went 'Oh, do I go to L.A.?' and I thought, 'No, I'll stay in New York and do theatre.'"

Okay, that was one smart decision. What was the other?

"When I said to myself, 'You know what? Maybe I've finally got to leave the piano shop.'"

McKinney wasn't speaking just metaphorically. He actually did support himself for a while by refurbishing old instruments at the Foothills Piano Shop in Calgary, and it was the last full-time job he held before deciding to make his living in show business.

But he had to travel around the world before he got there.

Mark Douglas Brown McKinney was born in Ottawa in 1959. His father was a diplomat, which meant (as McKinney now sourly admits) "that we were travelling around all the time. It made me feel like a dislocated kid. It got tough. I was kind of neurotic, because there weren't a lot of explanations in those days."

And instantly, McKinney becomes his father, a career foreign service man whose lips never move when he talks.

"'Well kids, here we are in Trinidad, and now we're moving to Paris.' 'Okay, Dad.'"

McKinney's eyes gleam wickedly. "In retrospect, I guess he was posted there at a very propitious time for me in terms of this play. See, there I was in Paris from ages ten through thirteen, a time of great sensual awakening — which is usually sexual, but in my case it was food. I was a very adventurous eater, but I kept my North American roots."

Another McKinney character — this time a silicone-smooth French headwaiter — instantly comes to life: "Here is the young monsieur's *escargot bourguignon* and his chocolate milk."

I ask him if he now views himself from those days as a character.

"Very much so," he readily agrees. "A multicultural, utterly enthusiastic, socially inept nerd with his nose pressed against the glass. Kind of like Darill."

McKinney has just invoked one of his most esteemed comic creations — the Belgian dingbat, with slicked-back hair, leather jacket, and string tie, whose mouth usually hangs open wide enough to catch field goals.

He snaps into the character, waits for the laugh of recognition, and then slides back into McKinney, twisting the knife on himself.

"I think people gave up on me after a while. They tried sending me to all kinds of schools." He looks around and becomes a

Brooklyn wise guy with salacious information to disperse. "I even went to a boarding school in Port Hope. Nothing worked. I finally finished high school at night. I just wasn't a very good student."

His nostrils flare with disapproval, and he transforms himself into a chagrined Rockcliffe matron. "I mean, he wasn't going to be attending the Sorbonne . . . "

McKinney looks down at his drink and volunteers some self-analysis. "I didn't want to be a failure. I like certain things about success, but I lacked the fundamental discipline. I was really well read . . . but once they started adding letters to math, my future fell apart."

His next step was to go off to Memorial University in Newfoundland. Why? "Because I'd read *The Razor's Edge*" — Somerset Maugham's novel about journeying to Tibet in search of self-knowledge — "but that was as far away as I could get with the money I had."

When he got out there, he was supposed to be studying politics and economics ("I still thought I was going to be prime minister," he says in his best Pierre Trudeau imitation), but he wound up doing funny voices on the campus radio station and trying some really bad comedy.

"I had thought about me in the arts before, but always in a very Darillian way. You know, it's all out there," he waves his hand somewhere in the general direction of Corner Brook, Newfoundland, "and it's all about wisdom that must be received. I totally missed the point that it was supposed to be about self-expression."

"So I'd do stand-up, and I'd bomb and bomb and bomb again. I'd go out there with notes, for God's sake, with jokes the audience couldn't relate to. With material borrowed from *The Tonight Show*." He shivers at the memory. "I had no comic vision of myself."

And no academic vision, either. "I flunked out, and that was the end of that track. There was no going home." This time there's no humorous imitation of parental distress, just an embarrassed silence.

I look at McKinney in the pause. He strikes one as the kind of guy you'd like to have sitting next to you at a Parents' Night — warm, friendly, bright, capable of getting off a few good jokes. His slightly unkempt sandy hair and wire-rimmed glasses amplify the impression of a hip suburban dad who just happens to be a star.

He orders another drink and continues the story. "I had to work, so I went out to Calgary and then I wandered into the Loose Moose Theatre, which was a great place with a great artistic director, Keith Johnstone. You could walk in one day and the next day find yourself up on the stage."

So together with his buddy Norm Hiscock (now a senior producer on TV's *King of the Hill*) he plunged into the world of improvisation. "My early improvs made all the mistakes — unfunny, physically violent, scatological, every scene ending with a murder, but Keith was a real Pied Piper, we all worshipped him, and after a while I started getting better."

He also joined up with a certifiably demented young comic named Bruce McCulloch. "Back then, Bruce would do stuff like stick his head in a bucket and paint the stage. Naturally we started working together . . . "

By 1983, they were on the top of the heap as far as the Calgary comedy scene went, and so "we thought we've got to hit the big time, Toronto!"

But for a while, things were lean. "Splitting a basement apartment on Jarvis, temp mail-clerking just long enough to go on unemployment. I even worked at the Second Cup. I liked that."

McCulloch and McKinney joined up with another group called *The Kids in the Hall*, which featured Kevin McDonald and Dave Foley. "And after a while," McKinney recalls, "Scott (Thompson), well Scott just crashed the party and joined us."

The group soon became big, in that selling-out-midnight-shows-at-the-Ritz kind of way, and they drew the eye of the talent scouts from *Saturday Night Live*.

The upshot was that McKinney and McCulloch were hired, but as writers.

"It was a very bad year. It was the Robert Downey Jr. year. It was an object lesson in showbiz. Here we were in Toronto doing very hot great work, and then we went down to New York, sitting opposite Madonna, and everything fell apart."

But Lorne Michaels was impressed enough to put all *The Kids in the Hall* into development, and they finally hit the TV screen (courtesy of CBC and HBO) in the fall of 1989.

Five years of blissful comic anarchy followed. Everybody has favourite sketches from those shows, but if you asked most people to pick one McKinney character, it would be The Headcrusher — that dyspeptic geezer with an ersatz Polish accent who squeezes his fingers together while intoning the mantra "I'm crushing your head."

McKinney remembers the moment of creation perfectly. "I was with Kevin in the Atrium, Dundas and Bay, at one of Toronto's first café au lait shops, you know with the four-dollar butter tarts and stuff like that. We didn't really have enough money to go there, but we did anyway.

"I remember looking at all the Yuppies zooming in and out, and I was just sitting there saying 'Look at those bastards, they make so much fuckin' money, and we can't even pay for this hot chocolate. I'm crushing their heads. I'm crushing your head.'"

He goes from Mark McKinney to The Headcrusher without shifting a gear and it is hilarious and frightening at the same time.

After five seasons, the Kids finally split up amid rumours of great acrimony.

"When did the stress start? Oh, from the very beginning. Bruce and I screamed at each other the very first time we ever met. We were just young guys without guile or agendas criticizing each other's sketches cruelly, cruelly."

"Kevin and Dave weren't used to working that way, but they got into it, and Scott was, well, Scott. It was like that all the time. It was never 'Oh, that Dark Tuesday when it all fell apart!' It fell apart for five years."

So they went their separate ways, and McKinney moved down to New York to become a cast member on SNL, taking along Darill and The Headcrusher and other pet creations.

"I went in there thinking I could just continue doing my thing. I should've realized it was different, and that having a kid could be so distracting."

Yes, from *Kids in the Hall* to kids on the lap. McKinney married Marina Gharabegian in September 1995, and their son Christopher was born the next year. Their daughter Emma came along in July 2000.

"I always knew doing SNL was a grind. You go there to become a star and then move on. I was out of synch. So Lorne and I finally agreed that I should leave. It was mutual."

He appeared in a variety of largely unsuccessful films that he's quick to mock: *Brain Candy* ("I never thought it would tank that badly"), *Dog Park* ("My Genie Award-winning triumph"), and *Spice World* ("Let's not forget the classics").

Then he began doing theatre and "from the second I started, I loved the whole experience. The going to rehearsal every morning. Apples and soup for lunch. The kinder, gentler Mark." He raises an eyebrow in self-mockery. "I loved getting on the subway and going down to Times Square to do a show. How is it different from what I had been doing? It's a little friendlier . . . "

I realize that the closer we get to the present, the more McKinney has been talking without benefit of his other voices and characters. "I like this kind of work. I like my family. I like the fact that I get to come back to Toronto."

But just when it's getting too gooey for words, one last character appears, a nervous-on-the-service secret agent. "There's just one thing that worries me. I won a big debate back when I was in

Grade 11 because I made a girl from St. Clement's School cry with my heckling. I'm afraid she'll be in the audience on opening night."

He shouldn't worry.

The kid is all right.

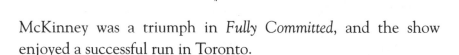

McKinney was a triumph in *Fully Committed*, and the show enjoyed a successful run in Toronto.

Since then, his career has followed his usual eclectic path, ranging from a 2002 reunion with the *Kids in the Hall* ("The Tour of Duty") to writing the live Scooby-Doo show, called *Stagefright*.

As of this writing, McKinney has just finished a role for iconoclastic Canadian director Guy Maddin in his film *The Saddest Music in the World*.

Scott Thompson
Colin McConnell /Toronto Star

SCOTT THOMPSON

Mojo Time for the Shih Tzu Man

Fans of *The Kids in the Hall* would have no trouble telling you who the most certifiably deranged member of that edgy group clearly was: Scott Thompson.

During the group's time together, he was always the one who went the furthest over the top, and acquired a large group of followers in doing so.

Afterward, he had a fair bit of success in American film and television, but then he seemed to pull himself off the radar screen.

I was surprised when I was offered an interview with him in December 2001 to promote his new one-man show, since theatre had never been Thompson's first love.

But I was intrigued (who wouldn't be?) and I showed up to see what had happened to the Kid who seemed least likely to grow up.

It took a firebomb to get Scott Thompson back to Toronto.

The popular star of *The Kids in the Hall* and *The Larry Sanders Show* was living in Los Angeles in 2000, when a terrorist attack nearly killed him and his then partner, director Joel Soler.

Soler and Thompson were working on a documentary about Saddam Hussein, called *Uncle Saddam*, when it started.

"People were phoning us, making death threats and I didn't think anything about it." Thompson is perched on a sofa at Starbucks, sipping a double espresso as he remembers.

"I thought it was all too dramatic. Joel kept warning me and I was sure he was exaggerating." His eyes still have their impish gleam, the corners of his mouth turned up in a puckish grin. Then his expression changes.

"Until one night when they filled up three garbage cans with gasoline and set them on fire in our driveway. We raced outside and discovered red paint all over the walls saying, 'In the name of Allah, the merciful and compassionate, burn this satanic film or you will be dead.'"

"That sure lit a fire under my ass." It prompted Thompson to create a one-man theatre piece called *The Lowest Show on Earth*.

"I had to write something new if I wanted people to see me in a different light," he admits. "I was in a rut where all I was ever going to be was the boring gay guy next door."

But wasn't *The Larry Sanders Show* more than that? "Not really," sighs Thompson. "I was still just the funny fairy — second verse, same as the first. Some of the jokes had a bit more edge, but I finally wanted to say to Gary Shandling, 'Look, sister, you think being gay is such a scream? Well, you try it for a while.'"

"But in the end, it was *Providence* that did me in," he says, referring not to divine intervention, but the popular NBC series.

"I spent nine episodes there, but I was just a lapdog. I had about as much mojo in that role as a Shih Tzu. The last time I put on my apron and helped the heroine spray her hair, I thought I might as well be an extra in *The Last Emperor* with my balls in a little basket, because at least eunuchs in imperial China had power behind the scenes."

Thompson was born on June 12, 1959, in North Bay ("Yeah, me and Mike Harris") and raised in Brampton, Ontario. After being asked to leave York University's theatre program for being "disruptive," he drifted into the world of sketch comedy, finally becoming a member of *The Kids in the Hall*.

He describes the years they spent together on TV as "five very intense individuals sharing the same hollowed-out tree. Five

Keebler elves making cookies that blow up as soon as you bite into them."

Thompson willingly embraces both the group's ongoing appeal and continuing personality conflicts. "We're planning another tour, unless I attempt murder on someone in the group."

Who would he murder? "It changes from day to day."

His most memorable creation from those days was Buddy Rich, the cocktail-sipping, lethally bitchy queen who brought down the wrath of straights and gays alike. "Political agitation marred my comedy in those days," he concedes. "I was hated on every side. But that's not what I'm into now. If you're looking for gay empowerment, stay home. There are other things besides sexuality in the closet."

Interestingly enough, Buddy does appear in Thompson's new show, which is a series of character sketches linked with a dramatic through line. In what has proven to be the most controversial scene during the play's tryout, the ever-swish Mr. Rich sexually embraces a nude actress representing Venus.

The wry Thompson smile is ever-ready. "Sure. It's Buddy . . . paying homage to the woman because, let's face it, everything revolves around them. He's just accepting the world as it is."

And right now, Thompson is ready to accept the world as well. "I'm happier than I've ever been before. It's discovering what's important and what's not. I know that I want to be taken seriously as a comic, but I can never forget that my agenda is an entertainment agenda."

If all that is true, then why give his play such a negative title — *The Lowest Show on Earth?*

"That reflects the past. I've been there, but you can go really low and still come back. It's like full survival after a stroke. Phoenix-type survival. Sure my characters show the ugliness in human existence, but I love them all, no matter what they do, how they misbehave. I never judge them."

Like everyone else, Thompson has had to live with the aftermath of September 11 (he cancelled a New York run of this show, for starters), but in his case there were different reverberations.

"Living with Joel and working on a film about Saddam, I was very aware of a lot of things ahead of everyone else. Joel's next project, in fact, was going to be about Bin Laden and he'd curl up at nights reading books about him. The first time I ever saw Osama's face, my gaydar went way off the edge. His fear of women is just '50s faggotry. You cannot overestimate what people do to prove they're men, to deny what they really are."

Thompson looks about conspiratorially, as if there might be Al Qaeda operatives sitting nearby, nursing their lattes.

"After our house was fire-bombed, I started to write this show and the first scene I created was Buddy Cole in Afghanistan, dressed as a woman, buying some anthrax to take on the Taliban. That was twelve months ago." His look mirrors my own astonishment.

"Then, a few weeks post 9/11, I read it again and thought, 'Who wrote this? Did Nostradamus decide to come up with some funny quatrains?' So I cut it from the show. I didn't want it to seem like exploitation. There's a lot of people already who are using that tragedy as a smokescreen for their own problems. They've gotten soft; they're wallowing in their emotions. Nothing is so big that you can't get back up again."

As an example, look at Thompson's bounce-back from the widely reported incident this past summer when he was forced off the podium in the middle of hosting the Griffin Prize for Poetry after celebs like Margaret Atwood and Anne Michaels found his bawdy monologue too excessive for their taste.

His gaze is level and his voice devoid of irony as he says, "In my heart of hearts, I never wanted to hurt anybody. I just misjudged the room and came on too strong. I thought they'd be cooler."

Any last words? "Yeah," Thompson pauses to finish his espresso. "Tell them I'm reclaiming my manhood. I've had it with the people who only want you when you're neutered."

Alas, *The Lowest Show on Earth* proved to be just that, earning unanimously scathing reviews from the Toronto critics, resulting in a quick closure after its opening in January 2002.

Thompson went on tour with The Kids in the Hall in the summer of 2002 and after that, kept busy with supporting roles on TV and in a series of Canadian films including one about the theatre industry, prophetically entitled *Ham and Cheese*.

Sandra Shamas
Rick Eglinton/Toronto Star

SANDRA SHAMAS

You Can't Eat a Flower

I n 1996, I began an interview show on TVOntario called *Dialogue*, which lasted four seasons, in which I spoke to 104 guests.

Sandra Shamas was the first, and I won't forget that interview quickly.

She had just finished a year's sabbatical in which she'd kept away from the media. This was her first public appearance, and when I asked her about her year off, she suddenly burst forth with a candid, unexpected, and fully detailed account of how her marriage had broken up and how, afterward, she had gone to pieces completely — if temporarily.

Ever since then, I approach our encounters with a bit of wariness, but this one, in October 2002, proved to be amiable.

Sandra Shamas has filled her new show — *Wit's End II: Heart's Desire* — with four-letter words.

Relax, it's not what you think. The words in question are "need" and "want."

We're having lunch at the stylish JK Restaurant at the Royal Ontario Museum, and the dining location was her request, because it's someplace she's always *wanted* to go, and that word is a recent addition to her vocabulary.

"I've been driven by need for so long that the issue of want comes up like an alien," admits the wide-eyed performer, whose

one-woman shows have made her one of the most popular entertainers in Canada.

"If you'd ever like to stop someone in their tracks, just ask
them, 'What do you *want*?' and a floodgate opens up. Because
your *want* is so huge, it's so colourful, it's so imaginative, it's so
sexy, so full of flavour, there's so much packed into it."

She snatches a piece of bread before discussing the flip side.
"But this is a world where if you say you want something, the
chances are you'll be argued with." She assumes an adenoidal
tone to nag: "What do you want that for?"

An ear-to-ear smile creases her features. "So I used to put all
my wants into the need column. Let's say I want a new dress for
opening night, but 'want' makes you vulnerable. Somebody's
going to say, 'Hey, you've got a whole closet full of stuff just hanging there.' So I'd give up and say I needed it and nobody would
argue with me."

She seems like a happy lady, and the smoked salmon and
potato salad appetizer makes her happier. ("It's very pretty," she
coos. "It looks like fairy food.") But it's taken her a while to get to
that point.

Born in 1957, in Sudbury (she once described it as "a place
where all the men were men, and all the women were men"), she
got out just about as soon as she could and landed in Toronto's
Second City in 1982. An assortment of work followed, including
a puppetry gig on *Fragile Rock*, where she met a guy named Frank
Meschkuleit.

Their relationship fuelled her first three solo pieces, which
began with the 1987 Edmonton Fringe hit that launched her
career: *My Boyfriend's Back and There's Gonna Be Laundry*.

A sequel followed (*The Cycle Continues*), but Shamas really hit
it big with her 1994 saga that chronicled the tying of their nuptial
knot: *Wedding Bell Hell*. It sold out its entire run at the Winter
Garden, which she now affectionately thinks of as "my theatre."

Shamas understands why that show was such a breakthrough.

"It's simple. There are a lot of weddings. There are a lot of wedding magazines. Recipes for the happy couple. There aren't many divorce magazines. What would their recipes be like? 'Make this, then cut it in half.'"

She knows what she's talking about. After the huge success of *Wedding Bell Hell*, she purchased a farm 45 minutes outside of Toronto, announced a year's sabbatical, and planned to settle in happily ever after with Meschkuleit.

He had different plans, however, and before she had even finished unpacking, he told her the marriage was over.

She still kept to her original agenda and took her year on the farm to heal and to think. She also grew to cherish her life in the country. "Oh my God, I do love it," she says, "but I never stopped loving being in the city. I like having options. I'm a big fan of options. I love where I live, and I love leaving where I live."

She also needed time for what had happened to get assimilated. "I don't talk about yesterday," she asserts. "I haven't had time to digest that yet. The evidence of daily events takes a long time to come to fruition."

As the table is cleared for the main course, Shamas puts some pieces together about how she works. "The situation I reveal to my audience always has a beginning, a middle, and an end. I always include the resolution. There's got to be a timeline, a space that's gone by between what happened and now. That's all past. I'm not there anymore."

The end result of her time off was *Wit's End*, which played to sellout audiences at the Winter Garden in 1999 after a tryout run at Buddies in Bad Times during 1998.

It talked about her divorce with humour and an amount of compassion that seemed amazing to audiences. But not amazing to Shamas. "You know, at the end of the day, I have to lay my head on the pillow and talk to God, and he's gonna say, 'So, Sandra, what did you do today?' and I don't want to answer, 'Gee, I really shit on a lot of people so I could get a laugh.'"

I ask if some of her acquaintances ever worry about being included in her material. She raises one eyebrow like a scimitar. "If they do, it's because they overestimate their importance in my life."

A Portobello mushroom sandwich arrives, as well as chef Jamie Kennedy's legendary french fries, served in a paper cone, with a dipping dish of lemon mayonnaise. Shamas is instantly in awe.

"Do you think people who live near here come just to eat these fries? They are absolutely astonishing!"

Her sheer sensual enjoyment of the food brings us back to her initial discussion of needs and wants, and I ask how her new openness to want has manifested itself.

She pauses over the lemon mayonnaise as the memory comes back to her. "I was standing in the seed store looking at all the flowers, wanting flowers, but only buying vegetables." She becomes a sharp-nosed biddy. "You can't eat a flower, dear."

Another mouthful of fries and she laughs. "I don't know who that voice was. Yes, I do. It was the denial of beauty. A small example, but so telling. For a long time I denied myself the joy of flowers — the colour, the beauty, the texture. I always wanted someone else to do it for me. Well, who the fuck is gonna plant them for you if you don't do it yourself?

"It's like a woman and guy are out driving, and the woman will ask, 'So are you hungry?' and the guy will say, 'No.' She's starving, but she's afraid to say, 'I want to stop and eat.' So what do you do, sit in silence and starve? Yes, apparently."

Shamas doesn't starve. She eagerly revisits her mushroom sandwich before continuing. "Ultimately, if you don't give your-self flowers, then you can never appreciate someone else giving them to you. And that was my lesson."

Another thing she learned about was turning 40, although it proved less of an ordeal than she had feared. "Honey, I love being in my forties!" she cries, dipping into the fries another time. (Shamas turned 45 the week of this interview.)

"I'm much freer, much more at ease. The things that I care

about, I care about. The rest? Forget it. I'm relaxed enough to let stuff go. That's a lovely gift. I realize who I am and what I'm doing. If I had known that this is what it would be like to turn forty, I would have done it twenty years ago."

There isn't a french fry in sight as the waiter clears the plates away. Shamas realizes that she's been in a fairly serious mood and wants to make it clear that "the description of the show has nothing to do with the execution. I know people want me to be funny, but all I've got to do is tell the truth. That's my job. If you laugh, then that's your response to it. I've always been wary of the comedian label. If they laugh, I'm a comedian. If they don't, I'm a dramatist."

It helps explain why she only performs her own work. She describes how she turned down an offer to do *The Vagina Monologues*: "I have a vagina, and I already do monologues, so what's the point?"

She is glad to be returning to her devoted audience. "They're happy friends who pay to see me, and I love every one. But let's not forget that I'm also paying to see them. I rent the theatre; I pay for the publicity. But we're in agreement. We're friends who really want to see each other."

Hecklers, however, are one thing she can do without. "I think if the ticket says 'Sandra Shamas,' then I should be the only one speaking."

As the double espressos arrive, Shamas finds a way to tie the pieces of our lunchtime conversation together with one story. "This spring, I took great pains to find thin-skinned heritage variety tomatoes, paid three dollars a plant for them at this chi-chi, poo-poo nursery. Planted them carefully, staked them, watched them, watered them, played Sinatra to them."

"Across the yard was a compost heap I started last year. And this summer, a bunch of wild tomatoes began growing out of it. I didn't do anything to them. Well, they came out nicer than the three-dollar fancy ones, better tone, better colour. They grew without any effort whatsoever."

Shamas smiles as she brings it all home. "There's a lot to be said for letting things go. Let them be what they should be, and just watch."

"Watch with some reverence. And delight."

Wit's End II; Heart's Desire proved to be the biggest hit for Shamas yet.

Lurking in the audience one night were some scouts from HBO and they invited Shamas to the U.S. Comedy Arts Festival in Aspen, held in March 2003.

Although she won the Best Theatre Award, she later confided to me that "working with 45 percent less oxygen was no thrill — it was about the same rate of exchange as our dollar."

Does this mean she might be taking her comedy away from her safe and secure home base? "If I was asked nicely," she says coyly. "It depends on the moment. It depends on the attention."

Oh, and don't go looking for the celestial fries at JK-ROM. The restaurant closed, alas, at the end of April 2003, as part of a giant renovation to the museum.

Milton Berle
AP/World Wide Photos

MILTON BERLE

Confessions of a Burger Queen

"Uncle Miltie" died on March 27, 2002. To my parents' generation, he was one of the biggest of all stars — the original "must-see" TV personality.

It's funny what time does, but I had totally forgotten that we worked together once, until the morning that I heard he had passed away.

This is what I remembered then.

He may have been known as "Mr. Tuesday Night," but I met him on a Monday afternoon.

When Milton Berle died this week at the age of 93, I thought back to the day in 1976 when we worked together, briefly but unforgettably.

I was toiling away as a very junior writer on an ill-advised television series named *Celebrity Revue*, a Canadian attempt to create a cheap daily variety program for the U.S. syndication market, shot at the killer pace of ten shows a week in a long-gone Vancouver nightclub called The Cave.

Although she would probably rather forget it was on her résumé, the current chair of the CBC, Carole Taylor, was the host and it's from her I learned what "grace under pressure" means.

An assortment of "celebrities," either on their way up (a very young David Letterman) or on their way down (a very tipsy

Robert Goulet) flew into Vancouver, learned comedy skits, sang songs, taped two shows a night in front of a rowdy crowd, and left town as fast as they could, clutching their paycheques for dear life.

Most of them came and went without registering on my radar, but when Milton Berle was announced as a guest, my ears perked up.

I was just a toddler when Berle had his glory days in television, but my family revered him as one of the "great" stars and that impression stuck with me. My dad was still alive then, and I knew he would have gotten a kick out of the fact that I had managed to work with "Uncle Miltie."

And so, consequently, I offered to write one of the comedy sketches for his appearance. The knowing looks my fellow (and more experienced) writers exchanged should have tipped me off, but I possessed the courageous ignorance of youth.

I knew that Berle still loved to dress as a woman, and that he always enjoyed topical humour. Burger King had just launched its "We always do it your way" campaign, so I combined the two.

In a stroke of political incorrectness that makes me shiver 26 years later, I came up with a routine where Berle would appear in full drag as a harassed counter-girl at a fast-food franchise called "Burger Queen," where the slogan would be "We always do it both ways."

It wasn't brain surgery, but I thought it was funny . . . until Berle burst into our office on Monday afternoon, four hours before taping.

At this point he was 67, and his face was already a sea of liver spots, topped by thinning hair dyed that orangeish hue we would become familiar with from Ronald Reagan.

True to form, Berle was waving a giant cigar, dressed in an outrageous plaid jacket, and loaded for bear.

"Who wrote this Burger Queen thing?" he wanted to know. My fellow writers melted into the woodwork, and I confessed my guilt.

After sizing me up with a withering glance, Berle admitted,

"It's not that bad, kid. It's a cute idea, but you got my rhythm all wrong. Let me show you what I mean."

He sat down at the desk and started tapping at the script like Morse code. "Dit-dit-dit-dot, dit-dit-dit-dot, dit-dit-dit-joke. You got it?"

My bewildered look indicated that I didn't, so he kept at me. "It's rhythm, kid: set-up, set-up, deliver. Say it in the right rhythm and it'll get a laugh — even if it isn't funny. I'll show you what I mean."

He struck a parody stand-up comic's swaggering pose and began: "I just came in from Frankfort." Pause. "You know what Frankfort is?" Bigger pause, then a rapid-fire attack: "It's the capital of Kentucky." It wasn't a joke, but I found myself laughing involuntarily. He was right. The rhythm did it all.

He pushed me toward my typewriter. "Go fix it. I gotta check on my costume."

Frantically tapping away like the telegrapher on the *Titanic*, I tried to rewrite my feeble little sketch. Then I ventured backstage, where Berle was terrorizing the staff.

"I can't wear white pantyhose!" he was screaming at them, "I gotta have sheer so you can see my legs. That's what's funny! Doesn't anyone around here know what's funny except me?"

That's how it went for the next few hours. Berle kvetched about the lighting, the set, the other actors, constantly nudging to get it right. You'd think he was back in his glory days at NBC, instead of doing a one-shot for an on-the-ropes Canadian series.

Just before showtime, Berle called me in for a last consultation. He was wearing full makeup, several inches thick, a curly blonde wig, and the Burger Queen outfit he had made them redesign to be shorter, bustier, and frillier. He never met a stereotype he didn't like.

"Let me see my intro," he demanded, and I showed him what I had written. He literally slapped his forehead in annoyance. "You've got it all wrong, schmuck! It's got to build, like this: 'Here he is, Mr. Tuesday Night, Mr. Television, Milton Berle!'"

He must have seen the look of wonderment on my face, because he explained, "It's got to be the best, kid, every time I go out there. I've got to make 'em laugh. I've got to."

For a split second he looked very old and tired, but then he revved up again. "What are you waiting for, a kiss on the lips? Go fix it!"

I suppose the sketch went well enough, because he clapped me roughly on the shoulder afterward. "Uncle Miltie says you did good, kid."

But as I turned to leave, he delivered the legacy: "Only never forget, it's all in the rhythm: dit-dit-dit-dot, dit-dit-dit-dot, dit-dit-dit-joke. You got it?"

I got it, Mr. Berle. Thanks for everything.

Within a few days after this article appeared in the *Star* (and, consequently, on-line), I received three separate e-mails from around North America, each from someone who had close to the same experience I did with Berle.

It seems that Mr. Tuesday Night, Mr. Television, Milton Berle, was in there slugging until the very end.

III

THE CREATORS

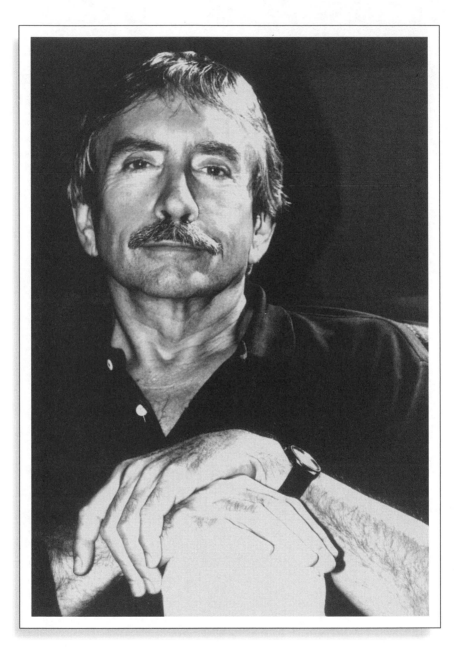

Edward Albee
Stratford Festival of Canada

EDWARD ALBEE

Fun and Games in Tribeca

I n May 2001, the Stratford Festival was preparing a production of *Who's Afraid of Virginia Woolf?* and I decided this would be a good excuse to interview the author, Edward Albee.

I was a huge Albee fan and had seen almost every one of his plays in their original productions. At the age of 12, I even precociously went to a matinee of *Virginia Woolf* on my own. A concerned audience member stopped me at intermission and asked, "Young man, where are your parents?" "They're at home," I ingenuously replied, "This play would be way too much for them."

Anyway, feeling that my credentials were intact, a mutual friend, Ron Rosenes, persuaded Albee to sit down with me to discuss his most famous script — "one he is heartily sick of talking about," I was warned in advance. That only added to my apprehension, which, you as you will see, was already in high gear.

Edward Albee doesn't suffer fools gladly.

That fact has been made abundantly clear through 40 years, during which unsuspecting journalists suddenly found themselves sitting with their heads in their laps, without ever having seen the razor.

Acerbic, sardonic, witheringly cynical. That's how he's usually described. Part Sweeney Todd, part Hannibal Lecter. Words to chill the blood of any journalist, especially one intent on asking him about his most famous play, *Who's Afraid of Virginia Woolf?*

Albee's 1962 drama deals with two couples in academia — George and Martha, Nick and Honey — who share a session of alcoholic "fun and games" late one night that turns into a scab-tearing exercise as to the limits of "truth and illusion," leaving its participants battered and broken.

It made me wonder if a similar fate was in store for me.

The journey down to the Tribeca district of Manhattan only serves to raise the anxiety level. A jumble of one-way streets and cul-de-sacs leads to an enclave where anonymous lofts alternate with the trendiest of restaurants. When I arrive at the designated place at the designated time, a disembodied nasal voice streams thinly through the intercom, urging me to wait.

Too late to turn and run, breathing deeply is the only option.

A freight elevator rattles down, the door clatters open, and there he is: Edward Franklin Albee III.

The 73-year-old playwright is dressed casually in a denim shirt; his salt-and-pepper hair is in slight disarray and his dark eyes are smouldering.

He makes small talk about how hard his address is to find as the elevator creaks and groans upward, reminiscent of something from an episode of *The Twilight Zone*.

It finally grinds to a halt, and he leads the way into an astonishing space. The generous expanse features the exposed brick and vaulting skylights common to many lofts, but Albee has filled it with a unique mixture of art: Primitive African, Russian constructivist, and modern abstract.

The eye catches on a piece by Wassily Kandinsky, some works by Milton Avery, as well as numerous paintings by young artists whom Albee has encouraged. He leads the way to a large black leather sofa, settles down, and waits.

No razor is in evidence.

I begin with the assurance that he won't be asked the same questions about *Who's Afraid of Virginia Woolf?* that he's heard 50 million times before.

He smiles — the twist of lemon over a dry martini — and says, "There are only three questions about the play that I've heard fifty million times, and here are my answers to them: "No, it's not based on any real people I ever knew. . . . No, it's not written about two gay couples. . . . Yes, the movie was all right."

Memories of the 1966 film (directed by Mike Nichols, starring Elizabeth Taylor and Richard Burton) flicker behind his eyes as he elaborates. "Not a bad movie at all. Nicely directed, well acted. Elizabeth was a bit young, but she did well.

"There was also the most extraordinary close-up I've ever seen. It happened near the end, when the camera moved in on Sandy Dennis (Honey). She had the most amazing bubble of saliva on her lip, and it seemed to stay there forever . . . "

He drags himself back. "Yes, the movie was fine, but it would have been better with the cast they had promised me — James Mason and Bette Davis."

When asked about the rumour that he had written the play with Bette Davis in mind (after all, it begins with the line "What a dump!" from her film *Beyond The Forest*) his gaze sharpens, and he almost seems to be wondering just where he put that razor.

"Absolutely not. I never think of actors when I'm writing a role. Because what if they refuse to do it? Then you're stuck with a character, and no one to play it. That isn't how I write at all."

The original production of *Who's Afraid of Virginia Woolf?* was a scandalous hit, denounced by as many critics as praised it, and denied the Pulitzer Prize for being "morally unsuitable" even after the judges had voted unanimously for it. (Albee subsequently had the last laugh by winning three Pulitzers in later years — for *A Delicate Balance*, *Seascape*, and *Three Tall Women*.)

Scholars back in 1962 had a field day searching the Woolf script for hidden levels of meaning, and Albee is now a bit more forthcoming than he used to be when asked if George and Martha could really be symbolic of George and Martha Washington.

"Well, I agree with the criticisms that the American

Revolution has long since failed and that our humanism has declined. How else can you explain the presence of George Dubya as our president?" The smile grows wicked. "You know what they say about him? He's only a heartbeat away from the presidency."

If George and Martha are the Washingtons, then what about the assertion that Nick stood for Nikita Khrushchev, at that time leader of the Soviet Union?

Albee keeps his equanimity. "It's true that there are arguments going on in the play between humanism and its opposite but, in the end, all it's really about is two couples, believe me."

Considering the worldwide success of the play over the past four decades, I ask him how many productions of the play he has had to sit through.

He flashes his evil grin. "I've had to see quite a few that I would have been much happier not seeing. The most common mistake people make is to get some failed middle-aged actress to play Martha." He grimaces at the memories.

"And some directors — I don't know how they manage to do it — some directors manage to stage the play without any humour. I don't know how they do it. I guess it takes a certain sort of talent."

So many years of seeing so many people impose their visions on his work induces a certain fatalism in Albee but, as he puts it, "I try to write a play that's director-proof and actor-proof. I haven't quite succeeded, but I'm working on it."

Albee also takes exception to the stylization some people impose on his most celebrated script. "It's a highly naturalistic play. Period. The intermissions are the same duration as the time spent by everybody offstage. And I keep saying to a lot of people who want to screw it up: Don't help, leave the play alone, it knows what it's doing."

He shares the full horror of the next observation in a whisper, almost as if he didn't want word of it to spread too far. "I saw a production done once by a company in Tokyo. Everybody was in dinner clothes, the set was black glass, and it was lighted from underneath. It looked like an ice show."

But was that the worst production he has ever suffered through? He shakes his head sadly at the memory of further agonies. "No, I once saw a production up near you guys in Canada. In a dead city on a dying lake. It was so terrible..."

He shudders as he tries to get the words out. "It starred one of these aging stock actresses, and they had me down in the front row. I wanted to stand up and say to the actors 'Stop!' and I wanted to turn to the audience and say, 'Go away, go home.'"

When asked why he thinks the play keeps being produced with such frequency after nearly 40 years, he offers two reasons: "It has become famous for being famous. And it's good, too."

Albee thinks of another reason for the play's enduring power. "Nick and George have an argument about genetic engineering, about cloning people. It sounds very contemporary, and I wrote it nearly forty years ago."

He has a gleam in his eye. "Well, isn't a good writer supposed to be ahead of his time? Historical inevitability. Nothing changes. I mean we playwrights are supposed to change the world but, in the end, I guess we just hold mirrors up, and if the audiences want to see themselves and change themselves, well that's their business, isn't it?"

"And my business is to keep writing. I believe in theatre that matters. Theatre that doesn't leave you the same person you were when you went in. Something that makes you question your values or examine your beliefs. Something that changes you in some way. Why waste sixty or seventy-five dollars to go into an uncomfortable building for two-and-a-half hours and come out unchanged?"

As for his work present and future, Albee refuses to categorize it.

"I never think about where a play fits in my career. I write a play to find out why I'm writing it, and then the characters take over.

"The trick to writing a play is knowing exactly where to begin and where to end it. Where to put the parentheses around the lives."

He puts the parentheses around this interview by leading the way back to the Rod Sterling-esque elevator.

While waiting for it to arrive, Albee is pleased to hear that some audiences during the Stratford previews had still found the play to be shocking.

"That's a good sign, because it *is* still shocking. The amount of truth being told; the amount of illusion being stripped away. That's still going on in our society.

The famous Albee fangs come out only once, at the very end, when I refer to the current production as a "revival" of his play.

"Revival?" he sneers, slamming the elevator door shut and starting the journey back down. "I hate that term. What does it mean? To bring back to life something which is dead. I hope that never describes my plays."

But then as we reach the street and the sunlight pours in, he smiles. "This has actually been quite pleasant. You see, I'm not so frightening, after all."

And I'd have to agree.

Albee's Tribeca loft was only five blocks north of the World Trade Center, and on 9/11, he was one of the first people I thought of. He later described the aftermath as "something out of a nightmare — smoke and dust, darkness and terror. I hated war before; I fear it now."

Despite some health issues, Albee had a new play on Broadway in March 2002 called *The Goat*. Proving that he hadn't lost his desire (or ability) to shock an audience, it dealt with a prominent architect whose life is torn apart when he has an affair with the barnyard creature of the title. Although fiercely dividing audiences and critics alike, it went on to enjoy a successful nine-month run and won the Tony Award for Best Play.

Stephen Sondheim
Courtesy of Stephen Sondheim

STEPHEN SONDHEIM

Something Just Broke

I first met Stephen Sondheim when he came to Toronto in 1993 to address a gathering of songwriters, and I had the privilege of interviewing him in front of a thousand people. Hardly the easiest way to begin a relationship, but it made for a memorable evening.

In the intervening decade, we would occasionally run into each other in New York, but I didn't have a chance for another sustained conversation with him until he was preparing a trip to Canada to accept an award being given him in the fall of 2001 as one of modern culture's "World Leaders."

A planned personal encounter fell through when a bout of flu sent him into hibernation, but he agreed to follow up on the telephone.

"Do you know why the first act of most musicals is better? Because that's all we ever had time to fix."

Stephen Sondheim is talking about his life's work in the theatre and the voice that crackles through the phone from his Manhattan home is electric with energy.

"I miss the road. God, how I miss the road!" He's referring to the network of cities — Boston, New Haven, sometimes even Toronto — where musicals used to go through their growing pains in the '50s and '60s when his career was in its early years.

"Look, every show needs to shake itself down in front of an audience and it's better to do that shakedown as far away from

New York as you can get. Because creative people are awfully anxious during tryouts and the one thing they don't need is friends coming backstage after every show saying, 'Darling, it's terrible!'"

The 71-year-old composer-lyricist speaks with the bitter voice of experience. Even though he's won every prize from the Oscar to the Tony to the Pulitzer, he recently suffered through a scenario that would have pained a man with a third of his credits.

His long-gestated and eagerly awaited musical, *Wise Guys*, went into a series of public workshops in New York, directed by Sam Mendes, starring the knockout duo of Nathan Lane and Victor Garber.

But when the smoke cleared, the planned Broadway run was abruptly cancelled in a cloud of acrimonious gossip. "A difference of opinion" is how Sondheim tersely describes it. "(Mendes) wanted the show to be something quite different from what I did."

He's more forthcoming about the actual workshop experience. "It was terrible. We were trying to rehearse changes during the day and then performing them at night in front of an audience."

"Look, a workshop can be a great thing. We actually started them with Jerry Robbins back during (*A Funny Thing Happened on the Way to the*) *Forum* when he was a little gun-shy about the project. We'd get some actors in to read the script and we'd learn an enormous amount."

"But over the years these things got bigger and more formalized, and now they're just glorified backers' auditions."

"No thanks. Send me back to New Haven, where you had audiences full of real people, not show buffs and vultures who were hoping for the show to fall on its face."

Perhaps he's overstating the case?

"No," you can practically hear Sondheim shaking his head in disagreement, "people actually enjoy watching other people fail. It relieves their own personal anxiety level."

The good news is that *Wise Guys* is back on track, now tentatively rechristened *Gold*, and the even better news is that it's reuniting Sondheim with his old colleague Harold Prince, with whom he worked on virtually all of his shows until the 1981 failure of *Merrily We Roll Along*.

When asked if it feels like two decades since last collaborating with Prince, Sondheim's wry reply is, "When you get to a certain age, everything seems short." But his tone abruptly changes and a genuine enthusiasm takes hold of his voice as he chronicles the progress he's making with Prince.

"Things are excellent. The show is three-quarters back to what we had originally. It's wonderfully revivifying to work with Hal again. He's so full of energy and forward motion." An image occurs to Sondheim and he lets it take shape: "Hal sees to it that the truck keeps going forward and I see to it that the brakes are on to keep it from going over the cliff."

But even before the reunion with Prince, things had been cruising along nicely for Sondheim. Although he hasn't had a new musical on Broadway since 1994's *Passion*, he's certainly been well represented with revivals of *A Funny Thing Happened on the Way to the Forum*, *Company*, and *Follies*, the premiere of his previously unproduced show from the 1950s, *Saturday Night*, a revue of his songs called *Putting It Together*, the television version of his *Sweeney Todd* in concert, as well as numerous salutes and tributes.

And to top it all off, six of his musicals will be mounted in repertory next summer at Washington D.C.'s Kennedy Center in an unprecedented "Sondheim Celebration."

It's especially gratifying to find Sondheim enjoying this kind of success because he's never written down to his audience. His philosophy has always been "my way or the highway," and that highway, to quote a line from his 1971 masterpiece *Follies*, "goes through rocky ground."

That rocky ground began with his birth in 1930 into a moderately moneyed New York family. Sondheim was the centre of an unusually bitter divorce when he was only ten. Thirty years later, in *Company*, he had a character describe one of the major joys of marriage as "the children you destroy together." He knew what he was writing about.

He wound up living with his mother, Foxy, a woman so terrible that she instantly explains all the horrific females in his work, from Mama Rose through Mrs. Lovett. Her psychological abuse of young Sondheim was legendary, and she treated him as a miniature mixture of husband, lover, and punching bag.

The poor kid would have probably never survived if Foxy's summer home hadn't been close to that of Oscar and Dorothy Hammerstein. From a friendship with their son, Jimmy, Sondheim gradually hooked up with Oscar, who was then riding high as the new partner of Richard Rodgers and the author of *Oklahoma!* Sondheim became a surrogate member of that showbiz family, showing up at the opening of *Carousel*, working as a gofer on *Allegro* and deciding that this was how he wanted to spend his life. By the time he was 16, he was writing full-length musicals, which Hammerstein criticized rigorously. But it would take another decade before he finally made it onto Broadway as the lyricist for *West Side Story*.

Sondheim now tends to denigrate his work on that show ("Why would a poor Puerto Rican girl sing, 'It's alarming how charming I feel'?"), but it got his foot into the musical comedy door in high style.

Another stint as lyricist on the 1959 classic *Gypsy* followed, and then in 1962 Sondheim penned both music and lyrics for the hit *A Funny Thing Happened on the Way to the Forum*.

His next two works, however, sent him into a slump. *Anyone Can Whistle*, although a cult favourite in 1964, closed after a week, and a 1965 collaboration with Rodgers called *Do I Hear a Waltz?* proved to be the kind of acrimonious failure that all parties ever regretted having gotten involved with. ("Let's not talk about that one, okay?" is how Sondheim still reacts 35 years later.)

A five-year fallow period ensued. ("Left to my own devices, I'm probably the slowest worker in existence," admits Sondheim.) But when it ended with the 1970 production of *Company*, an 11-year burst of creativity began that yielded six major musicals.

The catalyst was producer-director Hal Prince, who had known Sondheim since the early 1950s. The two of them sparked a unique synergy that brought out the best in each other and delivered such highlights of the modern musical theatre as *Follies*, *A Little Night Music*, *Pacific Overtures*, and *Sweeney Todd*, before a 20-year split that began with their 1981 fiasco, *Merrily We Roll Along*.

After that, Sondheim began working with author-director James Lapine. Since then he has produced the Pulitzer Prize-winning *Sunday in the Park with George*, *Into the Woods*, and *Passion*.

Working with author John Weidman, Sondheim also created *Assassins* and the long-gestated *Gold*. Then there's also the non-stop series of revivals in theatres, concert halls, and opera houses around the world.

After all this time, how does Sondheim feel about hearing his songs sung in different interpretations? He pauses, harrumphs, and then concedes that "it's fine if they're well, sung accurately, with the correct harmonies and melody lines. I have nothing against different interpretive approaches . . . "

The pause at the end of that phrase lingers and you wait for the other shoe to drop. It does. "But generally, the first time I hear a song is the way I like it best. I'm resistant to change. When I hear 'Send in the Clowns' in my head, I hear Glynis Johns singing it, not Judy Collins or Frank Sinatra."

Did the same thing happen when he sat through the recent controversial revival of *Follies* and heard Blythe Danner and Judith Ivey instead of Alexis Smith and Dorothy Collins?

"I found it . . . informative." The oddly chosen adjective and the beat before delivering it is as close as he comes to making a comment. Although known within the theatre as a plain-talking,

135

straight-dealing individual, Sondheim isn't anxious to burn any bridges publicly.

Later on in the conversation, he lets a few negative statements slip out about a colleague and then asks to strike them from the record. "Hell," he snorts, "you know this business. We'll probably be working together again next year."

Forget about next year. This year is shaping up to be a banner one for Sondheim. Besides the TV shows and the tributes, as well as a revival of *Into the Woods* scheduled to open on Broadway later in the season.

For a while, it even looked like this year would include a full Broadway production of his grim 1990 musical *Assassins* (all singing, all dancing, all shooting), which saw its original production cut short by the Gulf War.

This time it was supposed to go into rehearsal on September 24. But first came September 11.

The most moving moment in the show was added for the London version, a song called "Something Just Broke" in which people recall precisely what they were doing when they heard that John Fitzgerald Kennedy had been shot.

Where was Sondheim when "something just broke" on that morning?

It's a question he wasn't anticipating, and he hesitates a bit before answering. "I was in Connecticut, getting set to come into the city for a meeting about *Assassins*. I was crossing the yard to get to my car and then my neighbour said, 'My God, Steve, turn on your TV!' So I did." A long silence.

Sondheim cancelled the show. He had no other choice. Once again, it was the wrong time.

The scene comes to mind where a chorus of assassins is trying to convince Lee Harvey Oswald to pull the trigger on Kennedy and they promise him, "You can shut down the New York Stock Exchange. The world will weep. Grief. Grief beyond imagining. Despair. The death of innocence and hope . . . "

Could this show ever be produced again in New York?

"Yes," says Sondheim, "we're going to try and do it a year or so in the future." And then his voice drops. "Even though everything in the world seems to have changed and only time will tell how much."

He weighs the consequences and offers his considered judgment. "I'll tell you one thing. It will mean the end of a certain kind of smugness that this country has embraced for too long."

Or in his own words:

> *"Something just stirred like a shock,*
> *Something I wish I hadn't heard.*
> *Something bewildering occurred,*
> *Something just broke."*

Two years later, everything is still coming up Sondheim. The revival of *Into the Woods* won the Tony Award in 2002 and a new production of *Gypsy* starring Bernadette Peters opened in May 2003.

Gold, rechristened once again, now became *Bounce* and finally saw the light of day in Chicago's Goodman Theatre in June 2003.

But most memorable, was the Kennedy Center's "Sondheim Celebration" which showered praise on Sondheim's grizzled head from around the world.

That kind of re-evaluation and reappreciation of an artist's work usually doesn't occur within his lifetime, but Sondheim is different. What he's done is to create a body of work that can not only be enjoyed by audiences, but can also be examined seriously by scholars of music and drama.

If his mentor, Hammerstein, nudged the musical theatre into maturity, Sondheim has dragged it kicking and screaming into middle age — a time of troubled feelings and sober reflection.

The experience of going to see a series of Sondheim works in repertory at the Kennedy Center in the summer of 2002 will remain a major cultural memory for me.

To walk the broad marble terraces, and see the sun set over the Potomac River while fountains splashed with joyous abandon and sold-out audiences waited in eager anticipation, seemed the ultimate validation of the musical theatre as a serious art form.

The opening lines of *Sunday in the Park with George* could almost serve as a description of Sondheim's work and the glorious celebration dedicated to it:

> *"The challenge: Bring order to the whole. Through design. Composition. Balance. Light. And harmony."*

Twyla Tharp (with Billy Joel)
AP/World Wide Photos

TWYLA THARP

Sing to Me, Goddess

The piece of music theatre called *Movin' Out* that Twyla Tharp created from the songs of Billy Joel moved me deeply when I first saw it in the fall of 2002.

It had such a profound effect on me that I wanted to talk to Tharp about her vision and how she had arrived at it.

Bill Coyle, publicist for the show, warned me that Tharp didn't like doing interviews, but once he told her how much her work had touched me, she decided to give me some time. I could show up for a few minutes at the start of her dinner break.

When I arrived at the restaurant they had chosen, she was already in fighting mode.

"Bill says that the show got to you. Tell me why."

I talked about the legacy of Vietnam, the friends I had lost, the way it had even torn my own family apart. She listened. Then she flung out the challenge.

"Sing to me, goddess, of the rage of Achilles," she quoted, and then looked at me, waiting for me to recognize the allusion.

I thanked God for the years I spent studying the classics in high school, and said "Actually, Miss Tharp, it's even more effective in the original Homeric Greek," which I then proceeded to quote.

There was a pause. She smiled. "Stay for dinner."

Brenda and Eddie led the standing ovation.

Okay, maybe it wasn't the hero and heroine of Billy Joel's "Scenes from an Italian Restaurant" who jumped to their feet as soon as the curtain fell on the Broadway production of *Movin' Out*, but it sure looked like them.

He had an open-collared shirt with enough chest hair to stuff a sofa cushion. She was made up to a degree you don't see outside of the Golden Globes.

And when they yelled "Bravo!" their accents were pure Long Island.

As I looked around, I saw the rest of the audience rise to cheer along with them and even if they didn't all resemble our duo, they were their spiritual kin: people of a certain age who had lived through Vietnam, loved Joel's songs, and had come to see a show that brought those threads together.

"That's the reward for it all. Watching that emotional response to the show every evening."

Twyla Tharp is talking, which means you listen.

This brisk, bright 61-year-old woman has been one of the most respected and successful choreographers in the world of modern dance for more than 30 years. Works like *Deuce Coupe* and *The Catherine Wheel* not only impressed critics, but also pleased widely varied audiences.

Her musical theatre efforts, however, were less triumphant, consisting only of the 1979 Milos Forman film *Hair* ("It just didn't work") and the flop 1985 stage version of the movie classic *Singin' in the Rain* ("They told me the script was carved in stone. Well, the show sank like one").

It's no wonder that when she came up with the idea that the songs of Billy Joel would be the basis for a Broadway show told in dance, she felt a bit nervous.

"A bit? I spent two years staying awake at night thinking that people were going to stay away in droves. What do I know about commercial? I just know what I feel."

And what she felt was that Joel's songs held the key to unlock something that she had needed to say for a long time.

"I wanted to talk about betrayal on a grand scale, the betrayal of a whole nation. 'Sing to me, goddess, of the rage of Achilles.'" She's quoting the opening lines of Homer's *Iliad*. "Well, I wanted to say 'Sing to me, Billy Joel, of the rage of the generation that lived through Vietnam.'"

We're sitting on the West Side of Manhattan, in an Italian restaurant, but there's no "bottle of white, bottle of red" on the table. Just a litre of mineral water and a plate of angel-hair pasta that Tharp seems to inhale, rather than simply eat.

Her conversation only ventures into the past when she's dragged there, and when I mention something she said in her 1992 autobiography, *Push Comes to Shove*, she lowers her fork long enough to give me a no-nonsense look. "Forget that," she commands, with that drill sergeant voice of hers, "I change every ten years."

And so the woman who grew up in a stern Quaker family that taught her "storytelling was lying," finally learned "to go past that. I knew that I needed a narrative to communicate my vision."

But it all began with Joel's songs. "I sat down one weekend and listened to them again, everything he ever wrote." She lights up with a realization. "You know what his songs are like? They're like shards of pottery. You see, from a shard you can reconstruct the pot, from the pot, you can reconstruct the culture. And that's what I did.

"I finally understood that Billy's community was wrapped around two songs: 'Angry Young Man,' and 'Goodnight Saigon.' I also grabbed onto that lyric from 'Piano Man' about 'when I wore a younger man's clothes,' and I created the story of those men Billy was talking about."

She crafted a tale about three friends who serve in Vietnam and find their existences changed beyond recognition. While it's not the fun, *Mamma Mia!* sort of nostalgia ride some people might have been expecting, Tharp is unrepentant.

"If you stick your neck out to do something that has real content, well, that makes people nervous. Look, I'm all in favour of people being joyous about things, but real art offers you new perception, not just redundant entertainment."

She took her vision to Joel. "He said 'Go for it,'" she remembers, with one of her rare smiles. Tharp knew all along just where she was going to wind up with the piece,

"It's all about bringing these guys home. Many of them felt when they came back that they weren't really welcome. Sure, go on a journey, learn on a journey, suffer on a journey, but for God's sake, bring them home!"

The intensity she displays makes it easy to understand where the passion of the show comes from. But conveying it proved to be a problem, as she discovered when it opened in Chicago to confused audiences and negative reviews.

"Just before the first preview, I finally sat back, looked, and said, 'Oh shit, we don't have it!'"

The fatigue of that period resurfaces in her face. "You know what it's like when you're trying to open a big show? It's like you've got a recording with four hundred and eighty-three tracks, but you haven't had time to mix it down. Bring this up; take that down. Cut, refine, it's out, it's in."

She slams down her fork angrily. "I knew I'd need time to fix the show, but in order for my producers to get the revenue from all those performances in Chicago, I had to endure the criticism of trying out in a highly public place. I told them I wanted to go to Reykjavik, but they wanted Chicago. Guess where we went?"

If you looked in the dictionary under "feisty," it would probably say "See Twyla Tharp."

"First I told them to stop advertising it as a musical. This is not a traditional musical! There isn't a book that tells a story. This is closer to a film; it's cinematically structured.

"Yes, it has a beginning, middle, and end. Yes, it has characters with an arc. Yes, we want people to be emotionally affected. No, it's not a musical. That was the first problem."

Tharp is using a piece of bread to diligently mop up pasta sauce the way she cleaned up the show on the road. "The next problem? The beginning. I had forty-two hundred beginnings in Chicago; none of them worked very well. You see, the opening number of a show is a pledge, a contract to an audience. You're going to see great dancing, the music will be authentic, we're taking you on a voyage, and we promise to bring you home."

With only three days of rehearsal left in New York before previews, Tharp found the answer. She added Joel's "It's Still Rock and Roll to Me" as a prologue where the audience got to meet all the characters and understand their relationships. But how did she manage to create new choreography in that period of time as well?

She puts down the bread and almost looks vulnerable for an instant. "Okay, I'll tell you. I stole from myself, a piece I created in 1974 called *Ocean's Motion*, that was set to the music of Chuck Berry. I pasted the choreography from that directly into my opening number and I didn't feel guilty for a moment. Why? Because I figured where did Billy Joel get his ideas about rock and roll from? Chuck Berry."

She's practically trembling with intensity as she recreates the creative process she went through at the time. "But the number wasn't just necessary because it introduced everybody. It did something more important than that. We had to show that all these guys had something worth coming back to, something worth surviving for. That's the point of the whole damned show."

"So I fixed it," she says, jaw clenched. "I had all these little bells and whistles. I took them out. Stay with the story, Twyla, that's what will make it work."

She did just that, and when the show finally opened, the critics cheered, the audiences lined up to buy tickets and Billy Joel drops by to see it almost every Friday night.

But Tharp knows there's no such thing as a totally happy ending, and she pushes away her plate.

"I'm worried about this whole business going on right now with Iraq. Some people are taking our show as an allegory about the evil that war does and how we have to keep out of it at all costs. How fucking hard is it to pull yourself up and out again? Do we really have to go through this one more time? Haven't we learned anything?"

The question hangs in the air as the waiter brings our check. "Scenes from an Italian Restaurant." Curtain.

It was a great interview, but there was a tragic coda.

Knowing I was from Toronto, Tharp went out of her way to praise former National Ballet of Canada soloist William Marrié, who was alternating the lead in *Movin' Out* with John Selya.

"I picked him as the alternate," she said, "because I wanted someone with a different quality from Selya. Somebody tougher, with more capacity for danger. That's a great quality for a dancer to bring on to the stage, and I think he's going to go a long way with it. He's got a big future ahead of him."

I asked Tharp to describe the hard-living dancer personally and she shrugged. "What's William Marrié like? He drives a motorcycle, that's what he's like."

Two hours after having this conversation, Marrié was driving that motorcycle on the rain-slicked Manhattan streets when he slid into a taxicab and crashed.

He died the next morning, two days before his 34th birthday.

"Promise me you'll see him in the show," is one of the last things Tharp said to me.

There are some promises you never get to keep.

Baz Luhrmann
Diane Bondareff

BAZ LUHRMANN

The Renaissance Kid of Herron's Creek

After I'd been at the *Star* for two years, I got a new boss. John Ferri became city editor and Peter Scowen joined the paper as entertainment editor. Fortunately, Peter shared his predecessor's predilection for my interviews, and so they continued.

He even helped to shape some of them. Just before I headed off to interview Baz Luhrmann, he said to me, "Make this one special. Find out why he feels he has to conquer Manhattan, why he wants to wind up on the top of the world."

I was halfway out the door when he made his last request.

"And shoot the picture that way, too."

I did my best in the two hours I was given with Luhrmann and his wife, Catherine Martin, on an unseasonably warm November Friday in 2002.

The setting was the once shabby, now fabby, Royalton Hotel on West 44th Street. At the top. The very top.

Baz Luhrmann is on the edge.

Literally. And figuratively.

The man who revolutionized the movie musical with *Moulin Rouge* leans over the balcony railing outside his midtown Manhattan penthouse hotel suite, risking his life for the sake of a photograph.

"I can just see the headlines now," he shouts over the traffic din. "'Flamboyant Australian Director Plunges to His Death on the Eve of His Greatest Triumph.' Hell, it better be my greatest triumph," he looks down 15 floors to the street, "or I might as well wind up down there."

He's talking about *La Bohème*, his $10-million stage version of Puccini's opera, which is getting ready to open on Broadway, after a critically acclaimed tryout in San Francisco.

It's more than just another gamble for the artist, also famous for the films *Strictly Ballroom* and *Romeo & Juliet*. Combined with *Moulin Rouge*, they form a trio of works marked by incredible theatricality and over-the-top romanticism. Luhrmann refers to them as his "Red Curtain Trilogy," and he's just released a five-DVD box set to say "hail and farewell" to this period in his work.

Luhrmann is bringing down the red curtain on the first act of his life, and he knows you've got to send the audience off to inter-mission with one hell of a buzz. That's what he hopes *La Bohème* will accomplish.

It was a smaller version of this same production that launched his career when, at the age of 28, he staged it for the Australian Opera in 1990. He took Puccini's classic tale of starving artists, loving and dying in mid-19th century Paris, and boldly moved it to 1957.

Then he proceeded to do what he does with every project he's touched: cast it with attractive young performers, splash it with eye-catching colour, and stage it within an inch of its life.

The end result was a smash, and it launched Luhrmann into a 12-year trajectory that's allowed no time for looking back. But that's what he wants to do on this particular afternoon as he settles down into a chair in this achingly chic hotel suite.

His hair is stylishly trim, and he wears a well-cut dark suit with an open-collared shirt. The effect is part hip, part establishment. Would you buy a used opera from this man? He certainly hopes so.

He swigs thirstily from a vitamin-laced bottle of water, tinted a green you only expect to see in a Luhrmann movie, as he goes back into his past.

Mark Anthony Luhrmann was born in 1962, in the back seat of a car that was racing his mother to the hospital in a suburb of Sydney. When he was still a baby, the family moved to an isolated part of New South Wales.

"Baz" was a childhood nickname, a mocking allusion to Basil Brush, the bushy-tailed fox puppet that appeared on a popular television series. When Luhrmann grew older, he changed his name to "Bazmark," embracing the mockery and stating that the composite name "showed both sides of who I am."

"What kind of kid was I then?" Luhrmann thinks for a beat. "The same kind of kid I am now. Extremely busy. My father was a bit mad, you see. He thought that we had to be the renaissance kids of Herron's Creek.

"We had to learn commando training as well as photography, how to grow corn as well as how to play a musical instrument. We were up at five in the morning, and then we just went until we dropped. The town consisted of a gas station, a pig farm, a dress shop, and a movie theatre — and we ran them all. Well, we didn't start out running the movies, but the man in charge of it died of a heart attack. My dad had been a naval diver and photographer in the Vietnam War, and he knew how to thread film, so he took over."

He radiates energy as he remembers that time. "That was an enormous thing for us. Every night we would sit in the projection room and see the film. It made a huge impression on me."

It's no surprise that musicals had the greatest impact. "*Hello, Dolly!*, *The Sound of Music*, even dear old *Paint Your Wagon*. I saw them all and loved them all."

But while the nights provided him with a cinematic education, the days proved equally enlightening. "As a kid pumping gas, I saw an endless stream of humanity arrive from the big city, pass through, and then leave. Everyone from families, Hare Krishnas, lovers breaking up . . . and you're invisible to them.

"I guess that's why I've always been interested in people's characters."

He snaps his fingers. "Who's that person? What's that person? Where are they coming from?"

So, with an ever-changing cast of characters during the day and a constantly rotating series of films every night, it was only natural that Luhrmann would start to create on his own. "What I do now is exactly what I did then," he cheerfully volunteers. "I got an idea, put the kids together, pulled a sheet over the shed and made a story."

But this world Luhrmann found so entrancing ended abruptly after his parents' divorce when he was 12. He refers to it several times as a "schism" in the family, and it's obvious he still carries strong feelings about the breakup with him nearly 30 years later. His all-controlling father was grappling with alcoholism, while his mother wanted to make up for the years she thought she had wasted in the outback.

"I don't know just what Mum felt she had been missing," Luhrmann recalls, "but she sure let everyone know how unhappy she was."

The actual breakup was "horrible" in Luhrmann's own words, "a dark cloud that hung over our family for years and then suddenly burst." But when it was through, he chose to stay behind with his father.

After a few years, his father remarried, and the unhappy dynamics of that relationship drove the 15-year-old Luhrmann "down the yellow brick road back to the city and my mother."

"And as if things weren't bad enough for me already, she enrolled me in an all-boys school run by the Christian Brothers. For me, that was a retrograde step. It spun my world out."

For the first time, Luhrmann looks less than amiable, and his smile turns into an almost feral growl. "But that didn't stop me. There never was a time that I wasn't making something — magic shows, a modern-dress *Henry IV*. I also used to take TV shows and redo them as plays. *Starsky and Hutch* was a big fave."

More disappointment was waiting for Luhrmann when he

tried to enter the prestigious National Institute of Dramatic Art, only to be rejected for being too young (he was 17 at the time).

He turned the defeat into victory by getting himself cast in a major Australian film, *The Winter of Our Dreams*, opposite Judy Davis.

"I was Pete the Pimp." He flashes the Luhrmann leer. "Fancy that. Not old enough for theatre school, but old enough to play a pimp."

Luhrmann finally got into the Institute, landed a gig as Peter Brook's assistant on *The Mahabarata*, and then co-wrote and directed a play called *Strictly Ballroom*, which would later serve as the basis of his first feature film.

After leaving school, he took work as an actor to support a series of fledgling theatre and opera companies. He wound up directing a new experimental opera, *Lake Lost*, for the Australian Opera in 1987.

Looking for a designer to help with that production, he met Catherine Martin. Since then, they have been professionally inseparable, although it took a while for the relationship to morph into romance.

"CM" is what Luhrmann nicknamed her, and now everyone she works with calls her that. They prefer not to be interviewed or photographed together, and so it's down the corridor to another penthouse suite to chat with the woman who won two Oscars for her design work on *Moulin Rouge*.

Even the film's severest critics had plenty of praise for Martin's stupendous nightclub settings and her hundreds of eye-catching costumes. Her work manages to combine the seeming contradiction of being impeccably researched and outrageously indulgent.

"All musicals," decrees Luhrmann, "are about the lie that reveals the truth, and CM is absolutely brilliant at capturing that in her designs."

Martin is a pleasant blonde pavlova of a woman — sweet and seemingly fluffy, but with some real crunch underneath. She sits calmly sipping tea, dressed in a symphony of earth tones arranged with a designer's eye.

At 37, she's three years younger than Luhrmann and has been drawn to the visual arts since earliest childhood. "I loved painting and sewing and knitting and making candles," she giggles in her broad Australian accent. "I was a craft kitsch child. I still love a bit of craft."

While Luhrmann was pumping gas in the outback, Martin was being buzzed around the world by doting parents who took her to New York and Disneyworld and who remained philosophical during her difficult adolescence.

"I was extremely rebellious, very badly behaved. Played hooky for an entire year. Did everything my parents didn't want me to do." She hastens to minimize the damage. "It wasn't like I was injecting heroin in my eyes or smoking crack on the streets."

Then what was she doing? "Well," she admits shamefacedly, "going to the movies, mainly."

She seemed like a mate made in heaven for Luhrmann, but when they first met, "I didn't know it was going to be a life-changing moment."

Things started to change when "I saw how everything in the production we were working on came together. Then I said, 'That person is a genius!' and I realized he was very special."

Even after that, it wasn't what anyone would call a whirlwind courtship. They finally married in 1997 on the stage of the Sydney Opera House while music from their various productions played and the Australian Opera's technical director, Noel Staunton, was flown in on wires, wearing a tutu, to bless the happy couple.

It's back down the hall to Luhrmann, who recalls the first show they did together that rocked the world: their 1990 *La Bohème*. "The people at the Australian Opera said to me, 'Our audiences are dying off, and we want you to bring new audiences in here, young audiences, and we want you to do that by taking this beloved old dusty *La Bohème* and producing it as if it were being done for the first time.'"

Luhrmann laughs, gets up, and starts pacing around the room as he recalls how it all came together. "To do research we lived the bohemian life in Paris — me and CM and another designer named Bill Marron." The grin is positively wicked. "We were wildly out of control. Our young bohemian days were pretty bohemian!"

They rejected doing it in the original period. "How could kids relate to people running around in floppy hats and checkered vests and beards like ZZ Top?"

Eventually they settled on 1957 as being "a good social and political match," and after some initial audience complaints, Dame Joan Sutherland led a standing ovation on opening night, and all was well.

Within a year, Luhrmann had started making a film of *Strictly Ballroom*, and the enthusiastic reception it received on its release in 1992 paved the way for his 1996 modernization of *Romeo & Juliet* starring Leonardo DiCaprio.

But everything, in many ways, was a warm-up for *Moulin Rouge*, the romantic musical fantasy starring Nicole Kidman and Ewan MacGregor, which opened the Cannes Film Festival in 2001, grossed over $250 million worldwide and earned eight Oscar nominations.

All of Luhrmann's work — from *La Bohème* through *Moulin Rouge* — has been so hugely romantic that it's fascinating to ponder how he defines that word.

"I'm romantic," he declares after a pause, "because when I look at the world, I see it through my own perspective, with a heightened emotional distance. Sure, I've fallen in love a lot — usually with the people I create with in a variety of relationships." His eyes flash as he quotes one of his favourite lines from *Strictly Ballroom*: "There isn't only one way to cha-cha-cha."

Martin has a different spin on things. "Romance to me is

making something beautiful out of nothing. And the sadness of knowing those things will always end.

"It's not just love between men and women, or men and men, or women and women. It's closeness, it's dream weaving. It's going into the unknown, having an idea and pursuing it to the end."

Luhrmann returns to the world of *La Bohème* as he settles down in his chair again. "I relate to the journey of a young man who goes with his friends and lives the bohemian life and dreams of being creative. And then reality comes crashing down on him. Oh, I understand that on a very personal level.

"You see, when you're under thirty, you don't realize what a get-out-of-jail-free card you've got. Then slam! The door to the cage comes down at thirty. And if you try to hold onto your youthful idealism past that, it will destroy you."

For the first time, Luhrmann looks tired. "I've just turned forty. I look back on my life so far, and I think of what Strindberg said in *The Dream Play*: 'It's great, but it's not what I thought it was going to be.'

"Growing up is realizing that it's not about how many groovy hotels you stay in or how many wild nights you have. Ultimately, you have to let go of it and discover a new and interesting life."

All the flash is gone as he speaks simply. "If I don't make that transition, I'll be in a lot of trouble. Because I'll wind up getting it all and losing it all." Just like the hero of his next movie, *Alexander the Great*, which he starts filming next year in Morocco, again starring DiCaprio.

"I'm doing that film because I fear that I might be like him (Alexander). He keeps pursuing a horizon that never comes, but it's the pursuit that distracts him. Distracts him and destroys him."

He looks off in the distance, his mind already halfway to Morocco. "I won't let it destroy me."

All of that is still to come in the second act of Baz Luhrmann's life. "Right now, as soon as this is opened, I need a little intermission.

I'll put on a pair of jeans, grab my backpack and a credit card, and vanish out there somewhere. Until I'm ready to come back."

But first he'll take Manhattan, then he'll take *Bohème*.

The New York media flipped for Baz and his *Bohème*, with coverage like most people only dream of and reviews so glowing it sounded like the press agents had written them.

Then, as he had promised, he vanished from sight for a while.

Athol Fugard
Courtesy of Athol Fugard

ATHOL FUGARD

No Man Is an Island

For more than 30 years, I had been going to the plays of Athol Fugard. Every time, I came away moved and troubled. Fugard caused me to question my own values, my own beliefs, and for a few days after each show, I re-evaluated the way I was living my life.

But you know how it is — the world always calls you back to its daily rhythm, and the honesty of Fugard is forgotten — until the next time. This is all by way of explaining why, when I finally went to Princeton, New Jersey, to interview Fugard in the spring of 2001, I had mingled feelings of gratitude and shame.

But the man himself quickly made it clear to me that he shared those same mixed emotions, and I soon found myself at ease.

It seems a long way from Robben Island.

The cherry trees are blossoming on the Princeton campus, and as the late afternoon sun dapples the granite walls, you wouldn't be surprised to see the spirit of F. Scott Fitzgerald striding across the quad of his old alma mater.

But a different writer is on today's agenda.

Athol Fugard is waiting in a windowless basement room of the university's McCarter Theatre to talk about South Africa — past and present.

A revival of his revolutionary 1973 play *The Island* is opening in Toronto and the 68-year-old Fugard has been persuaded to put aside for a while one of his mottoes: "I never look at what lies behind me."

This production of *The Island* stars the two men who helped create the show nearly three decades ago — John Kani and Winston Ntshona — and it's a lifelong affection and respect for them that enables Fugard to open the book of memory.

He sits on a simple metal chair and stares across a battered wooden table. He's compact, wiry with grizzled hair and beard cropped close. But the eyes still promise hidden fire, and the face is creased with a lifetime of feeling things deeply, then expressing them openly.

Background facts are something he likes to race through quickly, and so he offers the briefest of sketches of the black theatre group he started in 1963 called Serpent Players, and of the two labourers — John and Winston — who told him they wanted to make their living as actors.

"At that point in South Africa for a black man to think of being a professional actor was the biggest joke there was," recalls Fugard, "but they persisted. We pooled our resources, our imaginations, and we delivered."

What they delivered was *Sizwe Bansi Is Dead* (1968) a play that increased Fugard's reputation and launched its stars into the world.

Fugard laughs at the memory. "After a while, they had so many offers to do the play that they were going mad, and they came to me again and told me they needed something else to perform as well, something darker.

"Well, if you lived in South Africa back then, there was nothing darker than Robben Island."

Over a period of four centuries, this small patch of land 12 kilometres from Cape Town served as a place of exile and imprisonment. During the apartheid era, it became an international symbol of hatred and oppression, most notably for the 29-year incarceration of Nelson Mandela.

"I had put together quite a dossier on the Island, because over the years a lot of our players had wound up there, arrested by the police on one phony charge or another, so when John and Winston were in need, I put it all on the table."

The years have dissolved, and Fugard speaks with the intensity of the present as he remembers what happened next.

"We were preparing for a production of Sophocles' *Antigone* when the police broke up rehearsals, confiscated scripts, and detained one of our actors — a young man named Sharkey who was going to play Creon's son, Haemon. A kangaroo court sentenced him to ten years on Robben Island."

Fugard's face contorts with pain as he remembers this young man losing his chance to go onstage in "the most beautiful play ever written about defying unjust laws," and feeling the most terrible frustration. Then the eyes almost twinkle as he adds, "but he found a solution."

It was customary on Robben Island for the prisoners to produce a concert at the end of each year, with each cellblock providing one 15-minute sketch. Somehow Sharkey persuaded one of his fellow inmates to join him in a version of *Antigone*, recreating the script from memory and concentrating on the climactic confrontation between Creon and Antigone.

"I knew that there was our play," relates a triumphant Fugard, "and the three of us created it from scratch in thirteen days."

A twisted smile crosses his face. "At first, we were going to call it *The Hodoshe Span*. Hodoshe was the name they gave the chief warder on Robben Island. It's a beautiful metallic little green fly that feeds on shit.

"But in the end we settled on *The Island*. It's a better name, a perfect metaphor for isolation . . . and separation."

In the final version of the script, two inmates of Robben Island — named John and Winston after their creators — go through the pain, the terror, the monotony, and the humiliation of imprisonment. And the play's climax is the performance of *Antigone* that Sharkey engineered for real. Life imitating art on a variety of levels.

Fugard's eyes seem to be focused very far away. "Our first performance was in a wonderfully courageous little theatre in Cape Town called The Space. From a window backstage, you could see Robben Island.

"We knew the police were coming to the performance, and we didn't know what would happen to any of us. We didn't get involved in any big speeches. Then the three of us just looked out the window at Robben Island and shared one thought: the comrades, the brothers.

"And then we went in and did it."

The play triumphed in London and New York as well as in South Africa. Audiences responded to the mixture of broad comedy and painful drama that the work contains. As the character of John says, audiences "laugh in the beginning and listen at the end."

Fugard joyously embraces those polarities. "I'm not frightened of the word *entertainment*. I don't think anybody ever puts their bum down in a theatre seat unless they want to be entertained.

"You see, an actor is a kind of prostitute. Their fundamental gesture is this," and then he crooks his finger as invitingly as the slyest of procurers. "I've got something good for you, stay with me."

He chortles from the bottom of his belly: "Of course, they're all holy prostitutes, because they're trying to give the audience truth, or beauty, or maybe both."

The world success of *The Island* bought a certain degree of protection for the work and the artists involved, but that didn't mean they got off free and clear.

"They tried to force me into exile," says Fugard, all misty memories gone now.

"They did to me what they did to so many over the years: taking away your passport, opening your mail, barging into your house in the middle of the night, frightening your wife and children, persecuting any black friends you had because they were infinitely more vulnerable than you because they weren't protected by a white skin. All of this is designed to make you leave."

Fugard pauses, out of breath. He waits, and then speaks calmly.

"It was an option I never chose. My wife begged me to leave for her safety and the safety of our child, but I never considered it. I was selfish. But then, creativity is selfish. There's no such thing as a generous artist. You'd sell your grandmother for a good line in a play."

He lowers his eyes for a moment. "One of the prices of creativity is what it does to your family. The career comes first." He raises his glance again, eyes blazing. "And by the career, I don't mean your name up in lights on Broadway. I mean that an idea comes for a goddamn play and you've got to write it. You have no choice. The inquisition of the piece of blank paper in front of you. You've got to take that on and go into it."

He has discovered something: "That's the paradox! It requires personal selfishness to say things that are important. The lie that tells the truth."

His openness gives me the courage to ask him about something that has haunted me for 20 years. In his admittedly autobiographical play *"Master Harold"…and the Boys* there is a scene where Hally (the Fugard surrogate) spits in the face of Sam, the beloved family servant.

"Did it really happen?" I ask him.

"Yes, it did," he says, looking right at me.

"Something so terrible, so painful to admit. How did you find the courage to write it?" That was the question he wasn't expecting. "This is the moment I have been dreading since the day I wrote that scene." I wait, giving him all the time he needs.

"I still remember the morning, sitting at my desk. I came to the scene and knew I had to do it, but I skipped by it, leaving the moment out. When I went back and read it, the hypocrisy of what I had done, made me blush. And so I took the pencil and wrote: 'Hally spits in Sam's face.'" Fugard is weeping himself, now, the tears flowing freely down his face. "But I couldn't face it, and so I erased it and walked away. But when I came back to the table, I looked at the paper, wrote it down once more, and prepared to live with it forever."

I try to tell Fugard how brave and important I have found his writing over the years, but he'll hear none of it.

"I don't know if there's anything good or significant to be said about my own personal career. I don't know what the evaluation will be in terms of the final product. But I know this — and it's no mean achievement for someone who is basically cowardly by nature — I haven't played it safe.

"If you want to play it safe, you're in the wrong business. If you want to deliver something that is meaningful to an audience you've got to be right on the edge all the time, and in danger of falling off. That's the only way you can stay alive."

He sits back, finding new energy. "I'm glad *The Island* continues to be done and that people are so moved by it, but I can't go back to it anymore. I don't want to go back. The future is so goddamn exciting.

"John and Winston, those two wonderful talents, should face the new South Africa. God do we have scenes to talk about now! Anyone who thinks it's a bed of roses has got another think coming."

He leads the way outside, to a garden filled with lengthening shadows as he discusses the present situation in his homeland. "Changing the laws is one thing. Changing the human heart is a much much bigger and more complex matter.

"There was a wonderful period of euphoria after the first democratic election. But it didn't take long for that euphoria to pass and for us to wake up and realize it's the morning after the party now and we've all got a headache because we've all got a problem."

"You see, I knew my fellow South Africans. I knew how much fear there was in the hearts of the whites. I knew the huge reservoir of bitterness in the hearts of the blacks. There was no way I could believe Mandela was going to wave a magic wand and heal it all."

He jams a Tilley hat on his head to shield him from the sun's rays as he takes stock of all he has said.

"Yes, there is a credit side and a debit side, but no matter how much greed and corruption we endure it can never equal what we have achieved as a nation. We have pulled off nothing less than the political miracle of the last century."

As he says goodbye, he reaches out and grabs hold of my hands with both of his to make one final thing clear.

"What kept me alive all these years in South Africa was being able to witness the magnificent powers of survival of the human spirit.

"That is what I celebrate."

The Toronto production of *The Island* once again proved the timeless power of Fugard's work, and audiences were profoundly moved.

Fugard continues to write and his plays — old and new — are produced around the world.

"Master Harold"...and the Boys was revived on Broadway in the summer of 2003, with Danny Glover in the role of Sam. Glover had played Willie in the Broadway production I originally saw in 1982.

Susan Stroman
Getty Images

SUSAN STROMAN

In Search of the Girl in the Yellow Dress

With actors and actresses — even with authors — you think you know what they're going to be like from what you've seen of their work.

But with directors, it can be different. Some are so used to creating their own private worlds that they don't let outsiders share their vision willingly. And others prove to be egomaniacs of such magnitude that it can ruin the pleasure of seeing their creations from then on.

People who knew Susan Stroman told me she wasn't either of those types, and her work on the Broadway stage was so spectacular that it definitely made you wonder what the woman who thought up all those magical moments was like.

We tried to get together in person for months, but we were never in the same city at the same time. I finally decided, in October 2002, to see how much I could learn in a phone conversation.

The answer was: a lot.

It took a while to make contact with Susan Stroman, yet it was definitely worth the effort, because she raised the curtain on her musical-comedy triumphs and real-life tragedy.

But the first trick was tracking down the award-winning director/choreographer. Was she in New York, keeping an eye on her

Broadway smash, *The Producers,* or in Toronto, where a new touring version of her hit musical, *Contact,* is about to open? How about Los Angeles, where the film version is scheduled for shooting this June?

I finally found her in London, where she was in previews, preparing the show to meet the British public and critics.

So many projects, with only a single "Stro," as she is universally known, to put them all together. She's one of those, like Bob Fosse and Michael Bennett, who does it all. She doesn't just direct these shows — setting the tone, look, and pace — but she choreographs them as well, creating unique moments of dance that drive audiences wild.

I've seen her around Manhattan's theatre district: a beaming blonde almost perpetually wearing her black baseball cap. She's got cornflower blue eyes you can spot at 50 paces and a CinemaScope smile I've enjoyed at a distance.

But I'd never spoken to her until now, though I've heard plenty about her from people who've worked with the lady.

Eric McCormack had the pleasure of stepping into the lead of her revival of *The Music Man.* "It's like she carries the whole show in her head. It's thrilling and inspiring and a little scary, all at the same time."

And Mel Brooks leads a whole one-man cheering section when her name is mentioned. "She's a goddess, the greatest, the most fantastic, stupendous, amazing talent who ever lived — with the possible exception of me."

With all that adulation and achievement surrounding her, it's just a bit intimidating to know that she is on the other end of the phone, backstage at the Queen's Theatre in London, right before a preview performance of *Contact.* "Thank you for taking all the trouble to call me from Toronto" is how she starts, radiating a warmth you can feel across the Atlantic, and suddenly, I'm another member of Club Stro.

Her voice fits the way she looks — bright and sunny — with a twang that Oscar Hammerstein might have described as "corny as Kansas in August," even though she was born in Wilmington, Delaware, in 1954.

"That's where it all began," she recalls. "I'd sit under the family piano while Dad played show tunes. I had that music in my bones . . . and I would visualize it. I would see hordes of people dancing through my head."

A bit of a rueful laugh. "I had no choice but to become a choreographer. I'd been doing it in my brain ever since I was a kid."

All types of music ruled in her home; one man was king. "Fred Astaire. His movies were a very big deal. Everything would stop for an Astaire movie, and we'd all just sit and watch. . . . He was so effortless and believable that he inspired me. He still does."

Stroman started taking dance lessons at five and was a part of all the high school shows she could be in. But the desire hadn't fully crystallized until, while a student at the University of Delaware, she saw a touring production of the musical *Seesaw*.

"I was watching that big number in Act II, 'It's Not Where You Start, It's Where You Finish.' There was Tommy Tune, all six-foot-six of him, surrounded by girls with balloons, and suddenly I just knew this was for me."

One year after graduating in 1976, Stroman beat out three hundred other dancers for a choice tap position in a revival of *Hit the Deck* in Connecticut.

"I can admit it now," she says sheepishly, "but I was never interested in being a dancer. I knew I wanted to be a choreographer from the start, but I also knew that I couldn't just waltz into Manhattan and take charge of things."

So she worked for Fosse as the Hungarian murderess in a tour of *Chicago*, hoofed her way through shows with names like *Whoopee!*, and finally found herself mired in a 1980 fiasco called *Musical Chairs*. "During one awful rehearsal, I turned to a pal of mine in the cast, named Scott Ellis, and moaned, 'Don't you wish we were on the other side?' and he said, 'Don't worry, we will be.'"

The chance finally came. In 1987 the tiny Vineyard Theatre on Manhattan's Lower East Side asked Ellis to direct and Stroman to choreograph a revival of John Kander and Fred Ebb's *Flora the Red Menace*, the show that had launched Liza Minnelli's career in 1965. Critics adored it, and all the hot showbiz crowd came to see it, including director Hal Prince, who asked Stroman to help him stage an opera, and Minnelli herself, who brought Stroman to Radio City Music Hall as her choreographer.

The next step was a 1991 off-Broadway revue of Kander and Ebb songs called *And the World Goes 'Round*. The show was a huge hit and got Stroman her first Broadway show.

Director Mike Ockrent was looking for someone to choreograph his next big Broadway musical called *Crazy for You*, with a score made up entirely of Gershwin classics. He checked out Stroman's work and asked her to join the team. She knew this was her big chance and gave it everything she had, including a show-stopping staging of "I Got Rhythm" filled with washboards, pickaxes, and everything but the kitchen sink. (Although I think that, too, finally worked its way in.)

Crazy for You knocked New York on its ear when it opened in 1992. Frank Rich in the *New York Times* offered Stroman the Gotham equivalent of sainthood when he hailed her as "extraordinary."

The success of that show brought her everything she'd ever dreamed of: professional credentials, lots of job offers, a Tony Award (her first of five), and — best of all — she got the guy. During rehearsals for the show, she'd fallen in love with Ockrent and they married in 1996.

She did two more shows with him, and she also worked with old partners like Prince and Ellis. Almost everything she touched glittered, and she became known as a kind of musical comedy Midas.

But Stroman knew that she was running out of steam, and felt that she needed to recharge her creative batteries. That opportunity came when Lincoln Center asked her to develop a dance theatre piece from the ground up.

Stroman had been carrying around an image: "An extraordinary girl I saw out dancing one evening, wearing a yellow dress. She moved with such confidence that I just knew she was going to change someone's life that night."

From that, she gradually built the show now known as *Contact*, which conveys a trio of complex human stories. Playwright John Weidman helped her fashion the scenarios, and she took the music from everywhere, from classical and jazz through swing and driving rock.

"Swinging" is a Gallic riff off a painting by Jean-Honoré Fragonard. A beautiful woman swings in a pastoral setting while two men fight over her.

"Did You Move?" is a scene in an Italian restaurant that Billy Joel never imagined, with a wife trapped in an abusive marriage trying to escape through fantasy.

And the title piece, "Contact," finds Michael, a successful but suicidal advertising man, at an after-hours club where he meets that Girl in the Yellow Dress and tries to save himself.

Where do all these characters come from? Is Stroman herself The Girl in the Yellow Dress, the woman out to change everyone's life?

"Sure," she laughs, "part of me is."

But then she pauses, and you can almost hear the locks opening inside. "There's a little bit of me in every character. There has to be in order for it to be real. Yeah, I'm that girl, but then I'm also Michael, coming home alone with an armful of awards and not knowing what it all means."

How about the wife in the abusive relationship?

"That's never happened to me literally, but it's one of my deepest fears, being trapped like that." But when asked where that fear comes from, she tightens up a bit.

"I get that from people in my family," she says abruptly and switches conversational lanes like a N.Y. cabbie.

"The girl on the swing with two men fighting over who's going to push her? I'll tell you," a world-weary laugh, "a lot of the time you've just gotta get out there and push yourself! But there's plenty of people waiting in the wings when you need them, people with good hearts, people who are nurturing."

Stroman knows what she's talking about. While she was working on *Contact*, Ockrent was dying of leukemia. He succumbed on December 2, 1999, at the age of 53.

When she won the Tony Award for her choreography six months later, her acceptance speech told the world, "Dance has lifts and dips and unexpected turns, just as real life does."

I ask her if it was hard to revisit the show, even three years later, and the pause that follows is its own answer. When she does find her voice, it's huskier, with tears just underneath.

"Yes, it's tough. In some ways, it's tougher. We had a benefit here for the Mike Ockrent Foundation, and I could barely get through the show or the ceremony. But I have to remind myself that I wouldn't have thought of *Contact* if I hadn't met Mike. I wouldn't have had this solace."

The words are flowing freely now, almost as though talking about it were a relief.

"When Mike was ill, I would just move back and forth — from his hospital room to the basement at Lincoln Center. I was able to lose myself there and find myself there, and that was a great blessing."

After the huge success of *The Producers* in 2001, *Newsweek* announced that "the musical theatre needs Susan Stroman," but she feels it's the other way around.

"I need the musical theatre. It's an art form that makes me very happy and gives me tremendous comfort. I don't know how other widows get along if they don't have something they can turn to like I do to my work. It's my partner now. And thank God, I love what I do."

The curtain is about to rise on *Contact*, but I ask her one more question to complete the picture in my mind. "What are you wearing?"

Her laugh is like a follow-spot illuminating a darkened stage.

"A black baseball cap. That's what I always wear!"

Sure. But somewhere, in the back of her closet, I'll bet she's got a yellow dress.

By the end of 2003, four different companies of *The Producers* will be onstage in North America, with British and Australian productions also in the works.

Despite a 2001 Broadway flop called *Thou Shalt Not*, Stroman is anxious to get a new show on in New York, and the latest reports have her working with Nathan Lane on a new version of Stephen Sondheim's *The Frogs* (based on the play by Aristophanes) for the Lincoln Center.

If all goes well, their work will open in 2004, 30 years after it was first seen in a production mounted at the Yale University swimming pool.

Neil LaBute
Bernard Weil/Toronto Star

NEIL LaBUTE

The Futon with a Carving Knife

This one was a challenge. LaBute is known to be a very sharp but very slick interview. A Teflon kind of guy, to whom nothing ever sticks.

I was anxious to get him to commit on the morality (or amorality) of some of the things he'd said in his plays, and I was also anxious to find out about his adolescence — a period that hadn't been touched on in depth during any of his previous interviews.

We met one autumn morning in 2002 in the lobby of a SoHo hotel, and fenced with each other for an hour.

You can judge the results for yourself.

"I don't trust anything that bleeds for a week and doesn't die."

Writer-director Neil LaBute hurled that misogynistic line from his first film, *In the Company of Men*, like a hand grenade into the 1997 Sundance Film Festival, and the explosion that followed launched his career.

It instantly marked him as "The Outrageous One," a reputation he's nurtured with subsequent works like *Bash* and *Your Friends and Neighbors*.

Although he's shown a mellower side in movies like *Nurse Betty* and *Possession*, it's the bad-boy image he enjoys cultivating.

"I never mean those lines as a cattle prod to the gut," he concedes, "but it doesn't hurt to use them to shake things up."

Well, Toronto theatre-goers will soon get a chance to shake their LaBute when his play, *The Shape of Things*, opens in town.

If you dealt strictly with the plot — a dangerous tactic with LaBute — you could describe *Shape* as a kind of college romance, about brilliant Evelyn, who turns schlumpy Adam into a veritable dreamboat, starting out by working on his physique and ending up by talking him into plastic surgery, videotaping every step along the way.

"I always find it amusing when women find a guy they're interested in and then immediately say things like, 'God, if I could just get him to change his hair!'" LaBute snorts, obviously knowing that changing his hair would be a lost cause. The 39-year-old Big Bad Wolf of American Arts has a coiffure that could best be described as early Brillo pad.

In fact, the unreconstructed Adam from *Shape* is not unlike LaBute himself, who resembles the young Francis Ford Coppola — a big, bearded futon of a guy with a mind like a carving knife.

We're sitting in a quiet corner of the lobby of the Mercer Hotel, one of those new boutique establishments in downtown Manhattan so chic that they don't have a name anywhere on the building. If you know it's there, babe, then you belong.

To be honest, it seems like a strange place to be chatting up this Detroit-born, Spokane, Washington–raised, Mormon-educated auteur, but contradictions aren't just the name of the game with LaBute, they're the game itself. No wonder our conversation went from biography to morality in the course of an hour.

Searching for a clue to his Rubik's Cube personality, I ask about his high school days, which haven't ever surfaced in the hundreds of interviews he's given.

"I was a constant moviegoer," he confesses gladly, "and the best job I ever had was ushering at a theatre that showed revivals. Not only did I get to go to all their attractions, but it made me welcome at every other theatre in town."

Having pegged him as a cinema geek, it then comes as a shock to hear that LaBute was "president of both my junior high and high school classes." When he sees my look of astonishment, he adds, "I was the only president who never went to the football games on Friday, because that was when the new movies opened and I didn't want to miss them."

How did he pull that off? "Well, in the same way that I write characters who have many faces, I was many people to many people. I was the quintessential actor; I could fit in very well. I had that whole Kurt Vonnegut 'who am I this time?' thing going for me. My personality was very adaptable to various groups — the bad crowd, the sports guys, the kids in the orchestra — I kind of fit in with everybody."

Since so much of his work centres on the male-female dynamic, I wonder what his dating life was like in those years. He grins. "Girls were and have remained good. They are the preferable gender. I was pretty normal in those terms."

He shoots back with rapid-fire honesty when asked if there was a particular type of girl he liked. "Yeah. The one you can't have. Everybody's favourite type of girl." The air of the unattainable still surrounds the love objects in his work, and he admits, "You only refine your foibles when you get older. You don't get any more suave or clever. You just take your greatest hits and repeat them, because there are new faces to try them on."

And then he seems to go back to a very specific place in his memory. "What if you walk across the dance floor and she says no? Do you have to pretend you were heading for the bathroom anyway, or walk back to where you were, publicly humiliated? How willing are you to risk that public shame to get something you're interested in?"

It's a question that's obviously haunted him for more than 20 years, and still resonates throughout his work, from the heroines of *Nurse Betty* and *Possession* through the romantically ambivalent quartet of characters in *Shape*, playing dangerous games of attraction and rejection on a Midwestern university campus.

College was a different scene for LaBute, and much has been made in the press about the fact that, although not a Mormon himself, he went to Brigham Young University for his drama training. ("Well, it was there, and they offered me money," is how he now dismisses it with a shrug.)

When he moved to Utah, however, LaBute found himself drifting into Mormonism, a situation that proved untenable once he started writing plays about gay-bashing members of the church. His current status is that of "disfellowship," which he describes as "the first step to excommunication."

In the years that followed, he worked as a grad student at NYU and a drama teacher in Indiana. He also married and had two kids, but his family life is absolutely not on the table for discussion. ("Some things," he insists with a strange rigor for such an outspoken individual, "are private.") For the record, they live in Ft. Wayne, Indiana, and she's a family therapist.

In the Company of Men was made for US$25,000, but it electrified the film community with its barbaric portrait of a reptilian young executive who seduces a hearing-impaired secretary, just so he can destroy her later.

His subsequent work is also so full of men who set out to abuse women — psychologically as well as physically — that the obvious accusation has arisen that he's a misogynist . . . perhaps "a soft-core misogynist," as one character in his most recent film, *Possession*, is described.

The denial is quick in coming. "I'm much harder on men than on women. If I were pushed, I'd have to say that I don't like men as much as I like women. Sure, women get abused in my work, but they never have it coming. The men are where the trouble is. Being a man, I know what we're capable of, so I call us on it all the time."

But Evelyn in *Shape* is a pretty cold-blooded piece of work, and her redo of Adam is much, much more than a mere Cosmo makeover.

"Women can be as ruthless and clever and duplicitous as men," LaBute allows. "It's just that they wear skirts, so they look better doing it." And he flashes one of his evil grins, knowing he's just lobbed another controversial curveball over the plate.

I decide to call him on it, and quote a line from the play that says "there's got to be a line out there somewhere, a line between really saying something and just needing attention." Does he feel he crosses that line?

He shakes his burly head. "I don't think provocation is a bad thing. I play a game with the audience of saying 'Closer, closer, it's okay, nothing is going to hurt you,' and then I whack them back into their seats. I don't think that's a harmful thing to do. I think the audience enjoys it. They're drawn to the unexpected."

LaBute's characters don't just behave unexpectedly; they often act in a way that many people would call immoral. But what is his own definition of morality?

"I would define it," he says leeringly, "with a great length of elastic cord. Very flexible. If no one hears the tree fall in the forest, did it really fall? Or is the important thing whether or not the forest ranger saw the blowjob you were getting behind the tree?"

Yet in the complicated and contradictory world of Neil LaBute, it isn't even acting on your obsessions that proves most telling. "What interests me is a person who stands in a store staring at the thing they want for hours, and even edges to the door holding it . . . but never actually leaves."

As he stands up to leave, he offers one last thought. "I don't believe desire is as bad as action. Does that make it true, or does it just make it convenient? I don't know. I just know what makes it for me. That's all you can ever go by."

Since our meeting, LaBute has released a film version of *The Shape of Things* and also had a new play off-Broadway called *The Mercy Seat*.

Continuing in his controversial groove, it casts Sigourney Weaver and Liev Schreiber as adulterous lovers who find that the disaster of 9/11 might prove to be the solution to all their personal problems.

The reaction — as usual, with LaBute — was widely mixed.

Ann Reinking
Courtesy of Ann Reinking

ANN REINKING

Keeper of the Fosse Flame

Bob Fosse was always high on the list of people I wished I had gotten to interview. He was a true original, finding new ways to tell stories with song and to allow dance to display our darkest dreams. Starting with *Redhead*, in 1959, I saw every show he every directed or choreographed that made it into New York, as well as all his films.

Given my obsession with his work, it only makes sense that any exchange I had with people who worked with Fosse, would turn out to be about him as well. That certainly was the case with Gwen Verdon (see p. 244) as well as this interview with Ann Reinking, which I conducted in June 2001.

Leave it to Bob Fosse to choreograph his own legacy.

When the master musical stager imagined a vision of his death in the 1979 film *All That Jazz*, he summoned three gorgeous women to send his alter ego Joe Gideon on his way. His brassy wife vamped him with "After You've Gone," his stunning mistress teased him with "There'll Be Some Changes Made," and his doe-eyed daughter brought it all home with "Some of These Days." And as he sparkled toward the afterlife in a gold lamé suit with an iridescence Elvis would have envied, they all promised to guard his memory in "Bye Bye Love."

Twenty years later, that's just what happened when Gwen

Verdon, Ann Reinking, and Nicole Fosse all served as directors/consultants on the musical tribute *Fosse*. This sizzling song-and-dance salute to the work of one of Broadway's late great showmen dazzled with numbers gleaned from his whole career — from the early days of *Damn Yankees* through his final show, *Big Deal*. It opened on Broadway in January of 1999, wowed the critics, and won the Tony for Best Musical of the Year.

"Where do you start to talk about Bobby?" Ann Reinking thinks about the question for a moment and then answers. "Go back to where *he* started, because that's what Bobby did all of his life — return to his roots."

He was born Robert Louis Fosse on June 23, 1927, in Chicago, Illinois. His mother spotted his talent as a dancer at an early age, and he spent his childhood years learning tap, ballet, and acrobatics. While in his early teens, he was part of a duo called the Riff Brothers that played burlesque houses and gave young Fosse a jaded view of human sexuality that he never really shook off.

After high school he spent two years in the navy and hit New York as a chorus boy in a revue called "Dance Me A Song" (1950). At this point, he was dancing as "Fosse and Niles" with his first wife, Mary Ann Niles, but he promptly dumped her for the show's leading lady, a hot musical comedy star named Joan McCracken.

A lifelong pattern was already established. Women fell for Fosse, and fell hard. He liked them too, but he liked to use them as well. And when they stopped being useful, he just moved on to the next. "I hate farewell scenes," he told one departing lover, a biographer, "they don't play very well."

McCracken herself was later to feel the sting of a Fosse betrayal and drank herself into an early grave, but she unknowingly did the world one great service: she talked the people who were creating a new musical called *The Pajama Game* (1954) into hiring her Bob as their choreographer.

Fosse was only 27, but that was old in dancer years, and he

wasn't making it big. He was too quirky. He couldn't do other people's steps, only his own. And even the hats he always wore couldn't disguise his rapidly thinning hair.

No, he couldn't go back and age into ignominy as Bobby Riff, the burlesque hoofer. He had to reinvent himself as Fosse, the choreographer, which he did with surprising ease.

His dances for *The Pajama Game* got raves, and he continued with the creative team on to its next show, *Damn Yankees* (1955), with its plutonium-hot, red-headed dancing star, Gwen Verdon.

"We didn't like each other when we first met," Verdon admitted to me in an interview more than 40 years later, "but there was an attraction there. Oh brother, was there an attraction!"

And it wasn't just sex. "It's like the two of us had been waiting for each other. I had the body made to do the dances that he'd been dreaming in his head for years."

And the results were there for all the world to see: sensuous, erotic choreography with an edge of wicked humour. Bob Fosse choreography.

The dancing grew so overtly sexual that when *The Pajama Game-Damn Yankees* team reunited a third time for *New Girl in Town* (1957), it precipitated a major fight between Fosse/Verdon and the rest of the creators.

The musical was based on Eugene O'Neill's *Anna Christie*, the story of a waterfront prostitute, and Fosse saw it as a grand opportunity for a no-holds-barred bordello ballet.

"It was magnificent," Verdon remembered, "full of sadness as well as sex. It was Bobby reaching for high art, for something more."

But the others, led by director George Abbott, called it "smut," and it never got onstage in New York. Fosse vowed not to be put in such a position again, and so he reinvented himself as Bob Fosse, Director.

Together with Verdon, he created the Tony-winning *Redhead* (1959), a celebration of each other and their vision of what musical theatre could be.

It was the show that paved the way for the later triumphs of Gower Champion, Michael Bennett, Tommy Tune, and Susan Stroman — a show where the entire vision moved from the world of dance. "Perhaps in the future, all musical comedies should be written by choreographers," wrote Brooks Atkinson of the *New York Times* with eerie prescience.

But once again, Fosse ran into a brick wall. He was fired from his next directorial gig, a quick flop called *The Conquering Hero* (1961), and he took two steps back as merely choreographer of shows like *How to Succeed in Business without Really Trying* (1961) and *Little Me* (1962).

The shadow of Bobby Riff loomed up again, and times grew tough in the volatile marriage. Even the birth of their longed-for and beloved daughter Nicole didn't ensure Fosse's fidelity.

"There were always other women," Verdon admitted. "Sometimes I knew about them; sometimes I didn't. I'm not sure which was worse."

As a love gift and an act of forgiveness, Fosse built one more spectacular star vehicle for Verdon, *Sweet Charity* (1966). Although the show was a smash hit, a cynical observer would have to note that once again Fosse was casting his wife as a whore, and the dance-hall girls who surrounded her were an echo of the women who had chipped away at his innocence during those teen years in burlesque.

Ups and downs continued, as erratic as the Dexedrine highs Fosse was now using to get through the day. The film *Sweet Charity* (1968) was a huge flop, and for four years he was virtually unemployable. At the bottom of this pit, he and Verdon separated, although they never officially divorced.

Strangely enough, once liberated from the bonds of a permanent relationship, Fosse's career went through the roof, and he exploded in all media, winning the unprecedented triple crown for directors in 1973: Tony (for *Pippin*), Oscar (for *Cabaret*), and Emmy (for *Liza with a Z*). And this is when he met Ann Reinking.

The stunning leggy brunette from Seattle was only 22 when Fosse cast her in *Pippin*, and the chemistry between them was immediate.

I spoke with Reinking on the phone from London, where she was rehearsing the European tour of *Fosse*, and her uniquely husky voice acquired an instant intimacy when I asked her what it was like to work with Fosse. "It was a dream come true," she began, "but every dream has a price. He was a taskmaster, but he wasn't cruel, not really. He just wanted 100 per cent from everyone, in everything."

The Reinking/Fosse relationship was to go through numerous ups and downs over the years, and in the midst of it all, he created one last show for Gwen, the 1975 *Chicago*.

During the problematic tryout period, Reinking was involved in her own troubled musical, as Joan of Arc in a show called *Goodtime Charley*. All of this would prove grist for the Fosse mill when he turned it into one of the pivotal sequences of *All That Jazz*.

Before their final breakup, Fosse and Reinking created together once more, in the 1978 hit *Dancin'*, which featured some of his boldest and toughest work — all of which saw Reinking front and centre.

She recalls the period. "He kept pushing me to go further and further. He'd taunt me with paradoxes. He'd say, 'You like yourself, but you don't like yourself. You know you're good, but you don't believe it.'"

There's an audible sigh as she lets go of the moment. "But that's what Bobby was like. A paradox. Fragile weight. Elegant but funny. Sexual but witty. Sophisticated innocence."

An ironic chuckle. "Innocence. That was something he kept examining. Innocence, the loss of innocence. And everything in between."

His final work explored this dichotomy, ever darker on the screen (*Star 80*, 1983), while onstage he retreated into the music and moves of his childhood (*Big Deal*, 1987). Unfortunately, none of his later work was successful, and when, on September 23, 1987, Fosse collapsed into the arms of Verdon outside the theatre in Washington, DC, where a revival of *Sweet Charity* was just about to open, he feared he would be forgotten.

But Fosse's art has long outstripped his death. In fact, it's now generally perceived that he was ahead of his time. The mordant cynicism and gritty reality he espoused didn't sit all that well in those days when guileless Jimmy Carter and clueless Ronald Reagan ruled America.

Today, in a post-O.J., post-Clinton, how-close-was-that-election-anyway world where the Bush twins almost seem like Fosse creations, his bracing worldview goes down like a tonic.

We need Fosse now, more than ever, to show us the decay behind the glitter, the darkness in back of all those twinkling lights.

"That's the one thing that makes me sad," admits Reinking. "Bob never got to see that he was a classic. But if there's a heaven, and he's up there, I bet he's having a crooked little celestial smile."

Verdon died last year, Nicole Fosse has stepped back out of the limelight to concentrate on her personal life, so now it's up to Reinking to be Keeper of the Fosse Flame, and that's just what she does, as productions of *Chicago* and *Fosse* criss-cross the globe.

She leaves me with her final thoughts on the man. "It was all about paradox again. He was self-effacing but self-promoting. Diffident, but confident. He was a master.

"He gave you the best he could possibly give, and it was superb."

Ann Reinking has continued to have a productive career as a choreographer, even venturing slightly away from Fosse's shadow as she did in the 2003 production of *The Look of Love* on Broadway.

Fosse's ghost continued to rule the entertainment scene — as his ahead-of-its-time *Chicago* proved to be the defining event of the musical theatre world onstage and later on screen.

IV

FROM TELEVISION

Bea Arthur
Ron Bull/Toronto Star

BEA ARTHUR

From Spit Drinks to Sitcoms

Aging stars and vampires dislike the daylight equally. I admit it was cruel to meet Bea Arthur at the Toronto Airport coffee shop at nine on an October morning in 2002, but I was flying in from Boston, she was heading off to Los Angeles, and it was the only way we could connect.

It did lend a certain slow-motion start to our conversation, but once she'd had some coffee to prime the pump, the memories started flowing.

And to be fair, I began by catching her off guard . . .

"God'll get you for that."

Bea Arthur glares at me with those hooded cobra eyes of hers as she spits out Maude Findlay's catchphrase threat.

I've surprised her by starting our early-morning encounter not by discussing her Emmy Award-winning performances in *Maude* or *The Golden Girls*, but by reminding her of one of her direst flops: the 1968 stage musical version of Bruce Jay Friedman's darkly comic novel, *A Mother's Kisses*.

"That's an awful thing to say to a seventy-nine-year-old woman before she's even had a cup of coffee," she scowls, reaching for some life-giving caffeine. "How the hell did you even know about it?"

When I tell her I actually took the train down to Baltimore to catch its final performance, her voice drops from its usual bari-tone to a pure bass in mock solicitude.

"You have my sympathy. That must have been as awful to sit through as it was to perform."

And then she laughs. It's a sound not unlike the Wicked Witch of the West crossed with James Earl Jones, but it's one of the things that's made her a star.

Her one-woman show, *Bea Arthur on Broadway — Just Between Friends*, has toured North America, had a successful run in New York, played to packed houses in Australia and is about to make its Canadian premiere.

"I have a deep and abiding bond with Canada," deadpans Arthur as she reaches for a bagel. "I appeared with Wayne and Shuster on *The Ed Sullivan Show*, and I did all those Shoppers Drug Mart commercials."

She's referring to the series of pitches she did during the 1980s for the Canadian pharmacy chain. Industry insiders remember to this day how acrimonious the taping sessions were, and Arthur doesn't deny it.

"They wanted me to be an old lady with a bun. They were stupid. I brought a very sexy evening gown, and there was . . . much discussion." Her voice scoops downward again on the last two words, one of her tricks of comic punctuation.

There's never been anybody else quite like Bea Arthur, with a 55-year career that's taken her to the top of the theatre and tele-vision worlds where she's created a gallery of great iconic figures: Yente the Matchmaker in the original stage version of *Fiddler on the Roof*, her Tony Award-winning triumph as Vera Charles in *Mame* as well as the title character in *Maude*, and the feisty Dorothy Zbornak in *The Golden Girls*.

Arthur's offered the public a lot of different faces over the decades, but what's the woman behind those faces really like?

She was born Bernice Frankel in New York City on May 13, 1923. When she was 11, her parents moved to Cambridge, Maryland, where they were practically the only Jewish family.

That, and the fact she reached her 5-foot-9 height by her 12th birthday, made her a bit of an outcast, "and so I started being funny to get accepted. I guess it happens to a lot of us oddballs."

Originally, Arthur trained to be a medical laboratory technician. A few years actually doing that work "bored me stiff," and so she decided to take a chance at acting.

She went to New York and enrolled in the drama workshop at the New School for Social Research, where renowned director Erwin Piscator took a shine to her.

"One look at me and he decided I was it," she laughs, "I must have been quite stunning at the time. I had enormous breasts . . . " she stares down at the ravages of time and quips, "I've since had them surgically removed."

"But Piscator believed in me and gave me the most amazing roles — Clytemnestra (in *The Oresteia*), Gertrude (in *Hamlet*), Katherine (in *The Taming of the Shrew*) . . . and I didn't know shit!"

Her fellow performers in the workshop included the likes of Tony Curtis, Marlon Brando, Harry Belafonte, and a young actor/director named Gene Saks, whom she would marry in 1950. They stayed together in an often-tempestuous relationship until 1978, and he directed her both on stage and screen in *Mame*.

But after leaving Piscator's company, Arthur went through some tough times and wound up earning her living in a place she'll never forget. "It was a joint called the 19th Hole in Greenwich Village, and baby, believe me, it wasn't near any golf course. I auditioned as a singer, and they told me I had the job. Some job."

Even 50 years later, her eyes look pained. "Sure I got to sing once a night, but the rest of the time, I worked the bar. We'd get guys to buy us drinks, but they were always spit drinks. You know what those are?"

She demonstrates with her orange juice.

"We'd order a shot of rye and a Coke chaser. We'd chug the rye and then spit it into the Coke. Then the bartender would give us a fresh Coke with no booze in it."

"The guys thought they were getting us plastered, and so they kept buying drinks. Nice, huh? I quit the night that three young Norwegian sailors who didn't speak a word of English spent all their money on me."

But a break was waiting for her, and she got cast as Lucy Brown in the legendary off-Broadway revival of *The Threepenny Opera*, starring Lotte Lenya.

"I adored her," says Arthur, snapping back into positive mode. "She taught me that comedy was just taking yourself seriously. I didn't think my role in the show was supposed to be funny, so I was shocked on opening night."

A distant smile as she remembers: "I sang my first line, 'I used to believe in the days I was pure . . . ' and I got a huge laugh. I paused and sang my second line '... and I was pure like you used to be,' and the laugh was even bigger. Lenya was waiting for me backstage. 'That's how you do it,' she said, 'You believe it.'"

Arthur had a less pleasant encounter with two other legends when she worked on *Fiddler on the Roof*. I ask her if there is any truth to the rumour that she tried to quit her role as Yente the Matchmaker during tryouts.

"It's not a rumour. It's true. When we opened, I got good reviews. Too many good reviews. Jerome Robbins — who was a genius and a bastard at the same time — started cutting my role to shreds. 'Bea,' he explained, 'this is not a show about a match-maker.'"

Producer Hal Prince persuaded her to stay, and she had the mixed blessing of continuing to work with the star, Zero Mostel. "I was lucky. I never had much to do with him. He was absolutely brilliant, but he was not a nice person. Haven't you ever noticed how many so-called liberals are really dictators?"

On the other hand, she remembers her time starring opposite Angela Lansbury in *Mame* as "pure joy, a lot of fun," tinged only by the regret that "musicals have changed. Now they workshop them forever, and they fail. We used to fling them together in three weeks, and they were hits. We did shows with no helicopters and no chandeliers, and we all won Tonys."

Norman Lear brought her to the small screen when he had her appear as Edith Bunker's outspoken liberal cousin Maude on a 1971 episode of his smash series *All in the Family*. The viewer response was so positive she found herself with her own series just one year later.

Maude was still a hit when Arthur walked away from it in 1978. "I thought we'd done everything we could do. But it was one hell of a series, the way we kept pushing the envelope — episodes on abortion, alcoholism, homosexuality. I was proud of it."

She's proud in a different way of *The Golden Girls*, which enjoyed an enormously popular run from 1985 to 1992. Arthur played Dorothy, den mother to a group of "ladies in later life" striking out on their own in Florida.

"It was a feel-good show," she recalls. "That's why it worked so well then and still works now in reruns. Besides, the relationship between me and Sophia (Dorothy's mother, played by Estelle Getty) is one of the great comic inventions of all time. Our differences in height, personality, everything."

The discussion turns to whether she had a favourite episode, and her smile grows bigger. "Yeah, the one where we entered a talent show dressed as Sonny and Cher. Guess who was who? I'll never forget doing it. We laughed so hard . . . "

Arthur's flamboyant personality has also included her offstage self, and over the years her fondness for considerable alcoholic intake has been noted by many of the people who've worked with her.

When I ask if she has any comment to make about it, her reply is immediate and unflinching.

"I believe that you're here on Earth for a short time, and while you're here, you shouldn't forget it.

"I enjoy my life. I always remember that line from *Mame*: 'Life's a banquet, and most poor sons of bitches are starving to death.'"

"Do I look like I'm hungry? Or thirsty?"

Arthur still continues to tour her show, appear on TV, and serve as a spokesperson for various AIDS-related charities as well as doing considerable work for PETA — People for the Ethical Treatment of Animals.

Eric McCormack
Louie D/LDP

ERIC McCORMACK

Triumph of the Will

As the following story reveals, I knew and worked with Eric McCormack long before he became famous as the star of TV's *Will & Grace*. Still, it was a kind of homecoming to meet him again on the set of the show, nearly a dozen years after we'd last parted company.

After saying goodbye at a Toronto restaurant on New Year's Eve, 1989, we renewed our friendship in Los Angeles on a Friday afternoon in February 2001.

"You're too modern, too American, too funny. Perhaps you'd be more comfortable on a television sitcom." Those are the words a young actor named Eric McCormack heard in 1989 to explain why he wouldn't be invited back for another season at the Stratford Festival.

Twelve years later, he's the star of the hit comedy series *Will & Grace*, which won three Emmys last fall (including Best Comedy Series) and sits proudly as the centrepiece of NBC's "Must See TV" Thursday line-up.

McCormack himself was also nominated for an Emmy and joined with his cast members in receiving the Outstanding Performance by an Ensemble in a Comedy Series Award from the Screen Actors Guild. With all that in his present, he can afford to smile wryly at his past and at the memory of then artistic director

David William's decision not to keep him on at Stratford. "I suppose I was grateful that he wasn't tempting me with security," McCormack says.

But he didn't feel that way at the time. I remember meeting McCormack a few weeks after that conversation. The past summer I had directed him as Demetrius in Stratford's *A Midsummer Night's Dream*.

When I asked if he was returning to the festival, he bit his lip, lowered his eyes and then looked at me with that hurt spaniel gaze Will offers Grace in unguarded moments. "They don't want me back. Maybe they're right. Maybe I do belong on television. Well, I'm going to find out."

He started to go, turned, raised his hand in farewell, and said, "Hey, I'll see you around."

It took 12 years, but here we are again.

This time the California sun is shining on the Studio City home of *Will & Grace* as I arrive outside the dressing rooms. I'm looking for the one marked "Eric McCormack" when I hear the voice, unchanged.

"Ouzounian, how the hell are you?"

He's moving across the parking lot, Starbucks cup in hand, and the first thing I realize with a rush of relief is that he hasn't really changed.

Okay, maybe he's gotten better-looking.

He's probably going to be one of those guys who hits his prime in his forties. (He turns 38 next month.) The face is more sculpted now, and gone is the youthful pudge of the Stratford days, as well as the hangdog look from too many late nights at post-show watering holes.

The Canadian stage actor's habitual pallor has been replaced by the sleek, omnipresent L.A. tan, and his hair has been styled so skillfully it looks as if no one has gone near it.

Clothes? Trimly tailored jeans, blue V-neck shirt, and navy zip-up sweater. Casual but classy or "rich but not gaudy," to quote Polonius.

In short, he's a TV star.

McCormack leads the way through the set, which looks like a bomb has hit it. Everything's pushed to the corners, and the walls of the various sets are all stacked up on top of each other.

"Jim Burrows," says McCormack by way of explanation, naming the legendary creator of *Cheers* who now directs *Will & Grace* as well as serving as one of its executive producers. "He hated the way the floor looked after last night's taping, and he ordered it all repainted today."

We find a corner that's still intact, a section of apartment belonging to Karen, the babe with the air-raid-siren voice played by Megan Mullally. She's not around, nor is Sean Hayes' irrepressible Jack or Debra Messing's warm-hearted Grace.

Today it's Will's World, and welcome to it. Will Truman is the uptight but endearing gay lawyer who stands at the helm of one of the most successful sitcoms in recent years.

Not bad for a kid from Hogtown, I think, as McCormack gets us seated, looks around, and smiles, totally at home.

"This is really where I've always wanted to be. You know how actors always have fantasies about their careers? Playing the title role in a network sitcom, being directed by James Burrows. That was my fantasy."

And although McCormack isn't yet 40, it took him a long time — in show-business years — to get where he wanted to go.

Born and raised in Toronto, he knew even as a kid that he wanted to be an actor. "I remember the first time I ever went to Stratford. Something happened to me, which is ironic in light of what I do for a living these days.

"We were being bused into town for a student matinee — I was probably in ninth grade — and we were driving towards the Festival Theatre when we passed the FAG Ball Bearings factory."

"One of the guys said, 'Hey, McCormack, is that where you work?' And I said, 'No, but if you wait a few minutes I'll show you where I'm going to work.' A self-fulfilling prophecy, I guess."

He smiles — humour, hurt, and hubris all in one — and you see the qualities that made series creators David Kohan and Max Mutchnick feel he was the right actor to bring Will Truman to life.

McCormack went on to study theatre at Ryerson Polytechnic University, where "I was way too serious. I remember they let us work as extras in one professional show, *Antigone*, and I was playing the Page.

"Well, I was inventing an offstage life for my character, filling my notebook with descriptions of how the Page spent his day. And this older actor asked me what I was doing, so I told him.

"He laughed, then he told some other actors, and they all laughed some more. I felt very young and very foolish."

In 1985, McCormack auditioned to get into the apprenticeship program at Stratford. He succeeded, and his first assignment was in British director Michael Bogdanov's edgy modern-dress production of *Measure for Measure*.

"I was expecting to hold a spear and wear a helmet. Not quite. I was in full drag — a wig, heels, makeup." He pauses, remembering it, and then a thought crosses his mind. "You see, everything was leading to *Will & Grace*, eventually."

McCormack was to stay four more seasons at Stratford under the wing of the next artistic director, John Neville. "Neville looked after me in those years, in ways I sort of almost took for granted. He brought me along slowly. At the time, I thought it was all happening too slowly, and I'd say 'John, I'm hungry,' and he'd go, 'Relax, relax, it will all be there.' It was his way of saying, 'I'm trying to figure you out. I'm trying to do well by you.'"

In 1989, which would prove to be both Neville's and McCormack's final season, the young actor was rewarded with two substantial roles: Demetrius in *A Midsummer Night's Dream* and Baron Tusenbach in *The Three Sisters*. Even though he performed excellently in both, he wasn't asked back.

Does McCormack now regret spending five years of his career playing basically a glorified collection of spear-carriers? "I've thought about this a lot over the years, because, you know, it's finally happening for me, but I'm thirty-seven. And when you're living out here in Hollywood, there are people at nineteen and twenty who have unbelievable things happening in their careers.

"Then I wonder why it took me so long. Well, I was way too Canadian, too Scarborough, too suburban. I just didn't have the balls to say dammit, here I am, get me while I'm young and hungry or you'll regret it. I just never thought that way."

Yet once he started thinking that way, he lost no time, and moved to Vancouver with its thriving film and TV industry.

By 1991, he was in Zimbabwe shooting the film *The Lost World*; 1992 found him as a regular on *Street Justice*; and then, in 1993, he began two years as the bearded heartthrob, Clay Mosby on *Lonesome Dove*.

Besides earning him a bevy of fans who still follow the show in its most obscure cable rerun, it introduced him to his wife, Janet Holden, who was working as assistant director on the shoot. They married in 1997 and honeymooned in Florida while McCormack worked on the Eddie Murphy film, *Holy Man*.

The years following their marriage saw McCormack almost constantly employed in L.A. by miniseries and made-for-TV movies, playing everything from an arrogant young stud (*A Will of Their Own*) to an uptight businessman (*Borrowed Hearts*).

Still, McCormack's grail, the weekly sitcom, kept eluding him. He came close to being cast as Ross in *Friends*, did six episodes of *Townies*, and made it into the pilot of *Jenny* but was soon back to doing guest shots on other people's shows.

Then, in 1998, came *Will & Grace*. McCormack once said: "The minute I read the script, I knew I was the only guy for the part. Not because of his sexuality, but in every other way, I'm just like Will Truman."

Talking to him, you see what he means. There's the wit, the polish, the I've-got-it-all-together surface. That's the McCormack who can banter with the best of them and is the sweetheart of the celebrity press.

But underneath there's the warmth and vulnerability of a guy who is just trying to make it through the minefield of contemporary life.

Like all great sitcom creations, McCormack's Will Truman has taken his own personality and fed it through the filter of a clearly defined character. The result is magic — or at least good enough for a five-year run and an eternity of syndication.

With ratings staying high, the sky is the limit for *Will & Grace*, and consequently, for Eric McCormack.

As he walks me back to the parking lot, he thinks of something.

"Remember how I told you about when I was a kid writing down the back story of the Page from *Antigone* and they made fun of me?

"Well, just before I came over to meet you, I ran into a young guy at Starbucks who has a small part in next week's show. He was working on his script, making notes, and I was about to tell him not to bother, but then I remembered how I felt when somebody did that to me, and I stopped."

He offers me one last thought. "I'd like to say nice guys finish first. . . . It just takes them a longer time."

Then he smiles and raises his hand in farewell just as he did 12 years ago, saying, "Hey, I'll see you around."

The series prospered, as did McCormack, finally winning his own Emmy in the Fall of 2001. He also journeyed to Broadway that year, taking over the lead in Susan Stroman's hit revival of *The Music Man* during his summer hiatus.

We met in Manhattan to talk about it, and he explained what was hardest for him. "Dialogue, blocking, songs, they all come easy to me. It's almost instinctual. But dancing? That's another story . . . " He laughs at the memory. "It took me an entire week just to learn the '76 Trombones' dance!"

But you'd never know it if you saw him glide around the stage. "That's what we're supposed to do: Work hard, and then make it look easy.

"The first time I ever did the show under performance conditions was at my first preview, with a full-paying audience out there. I'd had one dress rehearsal where I was the only one in costume, and one session with the orchestra where I just stood and sang along, but the whole thing — cast, costumes, music — didn't come together till that night."

Was he nervous? "I was petrified! But Deb (Messing) and Megan (Mullaly) came to see it, and knowing they were out there got me through it." His *Will & Grace* co-stars were generous with their praise, although Mullaly screeched one message of advice to him in her unmistakable voice: "Relax, honey!"

Yes, McCormack feels at home, on the musical stage, and on Broadway.

"I couldn't have done this five years ago, but now I'm ready. I'm thirty-eight years old, with twenty years in the business behind me, and three seasons on a successful TV series. It was the right time to make this move."

And would he do it again?

"In a minute. There's no way to describe the rush of playing the leading role in a hit musical. I've got over a hundred people around me, everyone working at their best, all of us making sure that the audience has a great time at every single performance. I love Broadway."

And judging from the response, it loved him right back.

But perhaps McCormack's proudest achievement to date is his son, Finnigan Holden, born to his wife Janet and him in July 2002.

Edie Falco
AP/World Wide Photos

EDIE FALCO

Wife, Mother, Pillar of Steel

Some interviews are obstacle courses: you get over the first hurdle, and another emerges. One star of a television series (name withheld to protect the guilty) who was starring in a Broadway show, made me go through four separate publicists, before she finally said no.

Then there's Edie Falco.

Even though she was in one of the most popular shows on TV and had just gotten a career-making set of raves for her latest Broadway show, arranging a meeting with her was a matter of one phone call.

Deal done, I prepared by seeing her most recent film, John Sayles' strange but gripping *Sunshine State* at 10 a.m. on a summer Sunday in Manhattan. (The movie hadn't opened yet in Canada.)

Then I walked uptown through the shimmering waves of heat to meet the only person Tony Soprano was really afraid of.

You know what would scare Edie Falco? A phone call from David Chase.

It's not that the star of *The Sopranos* doesn't get along with the man who created the hit series. Far from it.

There's another reason. Call it an occupational hazard of being on the Mafia-based program.

"David will phone an actor," Falco explains, "before he's

gonna kill him, so the poor guy won't have to just read it in the script for the first time. Can you imagine the conversation? 'Sorry, you've got three more episodes and then we're gonna whack you.'"

But it's not like that's about to happen to Falco. Her performance as Carmela Soprano — wife, mother, pillar of steel — is one of the strongest attributes of the wildly popular series. She has won two Emmys, a Golden Globe, and achieved "overnight stardom after 15 years."

We're sitting in her dressing room at the Belasco Theatre on a sticky summer Sunday afternoon, just before another soldout performance of *Frankie and Johnny in the Clair De Lune*.

Together with her college buddy, Stanley Tucci, she has turned Terrence McNally's 1987 play into one of the hottest tickets on Broadway. Part of it is due to the fact that the show got great reviews, and part of it is the buzz about Falco and Tucci's extended nude scene ("Oh, *please* . . . !" she says, dismissing that possibility with a disdainful wave of her hand).

But the biggest reason is the box office pull of Falco. She's become a celebrity, although the word makes her cringe.

"Look," she says in her no-nonsense voice, "it can really mess you up if you get caught in all this star stuff. I'm not cut out for that. I don't enjoy it."

It's easy to believe her. All you have to do is look at the biographical evidence. The 39-year-old Falco was born in Brooklyn but moved at an early age to working-class Farmingdale on Long Island.

Her dad, Frankie Falco, was a jazz drummer who provided her with the Italian heritage that has coloured her performance in *The Sopranos*. "Do I use my own family?" laughs Falco. "You bet! Those Sunday meals around the Soprano table? Look, every week when I was a kid, it was over to my grandmother's house — big, loud, lots of food, eating, laughing."

Mom was Judith Loney, a mainstay of the local community theatre, who gave Falco a love for the stage. "I would go with her to rehearsals, and there were all these grownups walking around in costumes pretending they were other people. It seemed like the coolest thing possible."

She soon found herself joining in and being drawn to it as a career. "My mom's little theatre group was pretty serious, so we'd do plays by Garcia Lorca, Ugo Betti, stuff like that. But in high school, I played the lead in the musicals — *My Fair Lady*, *Damn Yankees*." Whatever Edie wants, Edie gets?

"No, I got a kick out of musicals, and I respect the talent it takes to do them, but it's a whole different mindset, and I can't see myself fitting into it." A faraway smile creases the corners of her mouth. "They were fun, though. . . ."

When it came time for college, the Falco family couldn't afford the more high-end drama schools like Juilliard or Yale, and so she went to the State University of New York at Purchase, about an hour north of Manhattan.

Dressed in T-shirt and shorts, Falco becomes even more animated as she recalls those days. In fact, with her shining eyes and gym-trim figure, she looks like a college kid again.

"It was a relatively inexpensive school," she recalls, "but a good one. We were used to working our butts off and none of us came from money. So we made do, we thought on our feet. Hell, I remember that we used to put shows on in abandoned tunnels that linked the buildings together. We were a pretty feisty group."

In Falco's case, it was a talented group, as well. Her class came to be known as "the Purchase Mafia": Wesley Snipes, Parker Posey, Hal Hartley, and Stanley Tucci.

But as Falco remembers, "In school I was never the pretty one, never the ingénue. If they needed somebody over ninety or a whore with blacked-out teeth, those were the parts I got. And then, after I left school, I learned that if they want a ninety-year-old Italian grandmother, they go for the real thing, and so I got nothing. Nothing. Yeah, it was rough."

"I'd do anything I could get my hands on, lots of independent films that have never seen the light of day. But I never made any money. If I did score a small part, I'd use the cheque I got to pay off some debts and then it was back to waitressing."

The sunny woman who began the interview is gone now. "Waitressing . . . " she spits out the word, "waitressing in Upper-East-Side restaurants for snotty little rich kids who would never even look at me when they ordered. I'm staring at them, busted, broke, twenty-five years old. I was nothing to them."

She revisits the catalogue of pain, wanting to go deeper. "I worked in a factory, counting things, rubber-banding them, putting them in boxes and stacking them away. I'd get into a groove where my mind would go off on its own. I'd have some pretty trippy afternoons, watching the clock."

But one afternoon, it all went too far. Falco found herself in the middle of a full-scale panic attack, suffering from "real heavy-duty darkness," and she went home for help.

"Maybe that's why I usually play characters with a lot of baggage. I'm drawn to people who struggle, people who've gone through stuff. You see, they're on a journey someplace, but they haven't got there yet. They're still in the middle."

Her mother helped her get it all together again, and she returned to the city and her career, "I learned that it's not about a big break. It's about time and patience and a body of work."

So Falco kept building that body of work with directors like Hal Hartley and Woody Allen, appearing for two years on the tough prison series *Oz* and then finally being cast as a Mafia wife in a strange, but fascinating, 1998 TV pilot called *The Sopranos*.

But even that proved to be a bit of a curveball. "When we shot the pilot, David Chase looked at all of us and said, 'You know, it was a lot of fun, you guys are great, but unfortunately, nobody is ever gonna watch this.' And that was the end of that, and we figured we'd never see each other again."

Falco's smile returns as she recalls that, "A year later he called up and said, 'We've been picked up for thirteen episodes.' I remember that phone call; it's amazing how these memories stay with you. The first call I made after that was to my dad, to tell him, and the second was to my real estate agent. I said, 'Get me out of this apartment! Get me something bigger than one room!'

"Because that's what I had." She looks around her dressing room. "One room, this size. That's where I'd been living for seven-and-a-half years."

But the success of *The Sopranos* hasn't just given Falco a paycheque and star status. "I have feelings for everybody on that show," she says, "to an almost irrational degree, because they've been in my life for five years."

But no matter how moist-eyed she gets, Falco springs back to Carmela's Iron Maiden mode when asked to spill the beans about what's coming up on the show. "I really can't talk about it. I'm forbidden to."

She seems to soften a bit. "Look, we shoot it and then I don't see it till it goes on the air a year-and-a-half later. I don't even remember a lot of it. Okay, because they're the most recent in my memory, I could probably tell you what happens in the last two episodes in Season 4 . . . " then she twists the knife with a grin, ". . . but I won't."

"What's coming in Season 5? I have no idea. Except that it's the last one."

She raises an eyebrow. "Maybe we'll all start getting calls at night from David Chase."

The fourth season of *The Sopranos* finished with a firestorm of a battle between Tony and Carmela. Most major TV critics felt Falco's work in those scenes was some of the finest acting ever seen on television.

As I write this, the fifth (and supposedly final) season of *The Sopranos* is in production, and no one — the cast included — has any idea of how it's all going to end.

Paul Gross
Steve Russell/Toronto Star

PAUL GROSS

The Mountie Gets His Man

There are few Canadian stars who have an equally weighty presence on stage and screen, but Paul Gross is one of them.

Whether he's livening up the TV series *Due South*, or packing the houses at Stratford with his emotional *Hamlet*, Gross always makes good copy.

So, when he wrote, produced, directed, and starred in a film called *Men With Brooms* for his feature debut, it certainly warranted attention.

I even braved the non-smoking section of his favourite Toronto tavern to speak with him in March 2002.

"Direct a movie? Hell, I'd never even directed a two-car funeral."

Paul Gross grins at the circumstances that have brought him to within spitting distance of his first film's premiere.

Men With Brooms may be a simple comedy about curling, but it's being launched with the most extensive marketing campaign ever put behind a Canadian feature and it tends to make Gross more than a bit edgy.

"If I wasn't nervous, I'd be crazy, but then, hey, maybe I'm a bit crazy, too. You have to be crazy to spend a year or more of your life working on one film."

We're sitting in a pub not far from his Cabbagetown home. The air is thick with cigarette smoke, much of it generated by him, and he sips at his draft like any guy unwinding at the end of a hard day's work.

He doesn't look (or act) like one of Canada's biggest stars, but that's always been part of his charm.

Sure, he's handsome. Let's get that out of the way first. His 6-foot frame leans back in the chair with the inner confidence of a man who knows he looks just fine in a rumpled T-shirt and jeans.

Dozens of slobbering profiles have been written by journalists who turned into molten blobs of Silly Putty from his mere proximity.

They missed his more profound appeal. The secret weapon is sincerity. When you have a conversation with Paul Gross, he looks right at you, all the time.

His eyes, for the record, are blue, flecked with green, and remarkably clear for a man who's been spending long hours in an edit suite, getting his film just right, while the eyes of the Canadian industry are staring at him long and hard.

"It does feel right now that a lot of pressure is being brought to bear on what is basically a simple little film."

The "simple little film" that Gross and John Krizanc wrote deals with a group of small-town Ontario curlers who reunite after ten years to heal old wounds and win new money. Except for the curling angle, it's a pretty standard story, but since neither Gross nor Krizanc had ever curled in their lives, the choice of the film's central activity might seem a bit strange.

"Here's how it happened," relates Gross, moving in closer to seal out the ever-increasing noise of the Happy Hour crowd around us. "Robert Lantos started talking to me about doing a hockey film, but I couldn't see my way clear to writing anything about hockey without making it political. Our loss of stature, the selling of Wayne Gretzky, that kind of stuff."

"What I was interested in is the kind of sport that brings us together in a smallish way, a community way. A sport that didn't usually happen in an urban setting, that was free from cynicism, that hadn't been spoiled entirely by the managers and agents."

Gross was initially worried that his ignorance about the sport might prove to be a problem, "but it helped us tell the story more clearly. And I came to realize that one of the great things about curling is that you can see yourself on the ice. Look, I couldn't curl as well as (Canadian Olympian) Kevin Martin in a million years, but he's not like Vince Carter, not from another world. You actually feel you can talk with curlers."

"I know that some people are faintly amused by the idea of a film about curling. They think I'm going to be making fun of it, but nothing could be further from the truth. I don't embrace that kind of cynicism, that humour built on sneering. I don't like it much."

He stubs out a cigarette for emphasis. "Any pursuit done excellently is worthy. I respect anyone who does anything extremely well."

As Gross goes on about *Men With Brooms*, he engages you in such a beguiling manner that you start to understand what one of the film's crew said about him: "Every woman wants to be his lover and every man wants to be his friend."

Not bad for a 42-year-old military brat from Calgary.

As a kid, Gross changed his home every 18 months, following his father, Bob, who was a tank commander in the Canadian Army, around the world. By the time he was a teenager, he'd lived in England, Germany, Canada, as well as all over America and he'd developed a reputation as a bit of a hell-raiser that was to dog him well into his thirties.

Unlike many Hollywood types, however, who go off the deep end once they become famous, stardom has made Gross more responsible and he's now known as one of the hardest-working types in show business.

People tend to forget that Gross first broke onto the scene while still in his twenties as an award-winning playwright, writing serious Sam Shepard-ish scripts like *The Dead of Winter* (Toronto Free Theatre) and *Sprung Rhythm* (National Arts Centre).

But what really made him a star was his turn as the uptight but

215

endearing Constable Benton Fraser on the CTV/CBS series *Due South*. Seemingly overnight, Gross was a hot property internationally.

"Oh, I remember that well," chuckles Gross, exhaling a plume of smoke. "We got three hundred good reviews and two bad ones. The bad ones were from Toronto."

Is he worried about what the critical response will be to his film? "Individual reviews don't bother me. I wouldn't be surprised if the downtown critics in the big cities dismiss the film, but you can't make a movie thinking about them all the time.

"It's the aggregate effect you have to worry about. In other words, if everybody thinks you're stinky, then you're in trouble. Although I start to wonder if the twelve- to twenty-four-year-old demographic that movies are aimed at even bother to read the papers. The din of advertising is so loud it drowns out anything else."

Still, director Gross will be waiting eagerly to see what another kind of gross — the one from the box office — tells him after the opening weekend.

"I'd have to be psychotic not to be nervous about its reception. I never realized what a cutthroat business film distribution is! If you don't deliver on that first weekend, then sorry, buddy, you don't get a second."

For an instant, the pressure of what the success or failure of *Men With Brooms* could mean to the future of the Canadian commercial film industry seems to register with Gross, and his eyes momentarily lose their lustre.

Then he finishes his beer, shakes his head, and the smile returns.

"Look, strip all of the marketing aside and it just comes down to telling tales. I love the act of storytelling and that's why I love this movie. I watch it and I just sit there with this big grin at the end."

As he gets up to go, he stops for one last thought: "You wanna know the hardest thing about this whole movie business? It's how to make people aware that you've got something they might be interested in seeing."

Men With Brooms got kind enough reviews when it opened in March 2002 (even in Toronto!) and proved to be a fair-sized commercial hit around the country.

Since then, Gross has been occupying himself with TV guest shots, and plans for a new CBC-TV series where he'll play a novice politician suddenly thrust into the job of prime minister. For those who've been predicting an eventual career in public service for Gross, this is a logical intermediate step.

Stockard Channing
Peter Power/Toronto Star

STOCKARD CHANNING

The Heart of Darkness Bungee Jump

I t isn't often you get to talk to someone whose work you've admired on stage, screen, and television, but that was the case with Stockard Channing.

And much as I wanted to ask her about her stage performances (in unforgettable shows like *Six Degrees of Separation*), or her role on *The West Wing*, we were officially together to discuss her work in *The Business of Strangers*.

That was a fine job as well, so I had no trouble talking about it, but rest assured, we got into some of the other areas as well.

This interview was conducted in a Toronto hotel room in September 2001, far too early on a Saturday morning for Ms. Channing's taste.

The First Lady looks lovely in black leather.

There she sits, Stockard Channing, known to millions of *The West Wing*'s devotees as Abigail ("Abby") Bartlet, wife to Martin Sheen's imposing U.S. president Josiah ("Jed") Bartlet.

In a world where Internet sites are devoted to leaking plot details for popular shows like *The West Wing* to waiting fans, Channing has one "spoiler" of her own regarding Season 3 of the popular series.

"Abby's definitely in the hot seat this season." A liberating hoot escapes as she throws her head back, tossing her mahogany-coloured mane. "Oh yeah, she's in big trouble."

Channing was in town to talk about Patrick Stettner's offbeat but riveting black comedy, *The Business of Strangers*. In it, she plays a businesswoman named Julie with so frosty an attitude that co-star Julia Stiles keeps calling her "Duchess" on-screen.

Neither Abby nor Julie would be expected to wear the kicky black ensemble — heavy on the catwoman-like leather — that Channing is sporting, but that's what the woman is like: a study in contradictions.

The 57-year-old actress was born into a kind of *Upstairs, Downstairs* scenario on February 13, 1944, in New York City. Her birth name (Susan Williams Antonia Stockard) had that debutante-in-training air she still carries with her, although a raucous laugh and a salty vocabulary try to sabotage it at every opportunity.

Her father, Lester Napier Stockard, was a Brahmin-esque business executive and shipping magnate who died when Channing was six. Her mother was Mary Alice Stockard (née English) who came from a large Irish Catholic family in Brooklyn.

Channing went to Harvard University's Radcliffe College, majored in American history and literature and graduated *summa cum laude* in 1965. Despite those impressive academic credentials, she was drawn immediately into the theatre and then to Hollywood, where she scored her first on-screen role in 1971 as an unnamed ER nurse in Paddy Chayefsky's *The Hospital*.

Her work on several made-for-TV movies (including a 1973 Joan Rivers epic about plastic surgery called *The Girl Most Likely To*) brought her to the attention of Mike Nichols, who cast her opposite Jack Nicholson and Warren Beatty as a wacky heiress in his 1975 film *The Fortune*.

Despite its classy pedigree, the movie never took off, and Channing soon found herself mired in oddities like the disaster movie spoof *The Big Bus* (1976). Hollywood didn't seem to know what to do with this patrician broad who didn't fit any of their pigeonholes.

Even a turn as Rizzo in the 1979 hit adaptation of *Grease* failed to change her Hollywood luck, and things got worse after two failed sitcoms (*Just Friends* and *The Stockard Channing Show*) went down the tubes.

After contemplating leaving show business, Channing returned instead to the New York theatre, where her luck changed almost immediately.

A 1985 Tony Award for *A Day in the Death of Joe Egg* was followed by a Drama Desk Award in 1988 for Alan Ayckbourn's *Woman in Mind*, and then came her watershed role — Ouisa Kittredge, the society wife on the edge of despair in John Guare's *Six Degrees of Separation*.

This 1991 performance earned her both the Drama League Award and the OBIE, and when she repeated it on-screen in 1993, she was nominated for an Oscar.

"A part like that doesn't come along very often, and it fell into my lap at the last minute." Blythe Danner had been originally cast, but withdrew for personal reasons just before rehearsals started.

"The minute I started to read Ouisa's dialogue, it came to life for me. Those kinds of women have haunted me all my life. It was payback time for me, but — because I understood them — I thought I could offer some compassion for them as well."

"Let's face it," she says, laying her emotional cards on the table, "theatre has saved my professional ass time and time again. Movies make you famous, TV is a hoot, but I have to tell you, unless there's live people out there watching, there are times when I still don't think it's really acting."

Channing has worked steadily in big studio films such as *The First Wives' Club* and *Practical Magic*, but until she read Stettner's unsettling script for *The Business of Strangers*, she had never done a "low budget" movie (US$2 million).

It's easy to see why the part attracted her. Julie, a high-powered female executive on the road in an unnamed American city, begins to fear her CEO is flying out to fire her. She lashes out at

Paula (Julia Stiles), a young tech worker who's late for a presentation, and has her abruptly sacked.

Then, when the rest of the day goes in unexpected directions, she finds herself stranded in one of those eerily anonymous hotels with Paula, and the two of them embark on an insane journey of liquor and prescription drugs that brings them to the point of committing murder.

"Julie journeys into her own heart of darkness. She goes up that river. She becomes her own Kurtz for a second, and then it's like a bungee jump. She comes back again. There's a touch of the bad dream, the primal thing we get when we wake up at 3 a.m., what Scott Fitzgerald called 'the real dark night of the soul.'"

Channing relishes the role, and she's great in it. Her enthusiasm is contagious as she describes this puzzle of a woman.

"She's a character who's wrapped pretty tight. She has a lot of anxiety and energy, and that energy is fuelled by her anxiety. She hits the ground running, but when things don't go as she expected, it shocks her."

"It's kind of a curve ball to her. She's so used to fielding shit, dodging flack, that she can't quite absorb the good news. And that's what puts her off balance, and so she starts getting engaged with another person. It's an interesting logic. It makes a bizarre kind of sense to me."

And through it all, she has the support of Stettner's dialogue, which is clever in a cold and brutal way. "Look," she snaps at a headhunter who's just offered her a job in the Orient, "I don't have to go all the way to Japan to get slapped down because I have tits. I can do that right here at home."

Channing trusted her director, even to the point of being extremely vulnerable in the film's most telling sequence: a speech about how she experienced her first hot flash in subzero temperature at a football game she was attending to hustle clients.

She agrees how effective that scene is. "It's a very candid, open moment. That's when you see the person inside. Bit by bit."

Another thing she's done "bit by bit" is to become increasingly prominent on *The West Wing*. "I was in three episodes the first year, seven the second, and this year it's twelve."

Further signs of Channing's growing importance include the fact she'll be featured as a regular in the opening credits this year and that the scripts will concentrate a good deal more of the home life of Jed and Abby. A sunshine smile crosses her face. "If you're going to be on a hit television show, then this is the one to be on. She's such a great character."

Reminded of an episode late last season — when she corrected every attempt to call her "Mrs. Bartlet" by repeating "Dr. Bartlet" and ended with the explosion, "When did I think the American people were so stupid that they'd like me better if I stopped calling myself Dr. Bartlet?" — she savours the moment. "I love that line."

Channing guffaws at the Internet crowd that has announced she is to become hooked on prescription drugs later this season by self-medicating.

She waves a script. "I've got Episode 5 right here. We're shooting it next week. Nobody knows what's in Episode 6. If those cybergeeks know something else, then they know more than (producer-writer) Aaron Sorkin does."

And with that, the audience with the First Lady comes to an end.

Although the excellent *The Business of Strangers* didn't cause much commercial excitement, Channing continues to prosper on *The West Wing* and with three feature films scheduled for release in 2003.

In a March 2003 fundraiser in Los Angeles, she played the role created by Bette Davis in a one-night-only stage adaptation of the screen classic *All About Eve*.

The character is called Margo Channing, which gave an ironic edge to one of her big lines: "Miss Channing is ageless — spoken like a true press agent!

Chyna
Ron Bull/Toronto Star

CHYNA

Two Out of Three Falls Ain't Bad

This was probably the strangest interview I ever conducted. One Friday in March 2001, just before I was supposed to go on vacation, entertainment editor John Ferri called me into his office.

"How'd you like to have some fun?" is how he began, and I knew I was in for trouble.

It turned out that Chyna, one of the biggest stars of the World Wrestling Federation, was in Toronto for a one-day blitz to promote the tell-all story of her life. The Sports section didn't want to talk to her, because "wrestling's not a real sport." Okay, argued Ferri, then if it's all showbiz, why not have our theatre critic do it?

The idea of me getting warm and cozy with that buxom brunette man-killer tickled everyone at the editorial meeting, and so I got the job.

The only problem was that I knew *nothing* about wrestling. Less than nothing. When I went to the Internet to find some info, I even spelled her name wrong. (Well, wouldn't you start out with "China"?)

There were several other logistical problems connected with this assignment. Since Chyna was doing a lot of TV that day, I would have to go out to the suburbs where she was taping one interview, meet her there, and ride in a limo with her to the next session across town, asking my questions en route.

Oh yes, one more thing. I had to be there in an hour.

Well, I've never been known to shrink from a challenge, so I left the office, hailed a cab, and asked him to stop at the nearest Chapters. I ran in, grabbed a copy of her book, and proceeded to speed-read as much of it as I could in the cab as we raced to the studio.

If you told me in advance how this one was going to wind up, I never would have believed you.

How do you interview the bodacious star of the World Wrestling Federation who invented the man-mangling move they call "The Great Balls of Chyna"?

Very carefully.

Chyna and I are side by side in the back seat of a white stretch limo as it speeds across Toronto, and I keep reminding myself that this is the woman who broke the heart of former champ Triple H and cleaned the clock of pseudo-misogynist Double J.

One wrong question and I'll wind up out on the highway with a broken collarbone.

So I play it cautious at first, letting precious minutes tick away as the images of passing cars sail by through the smoked glass of our windows. For some reason, I've decided to let Chyna start talking on her own, without any prodding from me.

You can call me a coward, but it works. After a very short while, she turns to me and says, "Back when I was a kid, I never thought I'd be riding places in a car like this."

I pick up my cue. "Did you even dream about it?" She laughs. "Are you kidding? I wasn't allowed any dreams back then. 'Don't get too full of yourself, Joanie.' That's what my mother used to say." Joanie Laurer is the name she was born with 29 years ago in New Hampshire. "Trailer trash, that's all we were" is how she describes her childhood years.

But now she's known as Chyna, having survived a mother who killed her soul and a father who picked her pocket. She's even wound up as the first woman in the WWF to become an actual superstar.

"The fans know it's all fake," she willingly admits, "they know it's a story. That's why they love it."

And they love her, too. She entered the WWF in 1997 as "that oddball freaky girl who beat up people. I was the underdog who always got the shaft, but the fans didn't want me to stay that way. They're the ones who made me a success."

That's why she's in Toronto, like any good star, plugging her brutally honest autobiography *If They Only Knew*. It's written "with Michael Angeli," but it's hard to imagine he did much more than run it through spell-check.

"I fired two other writers because they kept trying to change my voice. I wanted it to sound like me."

And it sure does. Here's Joanie talking about her teenage eating disorder: "I'd binge on bags of sour-cream potato skins, hit the can, tickle the ole Adam's apple, do the Technicolor yawn into the toilet, and voila, I am thin again."

But there's a lot of painful material as well, especially about her dysfunctional alcoholic parents and how they used her as the prize in a series of vicious games that nobody ever won.

It's pretty tough stuff and the guileless way that she puts it all on the page somehow makes it even more horrific. Guileless, maybe, but clueless, no. She knows what grim reading it makes.

"I wanted to tell it all," she says.

"The good, the bad, and the ugly. I don't have anything to hide. Oh sure, it freaked me to read what I'd written — it seemed like a real-life *Dynasty* episode — but that's how it happened."

She looks out the window again and I study her. Her hair is the black of ink cartridges (as a child she was a natural blonde), the eyes a surprisingly pale green beneath the heavy makeup.

A pink knit sweater is open past the point of discretion to showcase the breasts she willingly admits have undergone numerous painful implants.

In an embarrassing moment, she looks back to discover me staring at her cleavage, but it amuses, rather than angers her.

"Go ahead and look," she encourages, "they cost me enough time and money." An evil gleam appears behind her eyes. "They even broke once."

"Broke? How?" This conversation is going places I had never imagined.

"Someone flung me face down on the mat, hard, really hard, and I landed just the wrong way. I could actually hear the implant splatter. Squuuiiissshhh!"

The smile vanishes. "The operation after that was the least fun of all. But I have to keep doing it. People expect me to look like this. Men especially."

We lock eyes and I ask her what kind of man she attracts.

"Guys who aren't intimidated by uniqueness."

She stretches out her arms and smiles knowingly. "They're not going to get this from the average woman."

Then the smile fades slightly. "But this fab diva female thing doesn't always keep them for long. I need a very secure person career-wise to be with me."

I'm just about to ask her to discuss her highly publicized affairs with several of her male colleagues, but she seems to read my mind and her gaze sharpens. "I'll just tell you one thing; it won't be a wrestler, ever again."

Chyna's career keeps moving past the narrow but popular borders of the WWF. In 2000 she did three guest spots on the sitcom 3rd Rock from the Sun, but now she insists she "doesn't want to be on other people's shows anymore."

How high is she aiming? She's had discussions with Arnold Schwarzenegger about co-starring with him in Terminator 3, and at the mention of that, her eyes light up. "I would make absolutely the best female Terminator. Believe me."

But, assuming she makes that leap and becomes a movie star, would she still be known as Chyna? She shakes her head emphatically,

"No way. I'll go back and call myself Joanie again. I'll always be Joanie. That's the real me, like it or not."

Looking for some other insights into her personality, I ask who her favourite musician is and she seems genuinely embarrassed for the first time in our candid conversation.

"You won't laugh at me?" she pleads, and I promise her that I won't. She bites her lip before softly whispering, "Barry Manilow."

I tell her that I interviewed Manilow last year and she breaks into a huge grin. "No way! Was he nice? Man, I love his songs . . . "

And then, swaying slightly, Chyna starts belting out one of Manilow's hits: "I can't smile without you, can't smile without you."

What else can I do but join in? "I can't laugh, and I can't sing."

And now it's a duet: "I'm findin' it hard to do anything . . . "

We keep singing at the top of our lungs until the limo pulls up to the studio where she's got her next interview.

She looks at me almost timidly. "Thanks. That was fun."

"It was my pleasure, Joanie."

She gives me a brief hug and I glance outside at the puzzled faces of the crowd who are waiting for a glimpse of that satanic superwoman they worship in the ring.

If they only knew, I think, if they only knew.

A few months after this piece appeared, Chyna became embroiled in a highly public and equally unpleasant rift with the WWF, which ended with the two of them parting company acrimoniously.

Since then, her career hasn't gone all that far. She didn't get the role in *Terminator 3* and no one's offered her a network series of her own.

She has launched a Web site, www.bodybyjoanie.com, and on it you can purchase memorabilia from her wrestling days and keep track of her public appearances at auto shows, etc.

Kaye Ballard
Rick Madonik/Star Photo

KAYE BALLARD

The Secret's in Her Sauce

Ever since I'd been a kid, I'd loved Kaye Ballard's work, on stage, screen, and my precious collection of vintage vinyl. She always radiated such warmth that I felt I knew her, even though we had never met.

That all changed in the summer of 2001 when the musical version of *The Full Monty* began its tour in Toronto and I was able to interview her.

The crowds coming to the touring production of *The Full Monty* to see naked guys in their thirties are saving some of their loudest cheers for a fully clothed gal who's going to turn 75 later this year.

But then, Kaye Ballard has always been an audience favourite, and her performance as Jeanette Burmeister, the feisty piano-playing senior is no exception.

Big bands, Broadway, television, movies, records, cabarets — she's made her mark on all of them during her 55-year career.

We met for lunch at a downtown restaurant, and after I told her how much I enjoyed her musicals from the past, she flung her arms around me.

"Love at first sight," she enthused, "and at my age."

Age isn't something you think of immediately with Ballard, because a force field of youthful vitality seems to shimmer around her. And the animated way she uses her hands to punctuate every detail of a conversation is something she comes by honestly.

"Sure, I'm Italian. I'm Calabrese, from down in the toe of the boot. I've got lots of energy because I eat tons of pasta, but I'm also always cold because I've got spaghetti sauce for blood."

That's an outright lie. The woman isn't cold. She's as incendiary as the plate of hot peppers in front of her on the table that she studies warily. "I'd love to eat one, but my stomach wouldn't love it so much. You try it and let me watch you enjoying it."

She was born Catherine Gloria Balota in Cleveland, Ohio, on November 20, 1926, and hit the road early as a singer-comedienne with Spike Jones and his City Slickers. "I played Calgary, Winnipeg, Buffalo," recalls Kaye, "but, thank God, not in the winter."

Early TV work with the likes of Henry Morgan and Mel Torme followed, and then she got her first big break on Broadway, starring as Helen of Troy in *The Golden Apple*.

This wildly ambitious 1954 musical (which moves Homer's *Iliad* and *Odyssey* to turn-of-the-century America) has now acquired cult status, and collectors kill for copies of the original vinyl recording that featured Ballard introducing the sensuous "Lazy Afternoon."

"We didn't know what he had when we were working on it," laughs Ballard. "Sure, it was good, but it was a little bit artsy. I think that's what killed it in the end. 'Too clever by half,' isn't that what they say?" She gets a dreamy look in her eye. "But I sure loved that big number of mine, 'Lazy Afternoon.' I still remember the set. A giant tree, with cutout pieces of lighting gel dangling from the branches, every colour in the rainbow. Cost a couple of dollars and looked like a million bucks. Kinda like me, huh?" Her self-deprecating barbs are always ready.

She chuckles ruefully when I call her lucky. "I've had *almost* luck. I was on the cover of *Life* magazine, but not the story inside."

For years, she utilized her smoky singing voice as equally as her deadpan wit.

"People always think of me as a comedienne," she admits, "but my secret weapon was always that I could stop the show with a serious number. I've also introduced songs like 'My Coloring Book' and 'Maybe This Time.' Both by John Kander and Fred Ebb. Great songwriters, and I did them first."

Broadway continued to be good to her with hit shows like *Carnival,* and she looks back on that as a charmed time.

"We had the authority of innocence. We used to do those shows in three weeks from scratch. Nowadays they have workshops for years, and the shows just keep getting worse. Whatever happened to reading a script and saying 'This works, let's do it?'"

Along with the musicals, Ballard kept recording and performing in cabarets, while guesting on television. When she was working with Perry Como from 1961 to 1963, she first met gifted comedian Paul Lynde.

"Paul was deeply troubled," she remembers, "and he must have gained and lost over two thousand pounds in the years I knew him. But Lord, was he funny!"

Ballard's eyes shine as she recalls a memory. "Perry would rehearse something and say 'What a nice song,' and then Paul would wheel on him and sneer, 'What do they do, tunnel the tunes from your house to the golf course?'"

Her Lynde impersonation is uncanny, but then she spent a season with him in 1968 on *Hollywood Squares* as well.

Another Ballard experience filled with unique personalities was the off-Broadway hit revue *The Decline and Fall of the Entire World As Seen Through the Eyes of Cole Porter — Revisited,* which opened in 1965.

"I adored that show," she enthuses. "It came at a time just after Porter's death when people thought he was a back number, out of date. Boy, did we set them straight!" She relished doing its naughty numbers and performing with the likes of the late William Hickey.

"Oh, he was an original, but you had to watch him. Never

trust guys who are that skinny. They don't eat enough. When he got nominated for his Oscar for playing the Godfather in *Prizzi's Honor*, people asked me if I was surprised, and I said 'No, I knew he was a killer. I shared a stage with him.'"

After that, she created the role that still causes instant recognition every night when she pops from behind her piano at the Elgin Theatre — Kaye Buell, one of the characters in the popular comedy series, *The Mothers-In-Law*.

"That was a happy time for me," recalls Ballard of the show's two-year run from 1967 to 1969, "and the best part was working with Desi Arnaz."

Besides appearing on the show, the legendary ex-husband of Lucille Ball directed and produced it "with impeccable taste."

I asked her about the self-destructive streak in Arnaz that led to his drinking himself into oblivion.

She looks at me carefully before answering. "I liked Desi. He was always good to me, a real gentleman. But sure, he was troubled. I would have liked to be able to reach out and help him, but the pain was so deep inside that nobody could go there. That's one of my big regrets."

There were some unhappy experiences too. She had two big musical flops. One of them, a version of *The Goldbergs* called *Molly* fired most of its creative team except for Kaye before getting to New York, but it died anyway.

"I was consulting a numerologist at the time, and she told me I should get rid of the 'e' at the end of my first name for good luck. I did. The day the reviews came out,, I put that 'e' right back where it belonged.

And then there was *Royal Flush*, which perished on the road shortly after its tryout at the Royal Alexandra Theatre in Toronto. Ballard looks like she's had too many cannoli after I raise that one.

"You know, years go by and I forget that show. Then someone like you mentions it, or I wake up after having a nightmare and it all comes back to me. It was one of those musicals where nobody knew what they were doing, including me, and Lord, did it show! We kept changing it so much we'd pin the rewrites to the big cuffs of our medieval costumes."

But one of her most ill-starred adventures occurred when she walked off during the first weeks of what would prove to be the long-running *Gary Moore Show* when she felt the other comedienne, an unknown named Carol Burnett, was getting preferential treatment.

"And then years later, I found out she had been sleeping with the producer, Joe Hamilton. She even married him."

Ballard allows a moment of regret at her own mistake. "Oh yeah, my timing was always great onstage, but not so great in real life."

Then she smiles again. "But what the hell, I've had a lot of laughs, and I plan to have a whole lot more." She raises her glass of iced tea. "*Salut!*"

Bad news: the production of *The Full Monty* never really caught on in Toronto, and closed after its next touring date in Chicago proved equally unsuccessful.

Good news: Ballard liked what I wrote about her and invited me and my wife to dinner. She had managed to discover an Italian restaurant in the West End of Toronto that I had never heard of, and we joined her there for an evening of reminiscences only slightly less spicy than the full-bodied red sauce that blanketed our rigatoni.

"This is good sauce," Ballard conceded, "but not as good as mine. One day, you'll come visit me out West and I'll make it for you."

Fortunately (or unfortunately) neither of us has had the time, and Ballard is still performing and touring around North America, as lively as ever.

Michael Palin
Myung Jung Kim/PA Photos

MICHAEL PALIN

130 in the Shade

I can admit it now. Michael Palin was always my favourite member of Monty Python's Flying Circus.

He wasn't the craziest, or the silliest, or even the funniest. But he was the sweetest and sanest. That's why I cherished him.

Nearly 35 years after the magical comedy series he had been a part of first appeared on television, Palin was happily involved in a new life as a travel journalist — on TV and in books.

It was in that role that he came to Toronto in April 2003 to promote his latest book, and we got together for lunch.

It all began with the Pythons.

Not the bone-crunching serpentine variety, but the rib-tickling comedians still remembered for the anarchic mirth they generated over three decades ago. That's when Michael Palin first contemplated a career in travel television.

Nowadays, he's made quite a name for himself as the gently befuddled host of popular series like *Around the World in 80 Days*, *Pole to Pole*, and — most recently — *Sahara*.

But back then, in the early 1970s, he was filming an episode of *Monty Python's Flying Circus* "while tromping through a muddy field in Yorkshire, all of us in full drag, and we couldn't find a place to wash."

"One of us wondered what we'd be doing in thirty years' time, and I think it was John (Cleese) who said he thought we'd all be making documentaries. I voted for *Great Swimming Pools of the World*, Graham (Chapman) refined this to *Great Gin and Tonics Beside Great Swimming Pools of the World*, and Eric (Idle) topped us all with *Death by Luxury*." Palin pauses wistfully. "I still rather fancy trying that one."

We're in Rodney's Oyster House — a Palin favourite from previous Toronto visits — to talk about *Sahara*, the book of his most recent BBC series. But as you might expect with "a self-styled polymath" like Palin, the conversation ranges as widely as the provenance of Rodney's mollusks.

He was born on May 5, 1943, in Sheffield, "a good grimy workers' place. My parents didn't have a great deal of money. They just wanted me to find a profession where I could be free of them and they could be free of me. I wanted to do something amusing that wouldn't tie me down."

No wonder he wound up with a "like-minded bunch of blokes" who called themselves Monty Python's Flying Circus and produced roughly three years of TV programs and a like number of feature films before finally disbanding (with allowances for the occasional reunion).

Looking back on those years, Palin now muses, "the wonder of it all is that we stayed together as long as we did. I always thought of Python as a centrifugal thing. One of us was always spinning off somewhere. And as long as we could control that, we were fine."

Palin stops with a glass of Chardonnay at his lips as he recalls, "sometimes that spinning off could be difficult and quite hurtful, but for the most part, it's happy memories."

With all those hundreds of sketches, can he nominate a favourite?

"As a matter of fact, I can," he smiles, shaking Tabasco on an oyster, "not a big one, or a famous one, but it's what I remember. The fish-slapping dance. Just John and me in pith helmets and shorts, hitting each other with fish until he finally whacks me with a big one and I fall into the river."

After the Pythons split off from the series, they went to make a series of films, sometimes together, sometimes separately. Palin was involved with many of them, including memorable entries like *The Life of Brian, Time Bandits, Brazil,* and *A Fish Called Wanda.*

He looks on that period with Palin-esque understatement as "quite a good run," but had come to the conclusion that "I wasn't going to get another decade like that" and then BBC approached him in 1988 about hosting a travel series called *Around The World in 80 Days.*

"At first, it didn't strike me as a likely idea," he confides, spearing a final oyster. "I mean the words 'intrepid' and 'Palin' don't really go together. Up to this point the most challenging place I'd been was the Scottish Highlands."

Still, he gave it a go, and discovered he liked it. So did the public, and since then, Palin's been in almost non-stop motion around the globe in a series of intensely difficult surroundings.

He learned that he had "hidden reserves of stamina. That's the word I use to describe the physical, mental, and spiritual resources I need to keep going. Now and then I get the usual twenty-four-hour digestive meltdown, but I just drink lots of water and let it pass through the system — sometimes with spectacular effects."

That's not to say that there haven't been frightening moments. Making *Pole to Pole*, they tried to land a plane directly on the North Pole, "but it was May and the ice was breaking up. The pilot had to touch down on an ice floe. The light was flat, he couldn't get his bearings, and if he'd flipped the plane, it would have been game over."

Palin builds the suspense by spooning some chowder down his throat before continuing, "He tried three times. No luck. Just before the fourth, I remember wondering what my kids would say if I died. Would it be, 'Our Dad was completely irresponsible.' Or 'Our Dad was a brave and great adventurer'?"

Another spoon of chowder. "I think they voted for completely irresponsible."

He survived that ordeal, but he met his next challenge at the other end of the temperature spectrum during the filming of *Sahara*.

"We were in Tirelli, a part of the desert where the sun beats down in the most unforgiving manner. For some reason, it was decided that I had to have a meal there, at the height of the midday heat. Just before we rolled camera, they told me it was fifty-five degrees Celsius.

"And then came the food. You molded little balls of millet and goat that had been cooking in a pit, and popped them in your mouth." Palin's face contorts at the memory. "It was like shoving hot coals down your gullet. And then, when it was too late, you realized the whole thing had also been bathed in an incendiary sauce.

"They watched me suffer and then they smirked, 'If you cannot eat a hot meal, you are not a man.' And I thought, 'Bloody hell, all this, and my virility being questioned as well.'"

But not far from the site of his culinary trial-by-fire, Palin had another kind of epiphany.

"We found ourselves visiting people who lived in a shack they had made out of pieces of tin and old sacks that used to hold explosives. I asked what made them happy and they said, 'We have our family, God is looking after us, and we have our beautiful home.' Spoken totally without irony."

Palin's face is usually crinkled with laugh lines, but now he grows serious. "I realized that you cannot assume because people are poor that they are unhappy. You want to see unhappy people? Go to Victoria Station during rush hour, and look at the executives making more money in a day than these people will see in a lifetime."

Another medley of feelings played in Palin's mind when he returned to the site in Tunisia where the final scene of the Pythons' 1979 mock biblical epic, *Life of Brian*, had been filmed.

"At first I was sad to go back," revealed Palin, "because it was all prettified and touristy now. Not like thirty-odd years ago. No point in pretending you can put the clock back and bring us all together once again."

His eyes grow a bit misty as he continues to remember. "A mixture of nostalgia and regret swept over me, but it was regret of the best kind. We had done something good once here, and I wish we could all feel that way together, just once more."

Since he has spent so much time in that desert world, I ask Palin what watching the images of the war in Iraq does to him.

"It saddens me immeasurably. I knew so much friendship and hospitality from those people. Now you see soldiers breaking down doors and grabbing people from their homes. You'll never recover the goodwill we once knew."

Next up for Palin is a journey to the Himalayas, which starts this May. He admits, "I like places where life hasn't been all tidied up by the tourist board."

And as he finishes his wine, he suddenly discovers why. "I think it all stems from growing up in Sheffield, where we got no favours from anyone. There was a kind of integrity about men making steel and surviving in appallingly polluted conditions, but they did survive, and they had a culture.

"That's what it's all about. Finding how people in difficult places make sense of their lives there."

As promised, Palin began shooting his series on the Himalayas in the summer of 2003.

After that, he surprised me by saying he wanted to journey up to Murmansk in Russia, on the White Sea. "I can't picture why anyone would want to go there," he confided to me, "which is exactly why it tickles my fancy."

V

FROM THE
THEATRE

Gwen Verdon
Dance Magazine

GWEN VERDON

Whatever Lola Wants

G wen Verdon, the four-time Tony Award-winning star of Broadway musicals, died on October 18, 2000, at the age of 75. I think the rest speaks for itself.

At least I got to tell her that I loved her.

Too often in show business you gaze at people from afar. They're up there on the stage, you're down in the audience, and never the twain shall meet.

Except sometimes they do, and then it's magic.

I first saw Gwen Verdon on Broadway when I was nine, in a musical called *Redhead*, a vehicle specially designed for the curvaceous redhead who held all Broadway in her thrall. There was one number she did — a Chaplinesque derby-and-cane vaudeville turn called "Erbie Fitch's Twitch" during which you could just hear the audience falling in love with her. She dazzled me, and I couldn't wait to see her again.

It was more than the early stirrings of male libido responding to those physical charms of hers that Bob Fosse (her husband and director) had put so lovingly on display.

No, there was something electric about her onstage that couldn't really be described or duplicated. She lit up the stage, that's what it was.

I caught up with her next on screen, recreating her signature role in *Damn Yankees* (released in 1958) through "Whatever Lola Wants, Lola Gets" and that was great, but I needed to see her live.

For that I would have to wait until 1966 and another triumph: *Sweet Charity*. This musical version of Fellini's *Nights of Cabiria* saw Gwen as Charity Hope Valentine, a dance-hall hostess looking for love.

By now I was old enough to go to the theatre on my own, and I stood at the back of New York's Palace Theatre on many Saturday afternoons, watching her with a hopelessly infatuated adolescent grin plastered on my face.

My favourite moment wasn't one of her comedy turns and it wasn't one of her hip-ratcheting dances. No, I waited for the big ballad, "Where Am I Going?" when she asked "Anger and hope and doubt, what am I all about?" and I wanted to be the one to tell her.

Long-necked, long-limbed, red hair piled on top of her head. She looked like the most sensual yet vulnerable giraffe who ever escaped from a musical comedy game preserve.

Fast forward to 1975, and her final Broadway appearance in *Chicago*, as an amoral murderess using publicity to escape the gallows. She was older then, but so was I, and I was learning to appreciate how worldly wisdom can be preferable to youthful enthusiasm.

She sashayed brazenly in her big number "Roxie," a piece that Fosse had custom-tailored to her skills, but once again, it's an offbeat moment I recall. In a throwaway intro to the song she talks about how she used to be seen decorating the arm of unattractive mobsters. "Ugly guys like to do that," she said, in a voice that combined pride and pain in equal measures.

After *Chicago*, Verdon coped with the onset of age the way many dancers do: she choreographed, she taught, she acted in films, and I reconciled myself to never seeing her in person again.

But then, early in 1998, Garth Drabinsky invited me to a Toronto workshop presentation of *Fosse*, his tribute to the work of Bob Fosse — Verdon's creative and life partner for so many years. I was thrilled at the chance to see some great Fosse dances recreated, but I remember saying to my wife as we drove downtown that I was going to miss Verdon's presence.

Little did I know.

There were two seats saved in the row in front of me, and I wondered who was going to fill them. Then, at the last minute, in came Gwen Verdon and her daughter Nicole, there to determine if Fosse's legacy was being treated well.

Seeing her so close was disconcerting, but then she laughed, with that unique throaty gurgle of hers, and I was nine years old all over again. My apologies to Mr. Drabinsky. I only saw half of *Fosse* that day. The rest of the time I was watching Mrs. Fosse.

I wanted to go up to her afterward and tell her how much her work had meant to me over the years, but I hesitated, and the moment passed. Then, about six months later, I was offered the opportunity to interview her just before the Toronto opening of *Fosse*. When the day came, I was as nervous as a kid before a first date. I even changed my shirt and tie three times, wondering which combo Fosse would have favoured.

I had vowed to be cool and professional, but when the cameras rolled, I looked into her eyes and spilled the beans: "Do you know I've been in love with you since I was nine years old?"

She laughed that wonderful laugh, threw her head back, and said, "My God, I don't think any man has ever been in love with me for that long!"

The ice was well and truly broken, and in the interview that followed she told me everything I wanted to know, including about that legendary opening night of *Can-Can* in 1953 when she stopped the show in a supporting role and became a star.

"I was naked in my dressing room when (choreographer) Michael Kidd came rushing in and told me they wouldn't stop applauding. He wrapped a towel around me and shoved me back on the stage. They had already changed the scenery, and I found myself standing in front of a set I didn't recognize, in a towel, while the audience just clapped and cheered."

"Then I caught a glimpse of (leading lady) Lilo, glaring at me with pure hate, and I said to myself, 'Gwen, there's always a price you gotta pay.'"

She talked about her difficulties with legendary director George Abbott on the 1957 musical *New Girl in Town*, where she played a prostitute based on Eugene O'Neill's Anna Christie. "Mr. Abbott was very rigid, very uptight. I think he didn't really like sex, and if you don't like sex, you don't like me."

Finally I came to talk about Fosse, the man who shaped her career, loved her and left her, but never really went away. (For some of the details, see *All That Jazz*.)

"He was the best. He knew what he wanted every single second of every show to be like, and you just did what he told you to. Then suddenly, when it all came together, you saw what he was getting at, and it took your breath away."

I asked her about the gossipy Fosse biographies with their tell-all details, and she shook her head in vigorous denial. "Honey, believe me, nobody will ever know what Bob Fosse was like, and I'll tell you why."

She leaned closer to me, and her eyes filled. "It's because Bob Fosse never knew what Bob Fosse was like. Believe me."

I did. I'd been believing her for 40 years.

And I got to tell her that I loved her. What I didn't get to say was goodbye, so let me do it now.

Goodbye, Gwen Verdon. You were the best.

For more about Bob Fosse and his legacy see the interview with Ann Reinking on p. 182.

Uta Hagen
Stratford Festival of Canada

UTA HAGEN

Truth and Illusion

S ometimes you go to the stars, and sometimes they come to you.

In the summer of 2000, the Stratford Festival invited Uta Hagen up to recreate her critically acclaimed performance in the off-Broadway hit *Collected Stories*.

The Stratford Festival's artistic director Richard Monette had seen Hagen do the play on a 1998 visit to New York. She co-starred with a young actress named Deborah Messing, soon to become famous as the distaff side of the hit sitcom, *Will and Grace*.

Monette wanted her to bring the play to his theatre and to offer some of her incredible teaching skills to his company.

His wish came true, and an added benefit was that I got to interview an actress I'd admired for nearly 40 years.

It was a case of life imitating art, but you'd expect that to happen with Uta Hagen.

One afternoon I saw the 81-year-old American actress and teacher give an amazing performance at the Stratford Festival in Donald Margulies' play *Collected Stories*. She portrayed a famous writer, and in the play's opening scene she greets a student who is a long-time follower of her work.

The next morning, I climbed the stairs to Hagen's apartment, another devotee of another living legend. "Don't call me a legend," the raspily commanding voice insisted. "It sounds like I'm not a real person."

And that's one thing Uta Hagen is: a real person. You know it from the warmth of her handshake, the eye contact she demands, and the almost tangible force field of energy that surrounds her.

I told her I felt like I was in *Collected Stories*. Her whoop of laughter put me at ease. "Don't worry, I'm not as scary as (the main character) Ruth. At least I hope I'm not."

She's right. This smiling woman in a long black housecoat was light years removed from Ruth Steiner, the acerbic author she played with such conviction.

We settled down to talk in the furnished apartment she occupied during her stay in Stratford. As I might have suspected, she had already imposed her vivid personality on its neutrality.

The kitchen was full of groceries waiting to be stored, a reminder that Hagen once wrote a most impressive cookbook, *Love for Cooking*, with a trick for cooking veal scaloppini that I use to this day. (Soak it in milk before proceeding with your recipe.)

There was also a well-stocked bar (after all, this is the woman who created the "liquor-riddled harridan" Martha in *Who's Afraid of Virginia Woolf?*) and the numerous ashtrays of an unapologetic smoker. (She uses her smoker's cough as conversational punctuation.)

A pile of jigsaw puzzles sat on the dining-room table. Were they simply distractions to pass the empty hours all actors encounter on the road, or a key to how she works? Is it all a question of making the pieces fit properly?

"Yes," she admitted. "Acting's a kind of puzzle. It has to come from the script through the actor."

Since *Collected Stories* deals with the theme of artistic appropriation, I asked her if she ever based a performance on someone in real life. She snapped her reply across the room.

"I don't imitate people — that's for nightclubs. When I'm playing Martha, I'm not stealing anyone's life . . . except my own.

Because when we perform, we're revealing ourselves, our own personal lives."

Warming to her theme, you could see why she's such an effective teacher. "In other words, if you really act well, you're using aspects of yourself which belong to the character. You're not somebody else. You are a different aspect of you. People come backstage talking to me about the character in this play and say, 'When she did that . . . ' and I say, 'No, she didn't do that. I did.' We have such a huge range of people who we are."

And Hagen learned to acquaint herself with those people from a very early age. Born in Gottingen, Germany, on June 12, 1919, she was the daughter of an actor-turned-professor and a singer. Shortly after her birth, the family moved to Madison, Wisconsin.

"I was lucky to have the background I did," she admitted. "When I decided at six that I wanted to be an actress, my father understood, and saw that I read the right things. By the time I was fourteen, I had read all of theatre literature — Ibsen, Chekhov, Shakespeare, O'Neill — I didn't know what it meant, but I had read it. I grew up with a sense of theatre in my bones."

At age 19, she made her Broadway debut as Nina in Chekhov's *The Seagull*, acting opposite the famous husband-and-wife team of Alfred Lunt and Lynn Fontanne. I wondered if her inexperience had terrified her.

"No. You see, the most powerful tool an actor has is his innocence. If he believes where he is and what he is, he has it made. I believed I was in Russia; I believed it was raining outside. I believed Miss Fontanne was a great actress, because she was. I believed Mr. Lunt was a wise and witty artist, because he was. That all made it easy for me."

After Chekhov, her next triumph was as Desdemona in *Othello*, playing opposite Paul Robeson and her then husband, Jose Ferrer. Robeson was known primarily as a singer and social activist.

In Hagen's words: "He wasn't a very good actor, but it didn't make a hill of beans of difference. His very being was Othello. He walked on stage and you believed he was a general, you believed he was brilliant."

And it served Hagen well as the smitten Desdemona. "Oh yes," she affirmed with a libidinous laugh. "Oh yes, indeed!"

When Hagen teaches students Shakespeare, she doesn't handle it any differently because of the verse. "The verse is there so strongly that you don't have to land on it or try to play it. You just have to fill what's on the page with yourself, and it's all there. If you make real to yourself what you have to say, it can be devastatingly wonderful."

Those last two words also serve as a good description of what may very well be Hagen's most famous performance: as Martha in the first production of Edward Albee's *Who's Afraid of Virginia Woolf?* back in 1962.

It didn't take her long to decide to accept the role when it was offered to her.

"After twenty pages, I knew I wanted to play it. It's that immediate. That incredible opening scene. Albee has such an ear for dialogue. We didn't change one syllable. We played it exactly the way it was written."

Nearly 40 years after creating the role, Hagen performed it again for one night as a staged reading in New York. Ben Brantley, the *New York Times* theatre critic, named it the top show of 1999: "The year's most dazzling evening of theatre . . . an 80-year-old actress shed decades to become a fierce middle-aged tigress with unsheathed claws."

Hagen is still stunned by the experience. "It worked like a charm. You could hear a pin drop. And at the end, they screamed for twenty minutes. What is it about the play that grabs people so much? It's the intensity. What the characters do to each other and how they do it," she said.

She takes a long drag on her cigarette as she remembers the original production. "God, we threw ourselves into it! There wasn't any other way to do it. Some nights I'd grab Arthur (Hill, who played her husband George) and say 'Truth and illusion, George, you don't know the difference'; he'd reply, 'No, but we must carry on as though we did,' and I'd think I was going to just fall apart right there."

Did she know the play was going to be such a big hit? She shakes her head emphatically. "We didn't worry about that; we were too busy acting it." She stubs out her cigarette in anger. "Besides, Broadway was different in those days. It wasn't just about having a hit. It was possible to do a good, solid drama then and people would come to it, because that's what they wanted to see."

She laughs, but it's more of a snort. "Not anymore, honey. It's all bells and whistles now, nothing but smoke and mirrors. You try to find a real script that could run as long as *Virginia Woolf* did. Go ahead, try."

But then, she surprised me. "Yes, it's a brilliant play, but ultimately, it's a distasteful one. Maybe I got carried away with it all when I was younger, but this time around I realized how truly ugly and unforgiving that final act is. I couldn't do a long run of it again — even if I had the energy."

In 1947, famed acting teacher and director Herbert Berghof invited her to join him as an instructor at his HB Studio. They wound up getting married and influenced several generations of actors — from Jason Robards through Matthew Broderick — with their teachings. After Berghof's death in 1990, Hagen kept the studio going in his memory.

As we returned to the present, I asked the teacher of *Collected Stories* if she had any advice to offer acting students today.

"See a lot of theatre, read a lot of scripts, perform in a few plays. Study modern dance, music, and decide what you really want to do. Everybody today is caught between commercialism and being an artist. I don't think the two go together. I think you can be a great artist and reach a lot of people, but if you're doing it by selling yourself to somebody, then it's no good."

And with that, the Collected Stories of Uta Hagen came to an end . . . for now.

In 2001, Hagen appeared at Los Angeles' Geffen Theatre with David Hyde Pierce (Niles from *Frasier*) in a play called *Six Dance Lessons in Six Weeks*.

It received excellent reviews and was set to come to Broadway, but Hagen suffered a stroke. She is still recovering and hopes to appear onstage again.

Cameron Mackintosh
Richard Ouzounian/Toronto Star

CAMERON MACKINTOSH

Sleepless in Shanghai

W hen Noel Coward wrote "Why Do the Wrong People Travel?" he obviously never went abroad with Cameron Mackintosh.

The world-famous producer decided to bring *Les Misérables* to Shanghai in the summer of 2002 as the first full Western production of a musical in China.

That was news enough, but once he cast three Canadians in the company, and had Toronto resident Colm Wilkinson returning to recreate his leading role of Jean Valjean, covering the show became a no-brainer.

What I hadn't counted on was that I would turn out to be the only English-language print journalist there, which meant that I was able to spend a lot of quality time with Sir Cameron.

The first thing you need to know about Cameron Mackintosh is that he has a wicked sense of humour.

Wondering how to break the ice with the world-famous producer of *Cats*, *The Phantom of the Opera*, and *Miss Saigon*, I told him I was recording his interview over a tape I had previously used for Alicia Silverstone.

"Cameron Mackintosh on top of Alicia Silverstone?" he asked with camp incredulity. "I'd like to see the pictures, please."

We both needed a bit of a laugh, having survived an intense 90-minute press conference with the considerable panoply of the media of Shanghai. The occasion was the Chinese premiere of *Les Misérables*, and although Mackintosh is no stranger to international press conferences, it did cramp his free-flowing style to have to pause every 90 seconds to allow himself to be translated by a terribly serious young woman with absolutely no gift for irony.

"I don't think she's telling them any of my jokes," hissed Mackintosh during one of the laughless pauses. He was referring to lines such as "I've brought you the best cast in the world, I've brought you the finest production team, I've brought you everyone except Victor Hugo, and I'm so sorry he couldn't be here."

Jokes are important to Mackintosh, because although he's very serious about his work, he doesn't want to be perceived as stuffy or solemn.

Stephen Sondheim — a personal friend as well as a composer he's produced on numerous occasions — described Sir Cameron (knighted in 1996) as "an overexcited, boundlessly and unabashedly enthusiastic child in the playground of the theatre."

And Mackintosh knew that was his playground of choice from a very early age. He was born in Middlesex, England, in 1946. At the age of 8, he saw the famous British musical *Salad Days* and sensed that he had found his chosen profession. He studied at the Central School of Speech and Drama in London, but never finished, choosing the practical world instead. By the time he was 18, he had been in the chorus of a touring production of *Oliver!* and worked as a stagehand at the Theatre Royal.

But what he really wanted to do was produce, and that's what he was doing by the time he was 21. His first few shows were dismal failures, and he slipped into the world of advertising to pay off his debts. But a few years later he was back in the theatre again, wiser and not sadder. As one friend quipped, "He's gone from rags to riches, but he had exquisite taste in rags."

Mackintosh bristles a bit at that description. "I've always looked on my taste as stylishly common. I can't stand shows about what I call 'privileged people,'" he says, sipping cautiously at a cup of green tea. "That's one of the problems I have with the characters in some of Steve's (Sondheim) shows like *Company* and *Merrily We Roll Along.* I want to slap their faces and say, 'Get a life.'"

Well, Mackintosh got a life (and a very good one, too) just before his 35th birthday, when *Cats* began its run at the New London Theatre in 1981. Not only did it unite him with Andrew Lloyd Webber, but it established him as the man who knew how to keep a show running successfully longer than anyone else. "He's a better promoter," says Sondheim, "than anyone else in the world today."

The subsequent successes of Alain Boublil and Claude-Michel Schönberg's *Les Misérables* (1985), *The Phantom of the Opera* (1986), and *Miss Saigon* (1989) saw to it that Mackintosh would never have to worry about where his next meal (or show) was coming from again.

Current estimates place his net financial worth at close to US$1 billion. It's hard to reconcile that with the jovial teddy bear who sits there in a button-down tattersall shirt, radiating a kind of placid contentment.

"I haven't gotten tired or jaded over the years," he says with a chuckle, "but I have become more philosophical. After all, I've been producing for thirty-five years, and I've learned how to cherish things. Take dear *Les Miz*, for example. I first started work on it with Alain and Claude-Michel nearly twenty years ago, and I never tire of it — unless I see it being done less than perfectly, and then I get down there with my whip."

Mackintosh isn't kidding. He's known as the man who can spot a substitute flautist in the orchestra after eight bars or will replace a performer who's been with a show for years if he feels they're letting down the side.

Sondheim again speaks from experience: "He loves to interfere in every department, but it's his major contribution. You feel there is a captain of the ship, a boss who is looking out for everyone's interests."

It was fascinating to watch Mackintosh in action in Shanghai. On Friday afternoon he was pleasantly paternal to the cast, amiably accessible to the press and socially available to his authors. ("Cameron, we will let you take us somewhere very nice for dinner tonight," smiled Boublil.)

And that evening, during the only dress rehearsal, he was a master of split focus. People slid up beside him all evening to discuss the Chinese surtitles, the opening night party, the sales for the rest of the tour, or a hundred other related issues.

But whenever a pivotal scene was on stage, Mackintosh gave it his full attention. As soon as the last note had faded, he was on his feet offering encouragement to the cast and crew, then turning firmly (but quietly) to deal with some technical problems.

At the end of the long evening, he seemed as fresh as he had more than 14 hours ago, and I asked him if he wasn't tired.

"I'm never tired," he said with a Cheshire cat grin. "Sleep is for other people."

On opening night, he clicked into even higher gear. First he addressed a pre-show reception for *le tout Shanghai*, and then he dashed back to offer cheer to the cast, returning to his seat to be near the dignitaries.

The show itself proved to be a highly emotional experience on both sides of the footlights.

It was at the end of the first act that the magic took place.

Up until that point the opening performance had gone well. There had been laughter and applause, but nothing to indicate why Mackintosh had laboured so mightily to make sure this show became the first Western production of a musical to play in China.

And then it happened.

The first act of *Les Misérables* finishes with a big ensemble number called "One Day More" where all the characters find themselves at various crossroads. Prominently involved are a band of student revolutionaries, and at a climactic moment in the song, their leader Enjolras, began to wave a huge red banner at the back of the stage.

All at once, a collective sound came from most of the 1,800 people in the audience. A sudden intake of breath, followed by a long, slow exhalation. For a split second, they thought it was the flag of China up there, calling them to revolution.

Yet even though they were quick to realize that it wasn't, a link had been forged between the Paris of 1832 and the Shanghai of 2002, and the cast sailed into intermission on a deafening wave of applause.

But soon the past and the present became too perilously woven together. The 13th anniversary of the Tiananmen Square Massacre had just recently passed, and the famous barricades sequence of *Les Misérables*, where the student revolutionaries are slaughtered in a hail of bullets was received in hushed silence.

The release came a few minutes later, during the song "Empty Chairs at Empty Tables" where Marius, the survivor, mourns his fallen friends.

> *"Here they talked of revolution*
> *Here it was they lit the flame*
> *Here they sang about tomorrow*
> *And tomorrow never came."*

As he sang that line, the woman behind me began sobbing. She wasn't alone. There was just a spattering of applause from an audience too moved to go through the conventional motions. But shortly thereafter, when the show came to its emotionally wrenching conclusion with the entire company joined together in "Do You Hear the People Sing?" the people watching could contain themselves no longer. They stood, they cheered, they clapped in time, they whistled, they wept.

At the curtain call he was suddenly on stage ("singing totally off-key right in my ear," admitted a distressed Colm Wilkinson) and then, like Mr. Mistofeles, "the original conjuring cat," he was slyly negotiating with Chinese theatre moguls in the lobby before heading on to the cast party.

I corner him there to ask about his future. There have been reports he might be leaving the theatre for television or film and that we're currently at a bad time for the musical.

He chooses his words carefully. "Right now," he admits, "we're between generations. It's happened before. Between *Show Boat* and *Oklahoma!*, between *Fiddler* and *Cats*, there have been gaps. Oh sure, there were hit shows, but there wasn't a whole body of writers.

"And that's what we need now. It's time for the next generation to invent what the next lot of theatre will be. I believe it's going to happen. There are a lot of talented people out there, but talent isn't enough. Brilliant things happen in a musical — when by some sort of divine inspiration the right authors get together with the right subject."

He smiles, a bit sadly. "I have an extraordinary situation at the moment. Three of the great songwriters who are all friends of mine are saying 'What the fuck are we going to do next?' Steve (Sondheim) wants to get *Gold* out of the way and move on to something new, but he doesn't know what. Andrew (Lloyd Webber) can't find a topic that excites him, and Alain and Claude-Michel are still looking for their next idea as well. It doesn't get easier. It gets harder and harder."

It's been an emotional evening, and Mackintosh is suddenly thoughtful.

"After all this time, I don't know what will be a success in the theatre. Until you try it, you don't find out. Because the theatre is dependent on bloody-minded independence. You come up with an idea which couldn't possibly work . . . and then it does."

Then he smiles, looking for all the world like a Harry Potter whose Philosopher's Stone hides a stack of show tunes.

"No," he says, "I'm never going to leave the theatre."

And he isn't.

Despite the disappointing Broadway run of *Oklahoma!*, and the final performances of *Cats* in London and *Les Misérables* in New York, Mackintosh plows ahead.

His next announced venture is something he told me about off the record when we were in Shanghai: a stage version of *Mary Poppins*. It's being produced in partnership with Disney and is expected to open in London late in 2004.

Cats
Reg Innell/Toronto Star

CATS

Up to the Heavyside Layer

On September 10, 2000, the musical *Cats* finally closed on Broadway after a run of nearly 20 years, and as I write this almost 3 years later, it still holds the record as the New York show with the greatest longevity.

Because of the importance the show had in the theatrical life of Toronto, and since a lot of people connected with it had shared their stories with me over the years, I thought it was worth pausing that September to note its passing.

Let's not have any more jokes about nine lives.

Cats closes on Broadway this afternoon after giving 7,485 performances, making it the longest-running musical in American history. Not bad for a collection of songs based on T.S. Eliot's quirky *Old Possum's Book of Practical Cats*.

This kitty caper's closest competition was *A Chorus Line*, which kick-stepped into oblivion after 6,137 performances, running three years less than its feline opponent.

The next two musicals on the list — *Les Misérables* and *The Phantom of the Opera* — are still going strong, but they would have to keep running about five years more to pass the total set today by Andrew Lloyd Webber's least likely hit.

You see, that's what we forget now. During its initial rehearsal period in England, nobody thought *Cats* was going to go anywhere. It was Lloyd Webber's first show without lyricist Tim Rice, and the replacement wordsmith, T.S. Eliot, was never known for musicals. Trevor Nunn was an esteemed classical director venturing far from his usual field, and the show's one star, Judi Dench, had to be replaced after she snapped her Achilles tendon during rehearsals.

Superstar director Hal Prince was initially offered the show to stage.

"I had just directed *Evita* for Andrew, and so naturally I was anxious to hear what he had written next," Prince once told me. "I listened to the score with interest, but couldn't figure out what it all meant. I finally said, 'Andrew, I think I've got it: Grizabella is Queen Victoria, Deuteronomy is Disraeli, and the junkyard is the British Empire. Am I right?' Andrew shook his head sadly. 'It's about cats, Hal, just cats.'"

Prince decided to pass on the project, but somehow it all coalesced. Superstar Elaine Paige was brought in to replace Dench, and everyone started working to provide her with a hit number. Lloyd Webber, as usual, pulled a melody from the air (or from Puccini), and after rejecting a lyric from Rice, Nunn cobbled together a collection of images from various Eliot poems. And that, children, is where "Memory" came from.

Toss in some outrageous costumes (fun fur would never be the same again), a spectacular set (with a giant tire that Firestone would envy), and hip-wrenching choreography (a windfall to chiropractors around the world), and *Cats* was ready to open in London on May 11, 1981.

The whole experience was an exciting one for a young British pop star named Sarah Brightman, making her legitimate stage debut. She began with the show as a dancer and later worked her way up the feline food chain to the point where she married the composer.

"We knew we had something exciting and different happening," she once shared with me, "but we didn't know whether or not the press and the public would take to it."

The British critics mixed condescension with commendation, but it didn't matter. *Cats* immediately proved to be an enormous audience pleaser and the stage was set for the British Invasion of Broadway.

Yes, it was with *Cats* that English musicals started their American reign. (And not the kind that stays mainly on the plain.) Of the five longest-running musicals in Broadway history, only one (that "singular sensation" *A Chorus Line*) is American. The other four (*Cats, Les Misérables, The Phantom of the Opera,* and *Miss Saigon*) are all British, and it began on October 7, 1982, when Rum Tum Tigger and his pals finally hit the Big Apple.

Like their London colleagues, the Gotham reviewers gave with one hand and took away with the other. "Breathtaking" and "spectacular" were frequently balanced by "vulgar" and "mechanical."

Frank Rich, then the critic for the *New York Times*, got it right when he predicted in the opening paragraph of his review that "*Cats* is likely to lurk around Broadway for a long time." He went on to criticize the show for its "failings, excesses and banalities," but concluded that the show took us "into a theatre overflowing with wondrous spectacle — and that's an enchanting place to be."

The theatre-going public agreed with Rich. The Broadway production won seven Tony Awards (including Best Musical) and went on to sell US$400 million worth of tickets to 10 million patrons. The original cast album won a Grammy and sold more than 2 million copies.

"It's a dear little show," producer Cameron Mackintosh once said to me with wry understatement. "I can't stand it when people mock it. After all, it made me very rich and it made lots of people very happy."

Lots of people, indeed. *Cats* has been seen by 50 million audience members in 250 cities around the world. And one of those cities was Toronto.

To the theatrical community of that city, *Cats* will always mean more than another long-running mega-musical. It represented the first time that Canadian producers were allowed to take an

American or British hit and replicate it using Canadian talent. Without *Cats*, there might not have been local productions of *Les Misérables*, *The Phantom of the Opera*, etc. etc. and so forth (as the King of Siam was fond of saying).

Now, if you dislike this kind of musical, you might not consider that turn of events to be a good thing, but for the thousands of actors, musicians, stagehands, and other craftsmen who found years of gainful employment on these shows, it was a blessing from heaven.

And it all came about in a particularly serendipitous way. Tina Vanderheyden (O'Keefe Centre programmer turned fledgling producer) had gotten an inside track on the Canadian rights to *Cats*. The only trouble was there was no theatre to put it in. (Ironic footnote: Fifteen years later, there are now nearly a half-dozen suitable spaces, most of them sitting empty!)

The original production of *Cats* called for a stage that could be virtually gutted to install the elaborate junkyard set. At the time Vanderheyden was looking for a venue, the provincial government had just committed to the renovation of the Elgin-Winter Garden complex, placing it in the hands of veteran Toronto producer Marlene Smith. But before it could be renovated, it would have to be gutted, and wouldn't *Cats* fit in nicely during the interim?

Gina Mallet, the *Toronto Star*'s theatre critic at the time, thought this was a marriage made in heaven and put the two women together. At first, Smith and Vanderheyden worked amicably, but the partnership soon dissolved in a flurry of acrimonious accusations and what journalists at the time dubbed a "cat fight," with Smith the apparent victor.

But all that was in the future when the show opened on March 13, 1985, and ran for two sellout years in Toronto, leaving only to vacate the Elgin-Winter Garden for its renovations. *Cats* then toured and returned to Massey Hall for a total run of more than five years.

What made it so successful? Smith still feels that "*Cats* was the best of all musicals for overall family entertainment. It appealed to adults and kids alike."

Kathy Michael McGlynn, who sang "Memory" in the original Toronto production, recalls: "It was the excitement, that's what I'll always remember; excitement on stage and in the audience. Every time I heard that fabulous orchestra play the overture, I'd get goose bumps."

But that's all in the past. There will undoubtedly be many touring companies still to come, but when Grizabella ascends to the Heavyside Layer this afternoon, an era will truly have ended.

I remember attending one of the final previews of *Cats* just before it opened in New York. A typical Gotham nay-sayer was spouting forth on why the show just wouldn't last: "It's not a real musical. A real musical is about Laurey going to the picnic with Curly or Eliza going to the ball with Higgins, not some old whore going up to heaven on a tire."

You were wrong, buddy.

Just like the ad says: Now and Forever.

Since writing this, the long-run landscape has changed slightly. *Les Misérables* finally closed on May 18, 2003, after 6,684 performances. *The Phantom of the Opera* still keeps bringing that chandelier crashing down every night and will pass the record set by *Cats* if it continues to run until 2006.

In London, *Cats* finally called it quits on its 21st birthday, in May 2002.

As for my prediction about tours of *Cats* continuing to haunt us, it came true sooner than I feared and in February 2002, we were visited by a production performed by a group so callow that I described them thus: "The young women of the cast all blend into one squeaky composite — the Olsen twins in fun fur — while the gentlemen of the ensemble favour a cute and perky fuzziness that seems as though Martha Stewart had forgotten her depilatory."

David Friend & Simon Morley
Peter Power/Toronto Star

SIMON MORLEY &
DAVID FRIEND

The Dick Trick Duo

I first heard of *The Puppetry of the Penis* during its 2000 run at the Edinburgh Fringe Festival. I couldn't imagine what kind of men would want to spend an entire evening manipulating their genitals into funny shapes before a paying audience.

In the summer of 2001 the show (with its creators) came to Toronto, and I had a chance to find out.

They're two of the nicest guys you'd ever want to have lunch with — as long as they've washed their hands first.

Their names are Simon Morley and David Friend, and they seem like a pair of fun-loving Australian lads delighted to be paying a visit to Toronto.

All this is true, but it's hard to forget that they're also the stars of *The Puppetry of the Penis*, about to make its North American debut after both shocking and delighting London theatre-goers.

Are these smiling, beer-drinking blokes tucking into bacon cheeseburgers at an upscale pub really the "practitioners of the ancient art of genital origami" who have been making a name for themselves by turning their private parts into public sculptures with titles such as "The Hamburger" and "The Eiffel Tower"?

Yes they are, but any preconception you may have had about this duo being a pair of sweaty-palmed perverts is quickly dashed aside by the healthy laughter they generate at their own expense.

Morley was the one who started it all, a 34-year-old native of Melbourne who grew up as part of a prosperous Catholic family, with three brothers and two sisters.

"Dad was a big highfalutin businessman who grew up religious, left it all, and then went back to God . . . with a vengeance. Now he travels around preaching with a statue of the Virgin Mary. Once he was trying to have a prayer meeting in the same city where we were doing our show. That was amusing."

Morley shakes his shoulder-length curls as he remembers how the whole phenomenon began. "It was my younger brother Justin who used to invite friends over and do impromptu performances. My poor mum would see the boys lining up outside and chase them away saying, 'No dick tricks here!' But before too long, we all were doing them."

When it's suggested that the average North American kid would have been working on his curve ball instead, Morley laughingly admits it might be a cultural thing. "Australians are always getting naked. We have a more suitable climate for dropping our pants."

But despite his fondness for this kind of creative play, he never thought of doing it for a living. And he actually was succeeding rather well as a promoter of stand-up comedians. "But I always wanted to perform myself and had a sneaky feeling I was going to jump the fence one day."

He edged into it by publishing a calendar featuring 12 of his "installations" but sales were abysmal.

"People just didn't want to stare at a picture of my penis for a whole month. After about five days they'd tear it down in disgust. I had a whole garage full of calendars gathering dust, so I thought I'd better come up with a show to help publicize it. That's when I met Friendy."

"Friendy" is David Friend, 32, his partner in crime. While Morley's looks are retro '60s hippie, Friend opts for a mixture of

Edwardian gent and surfer dude. The moustache is curled, the sideburns thin and pointed, but the tan is richly groovy and the cool blue shirt is opened halfway down to Tasmania.

"I was born in Melbourne too," he starts, "but my family was different. My father was a major in the military. He was in Vietnam when I was born." A crooked smile crosses his handsome face. "My mother says he was the only person you ever met who actually wanted to go to Vietnam. He was a career officer and an asshole."

"Ah, I see a pattern emerging . . . "chuckles Morley.

"I used to do my tricks for my own amusement," admits Friend, "but it was when I got to uni, playing rugby and drinking beer, that I began to do them at parties. Just to hear them laugh . . . "

Morley concurs. "You never heard people laugh so long and so heartfelt. That's why you keep doing it, to hear them laugh again and again."

And so the two of them teamed up and bought a video camera to broadcast their activities on a giant screen. ("That doesn't speak well of your equipment," said one of their sisters.) They were having a good time, but they weren't making ends meet. They'd do comedy festivals, rugger events, and a series of bachelor parties at $300 a night. ("It seemed like a lot of money," Friend remembers sadly.)

Australia wasn't exactly treating them like the greatest thing since Dame Edna ("Hometown boys always need foreign approval," says Morley), and so, in the summer of 2000, they took every cent they had and headed out for the Edinburgh Fringe Festival.

"We didn't even have enough money to pay for our lodging," Friend admits, "and so our landlord let us stay on credit."

Morley gets more upbeat. "We knew we had to make our own publicity, and so we arrived a week early walking around the city screaming 'Look at our penises!'"

His voice is so loud that people all around the restaurant put down their forks to stare. And then this man who does eight shows a week buck-naked begins to blush and modulates his tone. "Well it worked, because we were almost totally sold out before we opened."

"And then," adds Friend with a wicked grin, "we got our manager. If Elvis had Colonel Tom Parker, then we have Dame David Johnson. He adores us."

"He adores you," observes Morley with a leer at Friend. Despite the joking, the men admit that sex — straight or gay — isn't part of their show's attraction. They take great pains, in fact, to point out that they work hard to make it all totally non-sexual.

After Edinburgh, Johnson booked them into London's Whitehall Theatre ("Just down the road from Buckingham Palace, but the Queen never dropped by") and they found themselves the toast of the town.

A successful British tour followed ("Every night we faced thirteen hundred screaming women and twelve men") now a limited run in Toronto, followed by a Broadway opening.

After that, they're already making plans to franchise the show with other performers taking over. ("Kind of like *Riverdance*, only with a sense of humour.")

And then?

"I'd like to make some films," says the practical Morley, while the dreamy-eyed Friend talks about taking his girlfriend Jane and retiring to "a little cottage on the beach, a healthy lifestyle — grow my own plants, make my own beer."

But for now, as Friend happily concludes, "We're having a great adventure. We're not working in a factory or programming a computer.

"We're travelling the world showing our penises to people and they pay us for it."

And what is the show like? Here's what I wrote after seeing "the boys" in action.

It's a birthday that Jackie will never forget.

She's a cherubic, cheerful lady of a certain age and she'd been out to celebrate with friends over a dinner at Swiss Chalet. Then she wound up on stage during the audience participation portion of *The Puppetry of the Penis*, and found herself holding a naked man's legs in the air while he twisted his genitals into the shape of an Australian fruit bat.

That never happens at *The Lion King*.

For the record, Jackie seemed to have a wonderful time, as did the entire audience. There were married women with slightly sheepish husbands who began by looking as if they would rather be at Canadian Tire but wound up laughing loudly.

There were packs of single women hooting and hollering to beat the band, all decked out in eclectic finery. One wore a top that looked as if it had been salvaged from the movie *A Knight's Tale* and carried a bag that proudly announced, "I'm fresh obsessed."

There were groups of young men with methodical tans and neatly trimmed beards who reacted a bit more quietly than the women but enjoyed themselves all the same.

There was even one strange fella with an impromptu dye job and a wrinkled fatigue jacket who found himself shaking with uncontrollable merriment as the evening unfolded.

We were all there with our various agendas to see two lads who practise "the ancient Australian art of genital origami," and none of us left disappointed. How often can you say that in the theatre nowadays?

There are several things to be made clear about Simon Morley and David Friend, who are the penis puppeteers of the title:

Yes, they appear for the entire show in full frontal nudity — except for socks and running shoes.

No, they never allow their activities to become explicitly sexual.

Yes, they turn their private parts into public "installations" as they call them, ranging from the Eiffel Tower to a piece of Kentucky Fried Chicken.

No, they never do anything gratuitously obscene.

Maybe it all began as party pieces for a bunch of beer-soaked rugby jocks, but it's acquired a life of its own that is really quite astonishing.

This assortment of what the boys call "dick tricks" is an inspired mockery of conventional role-playing, a joyous debunking of the "new masculinity" and a user-friendly reconnection with sexuality at its most primal roots.

It's a unique skill and one that can't be dismissed lightly (okay, you try turning your thing into the Loch Ness Monster), but by the end of an hour, it has just about worn out its welcome. What endures is the sheer liberating fun of it all — an experience that's pure and impure at the same time.

Although some commentators have suggested that the whole production indicates how decadent and shallow our society has become, I prefer to think it offers us a vision of how simple and uncomplicated it once was.

It's hard to hate when you're laughing, which once again proves the penis mightier than the sword.

Betty Buckley
Getty Images

BETTY BUCKLEY

The Independent Diva

Buffalo is only a few hours' drive from Toronto, so it makes sense to drop down there occasionally to check out interesting shows and people.

They don't come more interesting than Betty Buckley. One of the last of the free spirits, she's conducted her career for the past 35 years by marching not just to a different drummer, but to a completely unique band of her own.

TV, movies, musicals, concerts — Buckley has triumphed in them all, but always in her own particular way.

It was worth the trip to meet her in April 2002.

If they made a movie of her life, they'd have to call it *The Three Faces of Betty*.

First comes the Tony Award-winning Broadway diva, known for her flamboyant turns in shows like *Cats* and *Sunset Boulevard*.

Then there's the TV and movie star, radiating gentle warmth in series like *Eight Is Enough* and films like *Tender Mercies*.

And, finally, the Grammy-nominated recording and concert artist who dazzles audiences with her passionate intensity.

Will the real Betty Buckley please stand up?

The woman who strides across the stage of Buffalo's Studio Arena Theatre, hand outstretched in greeting, first seems unlike any of her professional selves but, after spending a few hours with her, you come to realize that they were all sides of this complex and fascinating woman.

She's made peace with this seeming contradiction years ago and, as she admits, "Any career in show business is going to be all over the map, but no matter how scattered it gets, there has to be a connection of life and truth in everything you do."

Betty Lynn Buckley was born in Fort Worth, Texas, in 1947 and on this bright, breezy spring afternoon, it appears as if she never really left her home state.

Her silver-blonde hair bounces casually in curls down to her shoulders (unlike the sleeker look she favours onstage), and the cotton blouse and jeans she's wearing belong to the Back 40 more than 42nd Street.

On the fundamental level, she's a no-nonsense gal and, as she sits at a downtown bistro, deconstructing her smoked-turkey sandwich, sipping at iced tea, and looking right through you with her cool, grey eyes, it seems like you've known her for years.

And maybe you have, if you've followed the career that began on Broadway in 1969 when she made her first appearance as Thomas Jefferson's wife in the hit musical *1776*, later going on to star in *Pippin* and the London company of *Promises, Promises*, before making her movie debut as the sympathetic gym teacher in the 1976 horror classic, *Carrie*.

The next step on her journey, however, bears an astonishingly close resemblance to her present assignment.

Buckley is in Buffalo to star in A.R. Gurney's latest play, *Buffalo Gal*. It's the story of an actress who returns to her hometown to appear in a production of *The Cherry Orchard* and then gets sidetracked by the offer of a role on a new TV sitcom.

And although Gurney wasn't aware of this when he wrote the play, art was imitating life with a vengeance this time around.

Back in 1977, Buckley was appearing in Buffalo as well, at the same theatre. The play was called *A Very Private Life*, and she starred opposite Celeste Holm as "a suicidal Oscar-winning actress with low self-esteem." When asked how the play ended, Buckley jokingly fires an imaginary gun at her head and then laughs "offstage, of course."

What actually happened offstage wasn't quite as comical. Diana Hyland, the star of the new hit NBC series *Eight Is Enough*, died of cancer after only five episodes, and the powers that be thought Buckley would be the ideal replacement.

All through rehearsals and performances of *A Very Private Life*, she was flown back and forth to L.A. and finally offered the role. "There were Broadway hopes for the play," Buckley admits, "but my departure ended them."

After plunging into *Eight Is Enough*, there were times when she wondered if she had made the right choice.

"The first two years on the series were really bumpy," she confides, spreading mustard on her smoked turkey. "It was like being a real stepmother. The rest of the cast really believed they were those people. I believed I was a New York actress playing a part."

"L.A. frightened me very much. If you bought into the lifestyle, then you were locked into the industry because you had no freedom, no independence. For a while, I kept flying back to New York for singing lessons, and one of the producers said to me, 'What for? You'll never star on Broadway again. All you're ever going to be is a middle-aged mom on TV.'"

Her normally benevolent gaze goes Medusa-like as she recalls the incident, and you wonder if there's a poor producer turned to stone somewhere in the Hollywood Hills. But Buckley was saved by the cancellation of *Eight Is Enough*, and she returned to New York, where she created the role of Grizabella in *Cats* on Broadway, singing "Memory" for more than two years, and winning a Tony Award.

"What a gift of a part!" she laughs. "They talk about you all night and then you show up and get to sing the big number. That's even better than playing the lead in *Hello, Dolly!*"

From then on, she was enshrined as one of Broadway's major divas, a reputation she solidified with performances like the cross-dressing title character from *The Mystery of Edwin Drood* and the religious fanatic mother in *Carrie*. That 1988 five-performance-and-out flop holds a unique place in Broadway history. It became such a notorious flop that Ken Mandelbaum called his study of failed musicals *Not Since Carrie*.

But was it really all that bad?

"It didn't have to be," sighs Buckley, putting down her sandwich. "The score was glorious, and I loved singing it. But Terry Hands, who directed it, was one of those British gentlemen who thought he would come over and show us Americans just how to do musicals. Well, it didn't work."

Her eyes start gleaming intently. "I tried to get the producers to let me fix it, make it work. I would've known how. But it was all too late. Might have been. Might have been. Let it go, baby."

Then came her controversial interpretation of Norma Desmond in Andrew Lloyd Webber's *Sunset Boulevard*, which eschewed the more arch theatricality of her predecessors Glenn Close and Patti Lupone to deliver a harrowing portrait of a woman in despair.

Buckley works closely with her own therapist to make sure her performances are rooted in psychological truth, because she believes "theatre's purpose is give the audience a mirror to itself, a chance to reflect on their own humanity."

She brings the same honesty to her recording and concert work (her album *Stars and the Moon* was nominated for a Grammy), and she explains that "there's got to be a personal resonance in everything I do."

In addition to *Buffalo Gal* (which hopes to hit New York this fall) and a busy concert calendar, Buckley is also a regular on the gritty TV prison drama *Oz*. ("I love the way they shoot it: rough and ready and fast — just go for it!") She's also always available to workshop a new musical.

"The old shows are great," she says, "but it's the new ones that make my pulse beat faster."

But as she walks contentedly down Buffalo's Main Street, she seems happy to wait for the next piece of the puzzle to fall into place.

"Life goes on, right?"

Buffalo Gal never made it to Broadway, but Buckley still kept busy.

She released a moving new album called *The Doorway*, continued on *Oz*, completed an experimental film called *Mummy an' the Armadillo*, starred in William Finn's song-cycle *Elegies* at Lincoln Center, and continued to live her life "however I choose."

Rod Beattie
Lucas Oleniuk/Toronto Star

ROD BEATTIE

Coming in on a Wingfield and a Prayer

You'd think that someone who made a living doing a one-man show would welcome the opportunity for some conversation. Not necessarily.

Rod Beattie was initially perplexed at my request for an interview. "I'm a middle-aged white male. They don't come any duller than that." Also, Beattie had a reputation as being rather taciturn when it came to discussing his personal life.

I looked on both those elements as a challenge, and finally convinced him to sit down with me in Toronto, just after Christmas in 2002.

There's more to Rod Beattie than just Walt Wingfield.

After 17 years and three thousand performances as the Bay Street lawyer turned small-town Ontario farmer, you might think that a certain identity crisis may take place, but have no fear.

Beattie is alive and well and slurping the foam off a very un-Walt-like cappuccino. We're joined by Rod's constant companion — a large chocolate Labrador named Chokydar — as we search for the man behind Walt Wingfield.

Beattie was born in 1948 and grew up in Scarborough, where his father was an administrator at Ontario Hydro and his mother a dietitian who became a stay-at-home mom.

But when I ask about his siblings, the surprises begin.

"There are four of us. My sister is the dean of mathematics at University of Waterloo and my older brother is a nuclear physicist." He laughs as my jaw drops. "Yeah, then it all went to ratshit."

He's talking about the fact that he and brother Doug, 50, both chose lives in the theatre. Doug, in fact, despite his junior status, paved the way.

"Doug was fascinated by theatre, especially by Stratford. When he was eleven, he wrote a puppet show in pseudo-Shakespearean style called *The Awful Tragedie of King Harolde the Fair*, played the title role, and got me to do all the other voices."

And was that what drew him into the theatre?

"Not quite." He looks at his shoes.

"It's actually a little embarrassing. I was going to an all-boys school, and Doug told me there were lots of girls in his acting class, so I tagged along."

But those endearing young charms were not enough to get him to commit. Lack of commitment, we will find, raises its head later in the Beattie saga.

"I entered U of T to study English and Philosophy, but I then proceeded to spend far too much time having fun doing theatre at Hart House."

And no wonder. One of his first shows there was Jean Giraudoux's *Ondine*, directed by William Hutt, with future stars R.H. Thomson, Clare Coulter, and Pamela Brook in the cast.

"At the end of that production," Beattie recalls, "Hutt told me I should audition for Stratford, but it took me five or six years to get up the nerve."

By then, Beattie was working as a teaching assistant and trying to keep his theatre habit going on the side — a combination he finally found impossible.

"I had to admit that I was really smitten with the idea of doing Shakespeare at Stratford, and so in 1974, I auditioned and got cast as a kind of glorified spear-carrier."

His first part, he chuckles to relate, was Peter of Pomfret in *King John*. "He's only got one line, and I had to read the play three times to find it. But it's not a bad little scene. You get a huge buildup, and then you enter and say: 'Foreknowing that the truth will fall out so.'"

Beattie has slipped into one of his galaxy of rude rustic accents.

"And after that, the king orders you to be taken away and executed. What a way to start!"

But the almost perpetual twinkle in his eye vanishes as Beattie soberly says, "I had thought that to be a member of a Shakespearean company, to live and breathe and walk around in those texts, is all that I would ever really ask of life if I could do it. And I still feel that, really."

That's not to imply that Stratford in 1974 was a dream factory. It was the last year of Jean Gascon's tenure, and "when I got there," Beattie remembers, "there was a terrible tiredness about the place. If you were replacing someone you didn't have rehearsal; they just sent you off to study the video of last year's production."

But the next year, Robin Phillips took over and things were totally different.

"At the end of the day, your head would be swimming and there would be electrifying insight after electrifying insight," is how Beattie describes rehearsals in those early days.

Beattie was a part of the company for each of the six Phillips' seasons, and what he remembers most is getting fired.

"In his second year, Robin cast me as the fop Witwould in *The Way of the World*, opposite Maggie Smith, and I was way over my head, thrashing all over the place. I guess Robin didn't want to see any bloodshed, so he let me go."

But the amazing part is what happened next.

"Right after that, I went into rehearsal for *A Midsummer Night's Dream*, also under Robin, playing Peter Quince. My confidence was just about shattered.

"Yet somehow, on the first day I tried something different, and Hume Cronyn grandly said, 'Robin, is he going to do that?'

"I felt like my future hung in the balance. Robin quietly said, 'I don't know, Hume, but I certainly hope so.'"

Beattie smiles, remembering the blessing of that moment.

"And from that time on, he just let me develop. It was stunning therapy for me. I don't know of anyone else who is as sensitive to what artists require."

Phillips left in 1980, to be succeeded by John Hirsch, and Beattie remained for one season. After that, "another low point in my life. I wasn't asked back. What really bothered me was that nobody even phoned." He laughs in donkey fashion, like one of his Wingfield characters. "I'm still waiting for them to call."

If things reached a professional slump for Beattie, his personal fortunes certainly took a rise. By this point he was 34 and by his own admission "had drifted through a series of relationships with women in which the eventual complaint about me was that I wasn't prepared to commit. And whenever I'd hear it, I'd say, 'That's fair.'"

Then along came Martha Henry, ten years older than Beattie, one of the great stars of the Canadian stage, and married to actor Douglas Rain.

"I first met Martha back in 1974 at Stratford," Beattie recalls, "and we became friends. I was friends with Douglas, too, but they were married and that was that."

But now it was eight years later, and as Beattie and Henry worked together under Phillips' direction on the Theatre Calgary production of John Murrell's passionate *Farther West*, they found themselves drawn together. "We were clandestine for a little while," concedes Beattie, "but we soon got over that."

After so many years of refusing to commit, he looked at Henry and decided "she was it for me. Something in the back of my head had been right to stop me committing before that."

Things have occasionally been stormy for the couple in the intervening two decades, and in fact, Beattie reveals that "we're not living together at the moment, but in many ways we're the best friends we've ever been now."

The other long-running relationship in his life is the Wingfield cycle of plays.

Brother Doug reappears as the catalyst, convincing Dan Needles in 1984 that his series of columns from the *Shelburne Free Press and Economist* could be turned into a play.

An early workshop with Needles' brother Reed in the title role showed the work had potential, but he decided not to continue with it, and Doug turned to his big brother.

"I only had a week to rehearse it," Beattie recalls, shaking his head, "so I memorized the script, prayed a lot, and then we opened it at the Orange Lodge in Rosemont."

That was in 1985, and there's been no turning back. The five plays (*Letter From Wingfield Farm, Wingfield's Progress, Wingfield's Folly, Wingfield Unbound,* and *Wingfield on Ice*) form one of the great upbeat stories in Canadian show business. They've sold out houses coast to coast and met with equal acclaim on radio and television.

"I'm still surprised by the extent of their success," admits Beattie. "It seems to have more momentum now than it ever had."

After all these years, I ask if such complete identification with a part is a blessing or a curse for an actor. Beattie thinks about it for only a split second.

"It's a blessing. I get to do something every night that I believe in, and I have the most fun that consistently I've ever had on a stage."

The Wingfield saga continues, with no end in sight, and yes, there's a sixth play being prepared for the series.

"But I won't tell you what we're going to call it," Beattie stonewalls me.

When I ask why he's being so uncooperative, he has a ready answer: "Walt wouldn't like it."

The Follows Family
Bill Sandford

THE FOLLOWS FAMILY

The House of Atreus Does Summer Stock

This was one of the most physically (and emotionally) exhausting pieces I ever had to work on.

Once I agreed to profile every member of the Canadian show-biz icons called The Follows Family (and their appropriate in-laws), all of whom were involved in a summer theatre production of *Hay Fever*, I became aware that there could only be one viable strategy: I had to interview everyone in a single day, as rapidly as possible, to prevent them all from comparing notes.

Easier said than done. In June 2001, I took an early morning bus from Toronto on the two-hour drive to Gravenhurst, Ontario, watched about a half-hour of rehearsal, and then set up shop on a sofa in the lobby.

For the next eight hours, I talked (a little), listened (a lot), and kept the tape recorder running.

Although some of it was like *Rashomon* (how many versions of the truth *were* there?), enough of it hung together to let me start to see the shape of the final piece almost immediately.

When I collapsed on the 7 p.m. bus back to the city, I fell into an immediate sleep, haunted by visions of various bickering Follows family members.

Transcribing the tapes was another struggle, but putting it all together offered me a certain kind of bizarre satisfaction.

I hope you'll agree.

Angry confrontations. Emotional embraces. Floods of tears. Gales of laughter.

And that's just the rehearsals.

The Fighting Follows Family is back together 22 years after father Ted walked out, leaving his wife and four kids, the youngest of whom, Megan, would shortly become Canada's sweetheart in CBC's *Anne of Green Gables*.

They've all finally reassembled in a production of *Hay Fever* by Noel Coward. In other words, you've got a family of dysfunctional actors playing . . . a family of dysfunctional actors.

Summer theatre will never be the same again.

Coward's play features Judith Bliss, a matriarchal actress in the grand style, her playwright husband, their stage-struck children, and all the various would-be lovers and guests who descend upon them during a weekend in the upscale British version of cottage country.

It's a fascinating group, but not as fascinating as the members of the Follows family who have assembled to play them.

There's actor/director/father Ted, a 55-year veteran of Canadian showbiz, mother Dawn Greenhalgh, a dramatic diva with coast-to-coast credits, and their children: Megan, one of the most successful Canadian actors of her generation; Laurence, a prolific theatrical producer; Edwina, an award-winning screenwriter; and Samantha, an accomplished television performer.

To this already bubbling cauldron, add the significant others of Megan and Samantha (Stuart Hughes, star of Stratford/Shaw, and Sean O'Reilly, a popular American film/TV actor, respectively), and you've got eight sticks of dynamite in search of a match.

That potentially lethal spark appeared in a heated argument between father and son that could have ripped this entire production apart early on in rehearsals.

The actual cause of the fight was trivial enough. Laurence had unwittingly given a visiting journalist a copy of a book that had been personally inscribed to Ted. On finding that out, the 74-year-old patriarch went ballistic.

"The argument was about nothing, that's what made it so dark, so personal," says Samantha, the 36-year-old mother of two who seems the sunniest of the Follows clan. "Everyone was watching. It was what we were all afraid of. I thought, 'Oh God, here it is . . . '"

Much the same feelings came from Edwina, who at 40 is the oldest. Quiet, reserved, she tugs at her Yankees baseball cap in moments of thought. "My reaction to the fight? The worst is happening already, and I was hoping it wouldn't."

Dawn, now 67, was the veteran of many such battles as wife and mother, and she laughs huskily to describe her immediate withdrawal. "I left the room, then stuck my head in and said, 'Save it for the documentary.' In the old days, I would have been right in the middle of it, probably punched out by both of them."

The usually hail-fellow-well-met Ted grows unexpectedly quiet as he admits the extent of his temper. "In normal circumstances, if I had gotten into a fight like that with someone, I would have walked out and not come back."

Laurence, 38, the perennial kid brother, shakes his thatch of blond hair as he remembers the moment. "I just stood there and said, 'You will stop being like this. You will not walk out that door.' And he didn't. That was the first time he had gotten angry and not walked away."

"You can't walk out," explains Ted, "it's the family."

When told his father has said that, Laurence loses some of his usual ebullience. "The last time he was that angry with the family and he walked away, he stayed away."

For 22 years.

It was 1979 when Ted Follows finally walked out the door from a rancorous marriage that had stormed since 1958. The children he left behind ranged in age from 11 to 18. How they felt about that break-up very much depended on how old they were at the time.

For Edwina, who was 18, "it was a relief. For years it had been a constant threat. 'I'm going, it's over!' Well, when it was finally over for real, we could all get on to the next step."

The then 16-year-old Laurence was blunt. "I thought, 'Get out of here, who wants this situation?'"

Samantha, 14 at the time, greets the memory with her usual equanimity. "I don't have any issues with my dad about that. At the time, I knew it was best. It had become so rocky that there was nothing left to salvage. Time for some peace."

But for Megan, at 11, it was a lot more complicated. "Working on this project has made more feelings come up around my dad and what I felt about his leaving. I suppose that's why I really wanted to do it."

She smiles with the calm strength of a grownup Anne Shirley. "I get to see my dad in a world that means a lot to him. Now that we've graduated to adulthood we have choices as to how we want to carry our baggage from the past."

There's another set of dynamics — personal as well as professional — resolved in putting together a husband and wife again on stage after 20 years of divorce.

Ted is smiling at first as he remembers the old days. "We were known as the Fighting Follows. Everyone used to love to come to our dinner parties because our arguments would be such fun to watch . . . like *Private Lives*."

Then his face darkens. "But after about ten years, it turned into *Who's Afraid of Virginia Woolf?* And, boy, you're into a different kettle of fish."

Edwina remembers those days. "Yes, the fighting was considerable, and from a child's perspective it was overwhelming, because you never knew when it would spin out of control."

"Booze, darling, that's what it was," Dawn's husky voice cuts to the chase. "I used to use alcohol to boost me up, so I could call Ted on all his bullshit."

And she launches into an impromptu impersonation of what

she was like in those days — voice strident, words slurred, arms waving. She ends it as abruptly as she began.

"I'm sober now. If I kept drinking, I'd be dead. I'll always remember when I stopped. Nine months to the day after Ted walked out. Nine months of absolute bloody hell. Then I went to an AA meeting, and for the first time in my life I said, 'I'll do what you're telling me.' And it worked."

But even with two decades of serenity under her belt, Dawn had her worries about working with Ted and the family. "I thought he might try to bully me. We did a play together a few years ago, and when I forgot a bit of blocking he'd turn to the cast and say, 'You see why I divorced her,' thinking it would get a big laugh, and there would be stony silence. No one was in the least amused whatsoever.

"I thought he might try it here, but I've got a lot of backup with my family. He won't get away with it, noooo he won't," she concludes, giving that final "no" a melismatic intonation Tallulah Bankhead would have envied.

The two outsiders have a tricky role to play in this equation. Stuart Hughes is a veteran of the Canadian theatre scene as well as Megan's partner, so he knew what he was getting into.

"Meg and I sat down before we came here and said, 'What are we gonna do when the fur begins to fly?'" He laughs heartily. "I actually think this is a great play for us to be doing, because its theme is: How do I treat people I invite into my house? Which is a very good question to ask when you're working with this family."

"It's not about closure," insists Megan, "it's about making a choice to appreciate what you have." Although Sean O'Bryan has been Samantha's husband for six years, he'd never encountered any of the Follows gang professionally. "But it's not as crazy as I thought it might be," he admits in his Kentucky accent, "because I've already worked with plenty of lunatics like Nathan Lane."

"Hey," he chuckles, "so far it's been a blast."

And inside the rehearsal, on this muggy summer day, it certainly does seem like fun. The hurts of the past are set aside while everybody concentrates on the work at hand. After all, this is theatre, the only thing stronger than family to the Follows clan.

"I always believed in the theatre," affirms Dawn, "it was my religion, my higher power."

Laurence agrees, "I never grew up with a religion. There was no conversation about a divine force. If divinity existed, it existed on the stage."

Ted crosses over and wraps a compassionate arm around his son's shoulder, their quarrel forgotten. "This is where I want to be, back in the bloody old theatre."

His career began here in Gravenhurst more than 50 years ago with a production of *Hay Fever* for the Straw Hat Players, and he feels the circle is finally complete. "This is my home, and if it's my home, that's where I want my family to be."

Laurence looks around at how smoothly things now appear to be going, and smiles. This production was his dream, and — problems and all — it seems to be coming true.

"Not many people can get together as a family and put on a play," he asserts, and then laughs. "Hell, most people have trouble getting together as a family for Sunday dinner."

"Oh, it's going to be exciting," Dawn concludes, "we've got that great rapport. Darling, we're a family."

With Stuart assisting, Ted directs quietly, but firmly. He lets Dawn find her way, offers Sam and Laurence some practical staging advice, and helps the action build up to the big moment at the end of Act II when Megan's character, the outspoken Myra, turns on the Bliss ménage.

"It's a great pity you ever left the stage," her character says. "It's your rightful home. You can rant and roar there as much as you like!"

And as the rest of the clan launch into the free-form argument that brings down the curtain, you start to wonder if Noel Coward might have ever met the Follows family.

The reviews for the Follows' *Hay Fever* were generally good and the show toured Ontario over the next two summers.

Most of the family still speak to me, although I did hear one amusing story from a member who asked to remain anonymous.

The day the paper was published, they each read their separate copies of the article in the rehearsal hall. One member of the family flung it down in disgust. "He makes me sound like an asshole."

"Well, darling," Dawn reportedly said, "maybe that's because you *are* an asshole."

VI

FROM THE SCREEN

Kathleen Turner
Tannis Toohey/Toronto Star

KATHLEEN TURNER

Are You Trying to Seduce Me?

My first meeting with Kathleen Turner came under odd circumstances.

The American actress was appearing as Nina in the Manitoba Theatre Centre's production of *The Seagull* in Winnipeg in 1980.

It wasn't a very good production and the artistic director was fired just after the opening. I was being interviewed to replace him (yes, I later took the job) and dropped by to see the show, hanging around afterward to meet the cast.

Turner was a very nice young woman who acted well enough, and seemed pleasant offstage, but there was none of that va-va-voom she was later to make her stock in trade.

Consequently, when a sexy movie called *Body Heat* started generating attention a few years later, I didn't think the same Kathleen Turner could be the star.

She was, and my jaw dropped when I saw the change in her.

It took me 20 years to catch up with her again, this time in a bar on Manhattan's West Side. And once more, it was a stage show that brought us together.

It's a scene straight out of *The Graduate*: the innocent guy and the worldly wise woman sitting cozily in an intimate bistro while she lays down the rules.

"Sexuality is at the bottom of everything I do, but I'm very funny, too. I want to be clear about that."

Only it's not Benjamin Braddock and Mrs. Robinson. It's me and Kathleen Turner.

But it's hard to treat Turner dispassionately. Two decades after scorching the screen with her film debut in *Body Heat*, the opportunity to see her naked on stage as Mrs. Robinson in *The Graduate* shattered all sales records for non-musical theatre in Toronto.

And for the next hour, at a corner table, it's just the two of us.

She flicks her Courvoisier-coloured hair and fills the conversational snifter with another slug of that VSOP voice of hers. "Look, I don't believe that I walk around like a sexy woman. Not all the time. But on days when I feel hot, baby, then watch out."

She puts her hand on my arm, and I get a vision of all the guys who've been here before: William Hurt in *Body Heat*, Michael Douglas in *Romancing the Stone*, Jack Nicholson in *Prizzi's Honor* — it's pretty heady company.

Her hand stays there on my jacket and I have to ask the question: "Are you trying to seduce me, Miss Turner?"

Her laugh is a satanic rumble. "What does that fuzzy little guy Yoda say? 'Try? There is no try. There is only do and not do.' That's me, baby." Her hand moves away.

Some stars tempt the public with their availability; others intrigue them by being totally inaccessible. But Turner is something different. She's like Mount Everest — getting there might kill you, but think of the view from the top.

"What's she look like up close?" is what everybody wants to know. The answer is: Terrific.

Sure, at 47, she's 20 years older than when she first sizzled into stardom. Cut her a little slack, although it's not like many allowances have to be made. Her killer curves are a bit more ample than they were in the '80s, but everything is still in appealing proportion. She wears a black turtleneck sweater, dangling gold earrings and, bright-red lips aside, amazingly little makeup.

Yes, the eyes still flash, the skin still glows, and the voice — oh Lord, that voice! — remains a mixture of honey, gravel, wood smoke and Scotch distilled by time into a lethally potent blend.

"Did I sound like this when I was 16? You bet. You should hear my mother. We both sang baritone. When they split us up for the choir, they'd always say, 'Kathleen, you're with the boys.'"

But Turner wasn't casting her sexual spell back in adolescence. "Hell no, I was a complete tomboy — swimming, tennis, volley-ball. I've always loved sports, and I was very good at them."

She snorts in remembered derision. "Frankly, I thought boys were just competition. Unless one of them could beat me, it was a complete waste of time. I told my daughter that, from my experience, boys are essentially to be played with until you're 29. Then you can start to take them seriously."

Turner was also moving too much in those early years to form any kind of lasting attachment. She was born in Missouri in 1954, and her father worked in the foreign service, so her childhood was spent bounding around the world, an experience that gave her some useful skills.

"You have to adapt very quickly to new schools, new languages, new cultures. You're going to a country where nobody has ever seen you before, so you can be anybody you want."

And young Kathleen knew she wanted to be an actress. "We lived in Caracas when I was eleven or twelve, where we had a kind of English-speaking community centre that did theatrical productions, and I was always in their face . . . take me, take me!"

"Then, when I heard my father was being transferred and we were going to London, I was over the moon. I thought that's it now, I'm on the road for sure."

The forward trajectory of her story stops cold and her eyes cloud with regret. She takes a first sip from the iced tea she's so far left untouched before continuing. "Remember in *Peggy Sue Got Married*, that scene where she picks up the phone and hears her grandmother's voice? When I did that, I thought 'If only I could hear my father's voice again, what I would I give?'

"He's been dead 30 years now, and I still feel like I . . . " She looks at me, wanting to continue, but unable to find the words. I ask her how it happened, and she takes a moment before answering.

"It was very sudden. Actually, I'd run away the night before to Stratford-upon-Avon in rebellion. They told me I couldn't take the train to see these plays, and so I just went."

Turner speaks as if it were yesterday: "The next morning, I called to tell them I was okay, and found out he'd had a heart attack. I jumped on the next train I could, but by the time I arrived, he was dead . . . which is about enough to kill you when you're seventeen, but I got through it. And yes, I think about it all the time."

Some more iced tea, another flick of the hair and she tries to change the tone. "I was going to stay in England and study acting at the Central School, but all of a sudden we had to leave, because our diplomatic status was over. . . . They gave us four weeks to get the hell out. Yeah, they were lovely.

"We went back to Springfield, where my mother's parents lived, and I attended Southwest Missouri State University, which turned out to be a very good thing, but who knew at the time? It was just the best school that I could afford."

She's smiling again, and she leans in closer to tell me how it all started. "Suddenly there was all this fuss around me. Guys were all over the place, trying to convince me that I was gorgeous, that I had great legs. But I truly had never looked at myself that way. It wasn't encouraged in my family. Looks were nothing." She points one finger seductively toward her brain. "It was up here that was supposed to be important."

The power of not-so-positive thinking was to haunt her self-image for years to come. "When we were shooting *Body Heat*, I kept having this dream. I would cast a smouldering glance at Bill Hurt and then the audience would jeer, 'Oh, right.'

"I'd be naked in bed with him, and they'd start giggling and saying, 'Yeah, sure.'"

But now, after 20 years, the movie still retains its zing as the erotic film of choice for an entire generation. It's the story of a young lawyer (Hurt) lured into a labyrinth of murder, lust, and larceny by the Machiavellian Matty Walker, played with superb steaminess by Turner.

Getting the part was initially an ordeal for Turner. New York casting agents refused to consider her because she had no screen credits, only a stint on the NBC soap *The Doctors* and a handful of stage roles (including Nina in a 1980 Winnipeg production of *The Seagull*).

But after writer-director Lawrence Kasdan had failed to find anyone for the role, Turner was flown out to Los Angeles. She walked in and Kasdan handed her the most difficult scene in the film, where Matty confesses to her sordid past. He told the astonished Turner, "I want you to read it cold, right now."

The memory still provokes a wry smile. "My way of reacting to that kind of pressure is to go like this . . . " And Turner produces a middle finger salute. "I stretched out on the sofa, put my feet up, and proceeded."

When she finished, there was silence, and then Kasdan said, "I never thought I would hear that out loud as I heard it in my head."

If landing the film was tricky, making it was even more so. "We broke a lot of taboos, but then all my films do that," she grins. "I like to do that."

The seemingly explicit nude sex sequences were carefully calibrated, but that didn't make them any easier for Turner. "Working naked is extremely hard. I'd go through the scenes, and then I'd sob for half an hour. I would just start shaking and sobbing. No, sweetie-pie, not easy."

Not easy. But very successful. For the rest of the '80s, Turner never looked back. Commercial hits like her pair of adventures with Michael Douglas (*Romancing the Stone* and *The Jewel of the Nile*) alternated with outrageous serious films like Ken Russell's *Crimes of Passion*, in which she played a $50-a-trick hooker named China Blue. "That was some of the best work I've ever done. I went right to the edge on that one, which is kind of how I define acting. You've got to risk failure, or else you never move along."

What she moved along to next was *Prizzi's Honor*, a delicious black comedy in which she and Jack Nicholson played mob assassins who fall in love. "I always remember the scene where Jack and I keep rolling over and over in bed. 'Who's on top? I'm on top. No, I'm on top!' I just thought that a perfect manifestation of the whole male-female shit, and I loved it."

The hits kept on coming, including her Oscar-nominated turn in *Peggy Sue Got Married* and her never-to-be-forgotten voice of Jessica Rabbit in *Who Framed Roger Rabbit?*

But then, after she started appearing in duds like *Switching Channels* and *V.I. Warshawski*, fate dealt her another blow as well. "I developed rheumatoid arthritis, which is quite a serious disease. I'm doing extremely well now, but about six or seven years ago, I was doing extremely badly. I couldn't hold a pen. I couldn't feed myself. I couldn't walk. They told me I would be in a wheelchair for the rest of my life, and I said, 'No, I will not.'

"They put me on a cocktail of medications that was unbelievable. I was on chemotherapy, on prednisone, and my appearance changed. I blew up and I started to read all this stuff in the media that I was an alcohol abuser and it hurt terribly."

Turner the survivor raises an ironic eyebrow. "But at the same time, I knew that it was better that people think I was a drunk than they think I was mysteriously ill. Because I could get hired if I was a drunk. They do it all the time. But if you've got some sickness that they don't understand, then you can kiss it all goodbye."

Her family helped her through this time. Despite the sex-bomb image, she's been happily married for 18 years to real estate executive and sometime rock 'n' roller Jay Weiss.

The other joy of her life is her 14-year-old daughter, Rachel. "She's an amazing kid, a bit of a jock, too, I'm very happy to say."

For a few minutes, Turner sounds like any parent of a teen. "She's hitting the hormone wall now. You know, 'I love you, I hate you, I love you, I hate you!' I said, 'Honey, it's cool, everyone goes through it. You cannot help it. However, what you can help is who you inflict it on . . . your Dad is over there." And with that, she lets loose with a laugh that's witchy enough to send Dorothy running for cover.

The conversation switches to her performance as Mrs. Robinson in *The Graduate*, and I remind Turner that her last New York stage appearance was in *Indiscretions*, in which she seduced a very young Jude Law.

"You think I'm getting a reputation for young men? Onstage, maybe, but not in real life, because they're quite uninteresting. Conversation? They ain't got any. I can appreciate a nicely formed bod and that kind of thing, but once they start talking, it's over. Anything younger than thirty is just dull.

"Mrs. Robinson isn't like me. She's just there for the sex. She keeps telling him to stop talking. This is a woman who's intensely lonely and very angry. She got pregnant in college in the back seat of a car and that was it. The end of her life. And now the whole world is on the edge of a true social and cultural change, and she's missing it and she's mad. So she's gonna take whatever she can and that includes screwing around with younger men."

We finally get around to discussing the famous nude scene where she shows Benjamin her all. It was Turner's choice to include it, and she has no trouble defending it. "This is the moment that forces the action of the play. It's got to be big enough or shocking enough to move everything along, otherwise we all go home."

I ask her what it feels like to be playing the sex and nudity card again so many years after it started her career.

"Being out there naked at forty-seven isn't the easiest thing

I've ever done. It was a lot easier at twenty-seven, and even then it was hard, really hard."

Does that mean she won't keep doing this kind of role? "Oh no," she purrs, "I think I'd like to be the oldest living sex symbol on stage." And then she flicks her tawny mane one last time.

Despite decidedly unimpressive reviews, *The Graduate* went on to box office success in Toronto and New York — as long as Turner stayed with the cast.

An ironic footnote — especially considering her comments to me about how she "started to read all this stuff in the media that I was an alcohol abuser and it hurt terribly" — is that Turner checked herself into rehab for a drinking problem several weeks after she left *The Graduate* in December of 2002.

Renée Zellweger
Michael Crabtree/PA Photos

RENÉE ZELLWEGER

The Coulda, Woulda, Shoulda Girl

L ike many of my colleagues, I was skeptical about the casting
of Renée Zellweger as Roxie Hart in the film version of *Chicago*.
How could a woman who'd never sung or danced professionally
follow in the footsteps of Gwen Verdon and Ann Reinking?

But the buzz during the Toronto shoot was good, and when I
finally got to see the film, I was ready to eat my words.

No, she wasn't a musical comedy star, but she was one hell of
an actress.

When interview time in New York came around in December
2002, I knew I had to talk to her. Her dance card was full, but I
was patient as well as persistent, and we finally wound up spending some time together.

Renée Zellweger is an impostor.

The young woman who walks into the hotel room —
Starbucks cup in one hand, water bottle in the other — doesn't
look like Bridget Jones, Nurse Betty, or *Chicago*'s Roxie Hart.

She's blonde and petite, all right, yet the rimless glasses and
ramrod posture belong to somebody else. Maybe a nervous office
temp on her first day at a new job, rather than a major league
movie star.

The tentative smile seems like the real thing, but then she

opens her mouth to speak. "I am such an impostor. I am an impostor in this world. I am an impostor on the screen. I am an impostor in the role of Roxie."

When I try to tell her how much I enjoyed her singing and dancing in the film, she turns bright red — an instantaneous world-class blush — and stammers to find some words.

"You're very generous to say that, but whenever someone compliments me, it sends blood rushing to my brain and all I can hear is my discomfort. I don't know how to receive it and so I just go . . . " She makes an inarticulate gesture of surrender, and then turns to a therapeutic sip of coffee for support.

This is a woman known as one of the nicest stars in the business. While filming *Chicago* in Toronto last winter, she used to drop by the set on her down days with coffee for the crew or drive around the city buying meals for the homeless.

And when Gucci kicked her out for daring to bring a Starbucks into their hallowed premises, she left without a single divalike scene.

If the lady is that together, then why can't she handle a compliment?

I mumble an apology and she measures me with those blue-grey eyes that have done the same to Tom Cruise and Hugh Grant. Her sincerity meter is ticking. Will I pass? As the heat in her face subsides, she decides to continue, but drops her voice to a whisper.

"Do you know why I'm an impostor? Because there's a lot of people out there who've worked in this medium for a lot longer than me who deserved this beautiful experience."

It's true that when she was first announced for the role, there was a certain amount of showbiz eye-rolling about her lack of musical credits, and leading the pack was Zellweger herself. She loves to tell about how her brother screamed at her to stop singing in the shower when she was six; but to tell the truth, no one clamoured for her vocal renditions in later years, either.

She relaxes a bit when asked about the next time she tried to sing publicly. Unlike most stars, she loves telling stories that put her in a bad light. Self-esteem? You wonder if she knows the meaning of the term.

"Okay," she giggles, "I tried out for *Hair* in college . . . and I watched *Hair* from the audience. I enjoyed it very much. I was in journalism school. What was I doing trying out for *Hair* anyway?"

That was 1987, at the University of Texas, in Austin, where Zellweger went after living the first 18 years of her life in what she calls "the little bitty town of Katy." The more comfortable she gets, the more pronounced her Texas accent becomes.

Born on April 25, 1969, she grew up a bit of a tomboy and spent much of her high school years in cheerleading, gymnastics, and track — until a knee injury finished that for her.

While pursuing her journalism degree in college, she had to take a fine arts course and picked Drama. "That did it. The penny dropped for me. I wasn't sure if I'd ever be any good, but I knew I wanted to act."

She switched majors and graduated with a BA in Radio, Television, and Film, and then went off to seek her career in Los Angeles. But things were tough at first, and she found herself "waiting tables, bouncing cheques, and living on crackers."

A few breaks came her way, and by 1994 she was at the Toronto Film Festival with an independent film called *Love and a .45*. Other small movies like *Empire Records* and *The Whole Wide World* started to build her reputation as a young actress to watch, but it was *Jerry Maguire* that really put her over the edge.

Her performance as Dorothy, the single mom who greeted Cruise's plea for forgiveness with the classic line, "You had me at hello," catapulted her into the big leagues.

But it's vintage Zellweger that she described herself during filming as "the dork girl who got lucky." She returned to Texas during the filming to attend the wedding of an old sweetheart, "and everybody kept telling me how lucky I was to be working with Tom Cruise, but all I could keep thinking of was how I didn't get the real guy back home."

After that, she was offered a seven-figure salary to star in *Godzilla*, but wisely turned it down in favour of classier projects like *A Price Above Rubies* and *One True Thing*.

She did extensive psychological research for her role as the delusional heroine of Neil LaBute's *Nurse Betty*, which must have served as good preparation for working with Jim Carrey in *Me, Myself and Irene*.

Zellweger became engaged to the Canadian comedian Carrey after working on that film, and it's possible to see the attraction: "Jim's very bright and very funny and very sweet. He's also very vulnerable, which I look for in a man. But . . . " She looks from her water bottle to her Starbucks cup for support before continuing, but finally decides to do it on her own.

"But he's also very intense, like me, and uncertain, like me, and it's not such a good idea to have two needy people in love with each other."

So it broke up, as did her romances with actors Rory Cochrane and George Clooney. She tries to shrug her failed relationships off ("Things don't last. What can I say?"), but the insecurity still flickers behind her eyes, and the hurt is still so palpable that you're almost sorry you asked her.

The flap over her casting as Roxie Hart recalls the furor that greeted her landing the title role in *Bridget Jones's Diary*, best summed up when the London tabloids asked, "Why should a skinny Texan play a hefty Brit?"

But she's a skilled impostor, so she gained 20 pounds and worked on a flawless accent, which answered all the critics and won her an Oscar nomination for Best Actress.

Then she got a phone call from her manager saying Rob Marshall wanted her to read the script of *Chicago*.

"I didn't understand it. I'd never seen the musical, so it really didn't translate on paper to me. I thought there wasn't a thing I could contribute to this, so I decided to stay away. Far away.

"Then my manager called me back and said, 'Rob is down at the Four Seasons. He is one of the greatest people I've ever met and you should go meet.' And I said, 'I don't care how nice he is, it's still going to be singing and dancing and I can't make that convincing.'

"He screamed at me, 'You will get off this phone and you will go down and meet Rob and you will love him!'"

She looks sheepish as she continues. "So I had tea with Rob and he already had in his mind that there would be singing and dancing which would involve me and it would all be just fine. I bought into it, because he was so bright and generous and wise."

That he got her to actually start performing in this alien territory is a tribute to Marshall's ingenuity, and Zellweger now understands how artfully he roped her in.

A dreamy look transfigures her features as she describes the scene. "Sun's going down, light's coming through the skylight, there are shadows across the wooden floor and it's kinda dark. I'm watching them as they glide through a routine and I suddenly think, 'Hey, I can do that!'"

Her high school jock days return for a second. "You know, when you're playing basketball and you suddenly see that really easy lay-up you know you can make?" The woman is transformed, all hesitancy gone. In this instant, you see what happens to Renée Zellweger when the lights are on and the camera starts rolling.

"Then Rob tosses me a hat and a cane and says, 'Try this.' I started to follow him. It was an incredible moment. I was itching to try it, because it looked so fun. Sharing in the shadows in the dark, just quietly."

Time to move on to the singing. "That night, we had dinner. We talked about songs from musicals and he started to sing some of his favourites. I didn't know many, but I joined in. Soon we were belting out 'Over the Rainbow' together.

"Then, the next evening, I went to see my friend Meryl Streep in *The Seagull* in Central Park. Afterwards, I was so moved I had to sit down on a park bench by myself. A young couple walked up and tapped me on the shoulder and said, 'We were in this restaurant last night and we heard you and this guy singing together. We really think you should do a musical.'"

She beams. "And that was a big fat omen to me."

But there were still some problems to get out of the way. "Like the fact that I didn't know how to sing properly. I didn't know about breath, about enunciation, about anything."

Enter Elaine Overholt, Toronto vocalist, arranger, and Grade-A singing coach.

"God bless Elaine," says Zellweger, without a trace of irony. "She saved my life. She taught me everything, but she made it fun. We just enjoyed ourselves. It was playtime, her behind the piano, me at the microphone. Like a big karaoke bar, and we were the only two customers. Great. I didn't feel like such an impostor around her."

But if making the movie was such a positive experience and if her reviews have all been glowing, then why does she still embrace what she calls "my impostor syndrome"?

"Because I don't see what everyone else is seeing. All I see is coulda, woulda, shoulda. But that's okay. I don't torture myself with that anymore. I've resigned myself to the fact that I'm always going to be the girl who coulda been, woulda been, shoulda been something else. In life, in love, in the movies. It's all the same to me."

And it finally becomes clear that this contradictory mixture of incandescence and insecurity is the very thing that makes her a star.

She gets ready to go, picking up her coffee cup and water bottle, and then stops to ask, "Was that all right?"

Don't worry, Renée. You had me from hello.

The Coulda, Woulda, Shoulda Girl won her Second Golden Globe for *Chicago* and got her second Oscar nomination for Best Actress as well, but lost out on that one to Nicole Kidman.

Kidman is her co-star (along with Jude Law) in Anthony Minghella's *Cold Mountain*, slated for release in December 2003.

Before that, she romps through Doris Day Country in a tribute to 1960s romantic comedies called *Down With Love*.

Brendan Fraser
Myung Jung Kim/PA Photos

BRENDAN FRASER

More Than Just a Mummy's Boy

In October 2001, I was scheduled to fly to London to interview Dame Maggie Smith. That would have been exciting enough, but while looking through the London theatre listings, I discovered that Brendan Fraser was starring in a critically acclaimed West End revival of *Cat on a Hot Tin Roof*.

I recalled that Fraser had spent his adolescence in Toronto and wondered if that would want to make him talk to a hometown reporter.

After making a formal request through the usual channels, I was surprised to get a breezy e-mail back from Fraser himself, inviting me to breakfast while I was in London.

The night before we met, I saw his performance and (luckily) was blown away by it. When we sat down together the next morning, I suddenly had a lot more to talk to him about.

With Brendan Fraser, what you see isn't necessarily what you get.

Sure, the 6-foot-3 hunk who strides into the Sunflower Café in the Chelsea section of London is even more imposing in real life than he is on the screen.

His enormous blue eyes look right through you, he has a handshake firm enough to build a fortress on, and the trademark shock of brown hair that falls over his forehead makes him look younger than his 32 years.

He's wearing a navy cable-knit turtleneck and, as he sits himself down at a table meant for someone much smaller, he radiates the nonchalant cheerfulness of a college guy enjoying a late breakfast with one of his frat brothers.

You'd have to look hard to find the $11 million-per-picture star whose last big release, *The Mummy Returns*, grossed an unheard-of $90 million in its first weekend out on VHS and DVD.

This even surpassed the film's record-breaking US$68 million take during its first weekend in movie theatres in the spring of 2001 and proves that Fraser is still a sizzling screen commodity.

When I spoke to him, he was dispensing that heat in the West End theatre district, where his high-voltage performance as Brick in Tennessee Williams' *Cat on a Hot Tin Roof* earned rave reviews from the British critics and had a solid six-month run, despite the post-9/11 slump that badly hurt many other shows.

With all that's going for him, I expected to find a micromanaged Hollywood star holding court in a carefully controlled environment with a phalanx of handlers and a series of pre-packaged sound bites on any topic.

Instead, I get a one-on-one encounter with a straight-shooting, well-spoken iconoclast who meets me in a postage stamp–sized café that is the favourite hangout of Jamie (*The Naked Chef*) Oliver.

"I like it here," Fraser says, grinning. "They know me, and they make great poached eggs."

While waiting for the highly praised eggs to arrive, I ask the American-born, Canadian-raised, dual citizen how he wound up on the stage in London. He thinks a second before admitting, "It was actually a decision I had made years and years before, when I lived in Europe. My dad worked for the Canadian government in the tourism office, and for a while he was stationed in Holland."

He chuckles at the memory. "I was a typical TV baby living in Ottawa and then when we moved, wow, what a wakeup call! No television in English except for two hours of the BBC at night with subtitles. Those were my formative preteen years, but I didn't spend them in front of a TV, and I didn't have a lot of friends. So I became a storyteller. And when we'd go to London to visit, we'd always see some theatre — shows like *Oliver*, *Jesus Christ Superstar*, even *The Mousetrap*. I found myself drawn to them."

Did he ever tell his parents about his dreams? "No way. I wouldn't admit it to anyone. Imagine the audacity, the largesse of making that kind of a decision."

Perhaps, but you have to wonder if they got suspicious when — after moving to just outside Seattle — young Brendan stole the show during a Grade 8 production of *H.M.S. Pinafore* by allowing his Capt. Corcoran to become hopelessly entangled in his cloak, with highly comic results.

"No," insists Fraser, "everybody thought that was just a student activity, even when I continued doing it at UCC." Upper Canada College, a Toronto private school for boys, was his home-away-from-home as a boarding student from 1982 to 1986, and he still carries strong — if somewhat conflicted — memories of those years.

"It had quite a lot to offer," he begins positively. "I enjoyed myself and I liked the whole atmosphere. If something interested you, all you had to do was show initiative, and you could pursue it."

As he thinks about the past, his face clouds a bit and he takes a sip of orange juice as he thinks. "It's a preparatory school, but for what? For life? I didn't know it at the time, but I did wind up with a taste of what the world was going to offer me when I left that sheltered environment."

He broods some more. "I don't know if it was a good thing or a bad thing to spend so much time in a society of your peers. I'm not sure if I'd send my kids to an environment like that. You see, there were two kinds of kids there — with money and without. I was one of the 'withouts.'"

"Things worked out pretty well kid to kid, but parent to parent, I think some of the financial and social differences started to show. Yeah, when it got to the grownups, it could be a bit hairy."

The eggs finally arrive, and Fraser tucks into them with gusto. (You don't keep that build on black coffee.) I ask him when he graduated from UCC. He pauses, and puts down his knife and fork.

"I didn't graduate. After Grade 12, my father changed jobs and, quite frankly, we didn't have the money to send me back."

All of a sudden he's 17 again. "They weren't very forgiving about students returning who didn't have the dough. Some of the faculty were really nice and tried to make it happen, but the people in charge just weren't going to budge."

His jaw tightens in the way it usually does before a big action scene on screen. "I still miss a sense of closure about my time there. I never got to see things through to the end with my friends and I'm just a tiny bit bitter about that."

So he went back to Seattle a year early, got into college, earned a BFA in acting, and found himself heading down to California in 1991.

"Geography is destiny, they say, and I just crashed with a friend in L.A. for a month. I didn't have any aspirations to make films. I thought that it would be great to land a job and make some money to pay off my college loans."

He certainly did. Within a year he was working steadily in TV movies and had landed his first important part as an outsider at an exclusive prep school (talk about life imitating art) in the film *School Ties.*

His loincloth-covered presence helped him steal *Encino Man* right out from under Pauly Shore and, although the next few years were to feature their share of ups and downs, he hit pay dirt in 1997.

Another semi-clad turn as the lead in *George of the Jungle* provided him with his first US$100-million-plus box office hit, and he was getting known more for his physical appeal than his acting prowess.

An embarrassed flush rises quickly to his cheeks as he recalls those days. "You know something funny? All through my teen years, nobody thought I was good-looking, *nobody*. I was the big gawky one, the geeky guy, the nerd without a girlfriend. And when all of a sudden I wound up as this pin-up boy with hundreds of women chasing after me, I wanted to say 'Where were all of you back when I needed you?'"

He certainly didn't need them after he married actress Afton Smith in 1998. A sweeter look softens his features as he talks about her. "The first time I saw her, I knew she was the one, but it took me a while to convince her. But man, it sure was worth it," he grins.

Then came *The Mummy*, *Blast from the Past* and *The Mummy Returns*, hits so big that they more than made up for the not-quite-appropriate salute to his Canadian roots in *Dudley Do-Right*, the less-than-triumphant *Bedazzled*, and the out-and-out disaster that was *Monkey Bone*.

"Hey," says Fraser, with a gleam in his eye while wiping up the egg yolk, "it isn't everyday you get to make an eighty-five million-dollar art-house film! But I'm still wondering about that naughty, lusty evil *Monkey Bone*. Oh, he was a rotten little rascal, but I sure did like him. He was a ball of contradictions."

Not unlike Fraser, who alternates his macho commercial movies with more artistic entries like *The Twilight of the Golds*, *Gods and Monsters*, and *Cat on a Hot Tin Roof*, in which he plays characters either openly homosexual or dealing with conflicted sexuality. Is he saying to the audience, "Don't typecast me"?

"No," he insists calmly. "I'm saying it to myself. I'm trying to find a way to keep it all interesting and new. To diversify my choices. As Tennessee Williams said, 'Life leaves questions unanswered.'"

He relates to the tortured character of Brick in Williams' play so deeply that I prod him to find out why.

"A good actor," he begins, "treats every part as a key that he uses to unlock something deep inside him." Then he looks right through me, "And a smart actor never talks about what that something is."

He looks down, and I suddenly glimpse the true secret of

Fraser's appeal: no matter what kind of character he plays, there's always a part of it that he keeps to himself.

His next film up is *The Quiet American*, an adaptation of the Graham Greene novel about Vietnam, in which he stars opposite Michael Caine. It was made before, in 1958, but everyone told Fraser not to see the original. "Audie Murphy played your part," says Fraser in an astonishingly good Caine imitation. "He was a very brave soldier and a very cowardly actor."

Does it take bravery to stand up to a 9-foot mummy?

"Naw," snorts Fraser, as he takes a last sip of coffee. "It's about running and gunning. Just forget the acting. As (director) Stephen Sommers used to say to me before every take: 'Don't suck, don't die, action!'"

But after the expected laugh, he shifts gears and leans forward to make a final point. "You should do everything as if it's the last time you might ever do it. Because, you know, it may be. There's just too much uncertainty out there."

I take one last look at him: on the surface is the heartthrob, underneath is the serious actor, but at bottom is the kid who never got to finish UCC.

He walks me to the door, makes sure I know how to find the way back to my hotel, and vanishes into the London midday traffic.

Fraser has left the building.

Fraser's career has slowed down a bit following our interview. *The Quiet American* wasn't released until December 2002, with Miramax feeling its subject matter was too volatile in the aftermath of 9/11.

When it did open late in 2002, Fraser received excellent reviews for his work and Michael Caine, his co-star, got an Oscar nomination as Best Actor.

Also occupying Fraser's time is the birth of his first child, Griffin Arthur, born on September 17, 2002.

Kate Winslet
Myung Jung Kim/PA Photos

KATE WINSLET

Life after the Big Boat Movie

Sometimes life flings you a bonus. I knew that Kate Winslet was one of the most accomplished and intriguing actresses of her age range, and that was reason enough to interview her.

Teenage killers, mad Elizabethan maidens, Victorian heroines — she'd played them all.

But I had no idea what I thought of her personally, and so it was a pleasant surprise, on a frosty February Monday in 2003, to be ushered in to meet someone so refreshingly brisk, honest, and unassuming.

And chatty.

As Kenneth Branagh supposedly once asked, "Dear Kate, don't you have any *unexpressed* thoughts?"

Kate Winslet rolls her own.

She sits in a Manhattan hotel suite — peachy skin, honeyed hair, beige cashmere — and effortlessly juggles a pack of cigarette papers the way an actress of an earlier generation might have handled a silver tea service.

"I've been doing this for years," she explains in her take-it-or-leave-it voice, "and yes," she adds slyly, "it's just tobacco."

Cheeky, challenging, charming,

Those are the qualities that have made the 27-year-old three-time

Oscar nominee (*Sense and Sensibility*, *Titanic*, *Iris*) one of the most intriguing women in film today.

The official topic for discussion is her role in *The Life of David Gale*, and although Winslet is passionate about her admiration for the film, she's also equally willing to discuss the failure of her marriage, her current love interest, and her feelings over the digitally enhanced photo of her that appeared on a recent British magazine cover.

"It was such a brilliantly written script that I read it in one hit and immediately knew that I had to do it."

She's referring to Charles Randolph's screenplay for *The Life of David Gale*, whose title character (Kevin Spacey) is an anti–death penalty activist about to be executed for a rape/murder that he swears he didn't commit.

In the last 72 hours of his life, he grants a newsmagazine reporter named Bitsy Bloom (played by Winslet) a series of interviews that reopen the whole issue of his guilt or innocence with shattering results.

The political side of the film has dominated much of the advance discussion and Winslet is well aware that "the danger is that people will talk up the death penalty so much it might take away from what a marvellous thriller it is."

But it's interesting that what drew her to the character was "the enormous psychological journey she goes on. I've never come across a contemporary female character who changes her emotions and feelings so totally over the course of a film."

Bitsy begins as "a cold, hard-nosed bitch, out for No. 1," in Winslet's words — or as a fellow character describes her, "Mike Wallace with PMS" — but as the film goes on, she becomes convinced of Gale's innocence and winds up risking her life in an attempt to save his.

Her favourite moment, she recalls, was the scene when Gale says to her, "You know I'm innocent," and the script has her reply, "No, I don't."

"You see," enthuses Winslet, practically bouncing up and down, "I wanted to say 'Of course you're innocent!' but I couldn't. That's what made it so wonderful. The most challenging things as an actor are when you feel one thing and another has to come out of your mouth." She suddenly smiles a bit self-consciously. "When I feel strongly about a role, I still act the way I do when I was seventeen . . . "

That's how old Winslet was when Peter Jackson (director of *The Lord of the Rings*) cast her as a psychotic teenage murderess in *Heavenly Creatures* because "her intensity made everyone else pale in comparison."

Before that, she'd been growing up in Reading, England, daughter of an acting family, with a few TV shows and commercials to her credit. But after the extraordinary response to her film debut (which included a Best Actress Award at the Toronto International Film Festival), there was no looking back.

Over the next two years, she starred in *Sense and Sensibility*, *Jude*, and as Ophelia in Kenneth Branagh's *Hamlet*.

Then came *Titanic*.

"Ah yes," she exclaims, snuffing out her ciggy. "The big boat movie. No getting around that one, is there? I'm very grateful for it, but after a huge epic like that, one did want to do something rather different."

Which is just what she did, diving into quirky entries such as *Quills*, *Holy Smoke*, and *Hideous Kinky*.

It was while working on the last film that she fell in love with the assistant director, James Threapleton, marrying him on November 22, 1998. Their daughter Mia was born on October 12, 2000.

Her third Oscar nomination for *Iris* continued her upward professional spiral and everywhere you looked, there were articles about the happy couple and their beautiful baby.

"Of course," recalls Winslet, with a hint of bitterness colouring her voice, "the British press were huge fans of mine for a long time, 'Our Kate,' and that sort of thing, and then I committed the ultimate crime. I got divorced from Mr. Normal and they all came down on me like a ton of bricks. Because, of course, they thought it had to be my fault."

She spits out the last two words and then, for the first time, there's a silence.

"People fall out of love with each other. Marriages cease to be. It happened to me and it was a horrible thing in my life. I didn't want it to happen, I didn't think it was going to happen, I tried to stop it from happening. I didn't just wake up one morning and say, 'Oh this isn't working, I think I'll take my baby and go.'

"We spent a good six months trying to make everything okay, but nobody knew anything about that, of course. And we finally got to a point where we both realized it wasn't going to work for many deeply private reasons, and so we amicably separated."

She chooses her next words carefully. "It was heartbreaking and terrible, but an absolutely mutual decision."

She looks up again and a bit of the normal Winslet fire is back in her eyes. "Then, you see, I committed the one unpardonable sin. I fell in love again, I got happier than I've ever been and the media can't forgive me for that."

The object of her affections is director Sam Mendes, the wunderkind who ran London's Donmar Warehouse to critical acclaim for a decade, dazzled Broadway by re-imagining *Cabaret*, and conquered Hollywood with *American Beauty* and *Road to Perdition*.

"I met Sam shortly after my marriage broke up and we were both very nervous of the potential relationship lying in front of us. It took me a while to say, 'Okay, maybe — just maybe — I could do this again.'"

Her voice and face grow softer as she explains, "When you have a child, you can't make those decisions easily and once you've been through a painful experience, it takes a while to get over it."

Then she closes her eyes. "But oh, the mudslinging that went on in the press! They assumed that Sam must have been the reason for the separation because all throughout my marriage I had appeared to be happy. But there's a lot that goes on behind closed doors that people never know about . . . because I never talked about it." She pauses. "And I never will."

While we're on the topic of the media, I ask about the recent British GQ cover photo that digitally altered her image to make her seem slimmer.

She begins by laughing. "I thought it was a shame, because I felt I looked quite hot that day, but I obviously wasn't hot enough for them! Did I know they were going to do it? No. Did it surprise me? Also no. Magazines do things like that all the time."

Then she gets a steely tone in her voice, "What bothered me was that most of the young women who read these magazines constantly feel that they have to lose weight and I thought 'This is crap!' These women are aspiring to look like something they think is perfect and it doesn't exist. It was created by a computer.

"I didn't like what they did because they felt they had to make me skinnier. I don't look like that and I don't *want* to look like that. End of story."

Considering her relationship with one of the finest stage directors working today, I wonder if she'll be appearing on Broadway or in the West End soon.

She gives me a coy grin. "Here's what I usually tell everyone." And then she puts on a simpering voice that is decidedly un-Winslet-like. "Oh, I'd really *love* to, but I've never quite come across quite the right role."

Then she returns to her normal throaty cadences. "But you know what the truth is? I am absolutely *terrified* by the idea of doing theatre. There is no more revealing, horrifying experience for an actor than standing on a stage and staying in that moment. The second that I'm asked at a Christmas celebration or a family party to stand up and say a speech or sing a song, I just bloody die!

That is infinitely more terrifying than doing anything on the screen. What if it goes wrong and you don't believe me? On film, you can go back and do it again. Onstage you have to get it right the first time, every time!"

I end by asking her if there's any truth to the rumours that she and Mendes will be marrying fairly soon.

"No," she insists, "we're very, very happy the way we are. But . . . " She starts another sentence and then stops herself. "Before I played a journalist, I might have told you something more and then said, 'Off the record.'"

She grins.

"But now I know that no such thing really exists."

Winslet's career continues to move in interesting directions, with films as varied as *Neverland*, where she plays opposite Johnny Depp's James Barrie, and *Eternal Sunshine of the Spotless Mind*, another Charlie Kaufman brainteaser, where she and Jim Carrey are a couple who have the memories of their past affair erased from their brains so they can start all over again.

And yes, she's still with Sam Mendes.

Antonio Banderas
Diane Bondareff

ANTONIO BANDERAS

Desperado No More

When I first heard that Antonio Banderas was going to make his Broadway debut, I knew that I had to interview him. It's not that he was necessarily one of my favourite actors, even though I had certainly enjoyed his work in films as different as *Women on the Verge of a Nervous Breakdown* and *Evita*.

What intrigued me was that I felt there was a lot more to the man than the hot Hispanic image into which the media were anxious to pigeonhole him, and I wanted to find out if my instincts were correct.

He finally agreed to meet me right after a day's rehearsal, in the shabby lounge of the building in New York's West 40s where the show was being put together in February 2003.

Banderas was talking on his cellphone to his brother Chico in Spain as he walked into the room, but he ended the call as soon as he saw me, then greeted me warmly and sat down opposite to me, knee to knee, on a bench only meant to hold one.

Sometimes you click with a person right away. This was one of those times. When his publicist came by to take him to see *Les Misérables* an hour later, we were still talking intently.

And I was right. There *was* a lot more to him.

"This is a show about sex. Please set your phone to vibrate."

That sign is taped to the door of the rehearsal hall where the

Roundabout Theatre's production of *Nine* is currently preparing for its Broadway opening. It makes sense when you consider it's a musical version of the midlife-crisis-on-film that Federico Fellini called 8 1/2.

But it makes even more sense when you think of the show's leading man, Antonio Banderas.

Ever since he swivel-hipped his way into the hearts of millions of North American women in *The Mambo Kings* (1992), Banderas has represented a steamy Latin sensuality that he exploited in films like *Desperado, Interview with the Vampire*, and *The Mask of Zorro*, but which he now views as more of a curse than a blessing.

"Come on, look at me," he demands, sitting nearer than the most extreme close-up and pushing his face next to mine. "I'm getting older and I don't care. I believe that wrinkles are the medals life has given me."

Dressed in casual rehearsal gear, his hair matted with the sweat of a full day of singing and dancing, the 42-year-old Banderas still radiates energy as he hastens to close the topic of his physical appeal.

"You can fill your life with many things more interesting than sex. Sex is only a problem if you don't have it . . . like money. I think many people are worried about my sex life because they don't have one of their own."

The laugh that follows is so full of boyish exuberance that it instantly becomes apparent why Banderas is perfectly cast as *Nine*'s leading character, Guido Contini, the egocentric director whose "body's clearing forty, while my mind is nearing ten."

"Oh yes," he sighs, "I know what Guido is like. Every day you have to take on different roles — in front of your boss, in front of your wife, in front of your kids. You have to play the tough guy, you have to play the man, you have to play the father. It's hard to handle all those contradictions at once. I think many men can relate to that."

Most of them, however, don't seek the same escape Guido does, juggling a wife and two mistresses simultaneously. And Banderas? He throws up his hands as if to say "Guilty as charged" and admits "there was a time in my life when I was pretty messy in my relationships with women, but not anymore. I've changed since I met Melanie."

It goes without saying he's talking about Melanie Griffith, the tempestuous actress he's been married to since 1996. The ups and downs of their relationship have been tabloid fodder ever since, but Banderas has grown philosophical about it.

"It used to make me angry, but now it causes more indifference than anything else. Sometimes you get upset because of how it can hurt your kids, but time will put everything in its place."

Nine, the vehicle Banderas has chosen to make his English-language stage debut, was first produced on Broadway in 1982; Maury Yeston wrote the score and Arthur Kopit adapted the book from Fellini's 8 1/2.

With Raul Julia in the lead, it ran for 729 performances and won five Tony Awards, including Best Musical. A New York revival has been in the works for a long time and Banderas was first asked to play the part four years ago, when he turned it down.

"But now," he says, "the time is right for me to take on this role, because I'm ready to think about my whole life."

He was born in Málaga, Spain, on August 10, 1960. Young Antonio, like young Guido, knew what it was like to spend his formative years in a strict Catholic environment.

"I was studying in a seminary, even though I had no intention of becoming a priest. My parents thought I would get a better education that way, but all I saw was how repressive the Church could be, how manipulative. I saw young men who were torn apart because they were studying to be priests and yet they were in love with women."

"You see," he says with a conspiratorial grin, "I was taught that there were two kinds of girls: very good and very bad. On one side, you looked for someone to protect you, take care of you, almost replace your mother — that was the wife. But on the other side was the kind of girl that my father would look at and say, 'Go on, enjoy her. You will never regret it. But don't get too close to her, because this is not a woman you would marry.'"

The same duality exists for Guido in *Nine* and so he loses his virginity to Saraghina, a cheerful prostitute. Things were somewhat different for Banderas.

"There were a lot of female tourists in Spain back then," he begins tentatively, eyes lowered, "American, British, one from Sweden." His glance brightens with remembered youthful pleasures. "That was my first encounter with women who didn't have any attachments, didn't have anything to hide, because they were there for a week and then they went home."

He weighs the memory and offers his conclusion. "I think we both used each other." A distant smile crosses his face. "There are two I remember in particular. . . . They were way older than me. I don't know if that is when it all began, but I always liked women who were older than me." Griffith, by the way, is three years older than Banderas.

But before leaving the impression that his adolescence was a non-stop round of sexual games, Banderas is quick to shift to historical perspective.

"These were the final years of Franco's reign and everything was forbidden — listening to the Rolling Stones, kissing a girl in the street — everything."

"One day, near the end, when he was very sick, Franco came to our town and the square was filled with people calling out his name. I stood there and cried. Why? I didn't feel anything toward this man, but I could sense we were closing a chapter in my country that had taken forty years."

His face is filled with a political passion that he admits he hasn't allowed to surface in recent years. "We took the oppression for granted — visas, arrests, interrogations — they were all part of our everyday life."

340

"I was involved with a left-wing political theatre even though I was very young. I remember playing in Málaga and looking in the wings and seeing the shine on the helmets of the cops waiting for us."

Fear and hate mingle in his memory. "We took our bow and then they put us in handcuffs, brought us down to the police station and had us fingerprinted . . . for doing a play by Brecht."

He's quiet for a moment and then he points down to his left foot.

"I used to play soccer, but one day I hit the ground and broke that foot in three places. I had to remain still, wearing a cast. That's when Franco died and I just lay there watching it all on our little black-and-white TV." It was 1975.

When he looks up he seems to be realizing something for the first time. "I was fifteen then, and over the next five years, we went from a dictatorship to a democracy as I turned into a man. My country was growing up the same time I was."

Banderas quickly became a member of Spain's National Theatre, but by the time he was 22, his work had caught the eye of a young film director named Pedro Almodóvar. He offered the novice actor a part as a gay Islamic terrorist in his controversial film *Labyrinth of Passion*, but it wasn't an easy decision.

"Pedro was wild and daring. He was breaking rules and I wanted to break them with him," remembers Banderas, "but I pulled back and thought of my relationship with my family, the good Catholic boy I was raised to be."

Finally, his sense of adventure won out and he chose to make the movie, but "my mother never went to see it. Never. Not to this day."

Banderas went on to complete four more films with Almodóvar and he admires him, along with a canny appreciation of his strengths and weaknesses.

"He knows everything he wants to do. He is such a secure director that he takes possession of the whole project. He does costumes, picks the colour of the walls — everything. He even goes in front of the camera and shows you how to play your part. He is very, very clever. The only problem is that, as an actor, you feel like a pen in his hand that he's using to write a novel."

"I would go to Pedro and say 'I have an idea,' and he would say 'No, I'm the one who has ideas.'"

Their 1988 film together, *Women on the Verge of a Nervous Breakdown*, introduced Banderas to the North American public and to his first wife, Ana Leza — two events that would finally cancel each other out.

Banderas normally doesn't discuss his early marriage, but the relationship of Guido and his spouse Luisa in *Nine* makes him recall the past with fragility.

"What does she sing about him? 'My husband, he goes a little crazy.' Maybe that was me when I started to make it big in Hollywood." He stares off into the past, remembering.

There are two other women in Guido's life — the sensuous Carla ("Who's not wearing any clothes? I'm not") and the ethereal Claudia ("In a very unusual way, you've made me whole") — but Banderas thinks he has found both of them in Griffith.

"She is very sexy, but at the same time she is a great wife and mother. And she definitely is my muse, my inspiration."

Supposedly Banderas had recently forbidden Griffith to undergo any further plastic surgery, but he wants to set the record straight.

"Look, in a cruel world like Hollywood, once you cross the age of forty and you are a woman, you are in trouble. They are obsessed with fresh flesh and so an actress has to fight age every way she can."

"I would never forbid my wife to do anything. What I would do is say, 'Melanie, I love you the way you are. I don't care if you get old.'"

Age is not slowing down Banderas in the least, as he shakes off the fatigue of the day and seems ready to begin again.

"You know why I wanted to do this show? Because of Guido.

I love this character. He says, 'I want to be Christ, Mohammed, Buddha, but not have to believe in God,' and that's how I feel. I want to be everything, but I've come to realize that I can't. It's the time in my life to make choices. Break the ties with the past and make the journey into maturity."

Then, as if on cue, his cellphone goes off.

And yes, it vibrates.

The performance Banderas delivered in *Nine* earned him unanimous raves from the New York critics when it opened in April 2003.

I wasn't surprised at the natural way he took to the stage after our conversation about his past, but I was thrilled to see how effective he was. Where did Guido Contini end and Antonio Banderas begin? It was hard to tell.

Julie Andrews
AP/World Wide Photos

JULIE ANDREWS

In the Bleak Midwinter

As someone who grew up on *My Fair Lady*, *Camelot*, *Mary Poppins*, and *The Sound of Music*, Julie Andrews wasn't a performer to me — she was an icon.

By the time I started doing these interviews, it looked as though her career would never include live performances again, thanks to her well-publicized vocal troubles.

But something called *A Royal Christmas* was announced for the Holiday season, and I was informed that Dame Julie would be available for selected phone interviews. Although I wanted to meet her in person, I settled for an hour on the phone with her in late November 2002.

And considering some of the turns our conversation took, I'm glad in retrospect that I couldn't see her face.

When Julie Andrews steps on to the stage next week to perform *A Royal Christmas*, her heart will be filled, by her own admission, "with great joy and just a bit of sadness."

The great joy is due to the fact that she will be appearing once again (for only the third time in her entire career) with her legendary co-star from *The Sound of Music*, Christopher Plummer.

The sadness is due to a fact that plain-talking Dame Julie, last of the straight shooters, lays it on the table at the very start of our phone conversation.

"Please let everyone know that I won't be singing."

A botched 1997 operation to remove polyps on her vocal cords resulted in the loss of her ability to sing. There was a subsequent lawsuit against New York's Mt. Sinai Hospital and the two surgeons who performed the operation.

An out-of-court settlement was finally reached, and Andrews won't discuss that part of the proceedings, but the fact that one of the 20th century's most beloved vocal instruments has been silenced runs underneath our conversation like a melancholy cello line in an otherwise upbeat orchestration.

"I can't help it," she admits, "but when I think of Christmas, I think of the music of Christmas, those glorious songs that bring a family together."

The Andrews speaking voice remains a wonderful instrument — slightly husky, almost tangibly warm — the aural equivalent of dappled sunlight on an English country meadow.

The 67-year-old star is now officially "Dame Julie" after being honoured by the Queen last year, but she radiates such an approachable air that I have no trouble confessing that I still possess the autograph she gave me more than 40 years ago when she was playing Guinevere in the original production of *Camelot*.

She suddenly sounds concerned. "You're speaking to me from Toronto, but I hope you didn't see it there." I assure her it was later in the Broadway run. "Oh, thank God . . . then you got to see it after we had time to fix it."

The memories of 40 years whistle through her mind as she sighs. "Oh *Camleot*, poor, poor *Camelot*! We were four hours long when we opened in Toronto, and then Moss (Hart, the director) and Alan (Jay Lerner, the author) got sick and couldn't fix anything. We tried to cut it, but it was a fearsome task."

"Alan recovered just before New York, and started putting in changes, but we just ran out of time."

I ask her if she really did receive the words and music to "Before I Gaze at You Again" the night before the opening.

"Not really," she demurs, and then comes back with perfect timing. "It was the afternoon before the opening. I had to have a few hours to rehearse it before I did it at the final preview."

"Was I scared? Honestly, no. That's how I had been working all of my life."

She was born Julia Elizabeth Wells on October 1, 1935, in Walton-on-Thames, England. Her parents, Barbara and Ted, divorced when she was five, and Barbara married Ted Andrews. They sang in variety shows, and sometimes Julie would join them.

It soon became obvious that young Julie had an extraordinary voice, and by the time she was 13, she sang before King George VI at a Royal Command Performance.

"I wish I could remember more about those times," she admits, "but when they happened I was so young that I never realized how important they were, and so they never made the impression they ought to."

The rest of those youthful years are all part of a blur now to Andrews. At 19, she starred in *The Boyfriend* in the West End, and then travelled with it to Broadway. The great success of *My Fair Lady* followed, and then *Camelot*.

"Often I think I love *Camelot* best because it was the second child, the one that gets overlooked. Not the glorious triumph of *My Fair Lady*, but oh, it had heart and beauty!"

The years melt away as she confesses that "sometimes I would just stand on that stage and look at my two beautiful co-stars, Richard (Burton) and Robert (Goulet), and it would simply take my breath away."

"But then," as Andrews concedes, "I've always been lucky with my leading men."

At first you think she's being typically generous, but then the cast of characters unfolds in your mind: Rex Harrison in *My Fair Lady*, Dick Van Dyke in *Mary Poppins*, and, of course, Christopher Plummer in *The Sound of Music*.

Even upbeat Andrews is surprised at the continuing and

overwhelming success of the 1965 story of the Von Trapp Family Singers.

"We all knew that it had beautiful scenery, great kids, and that wonderful music. But none of us ever thought it would be such a big hit."

Andrews has her own theory why the film proved — and continues to prove — so popular. "It spoke to so many things we needed to have at that time, things we still need to have now — decency and beauty and generosity. But it did it all in such an entertaining way."

As for the recent *Sing-A-Long Sound of Music* phenomenon, Andrews would like to be "a fly on the wall one evening, just to see how it works, but I wouldn't want anyone to know I was there. I feel that might take the fun out of it all, somehow" (see p. 352).

Her co-star Plummer hasn't always shared Andrews' warm feelings about the movie, and for many years, in interviews, he would either refer to it as *The Sound of Mucous*, or refuse to discuss it at all. But, despite their difference in opinion about the film, Plummer and Andrews remained close.

She came to Stratford in the summer of 2002 to see his *King Lear*, which she pronounced "brilliant." But although they occasionally partnered at fundraising galas, they never actually performed together again until 2001, when they appeared in a live television version of *On Golden Pond*.

"When we did that," recalls Andrews, "we realized how much we enjoyed working with each other and when this project came up, I was delighted to get a chance to be with Christopher again."

A Royal Christmas tours 15 cities in 19 days, and it comes in the middle of Andrews' filming a made-for-TV movie, *Eloise at the Plaza*, based on Kay Thomson's famous children's books. "Some things never change," observes Andrews. "I'm playing a nanny again after all these years."

The recent seasons have demonstrated that Andrews still possesses box office magic, with 2001's *The Princess Diaries* grossing more than US$100 million, and her 2000 project *One Special Night* proving the highest-rated TV movie of that year.

Yes, Julie Andrews' life following the loss of her singing voice has been successful, but it hasn't been easy, and the memory of past glories makes it harder.

"All I can ever say," she begins tentatively, "is how blessed can anyone be? I look back at that period in my life when I had the chance of playing all those great roles and I think of it as a great golden decade. I was lucky enough to happen to be in the right place at the right time."

Her voice begins to throb with intensity.

"I would never knock those projects in a million years. They were so beautiful and so important and they gave so many people so much pleasure.

"And I don't regret coming back to Broadway in *Victor/Victoria*," she insists, even though it was during the 1995–96 run of the show that her vocal troubles began to appear. "I've always had an affinity for the Broadway musical, and I'm so glad I took the chance to appear in just one more."

You can hear her passion building, as the archetypal Andrews reserve finally crumbles, "Yes it was daunting, but I had such a ball doing it, heading that great company. Oh it was a joy, and then . . . "

Her voice breaks and she stops herself. "I'm sorry," she apologizes, "I didn't want to look back that way."

We return to *A Royal Christmas*, and she stresses what a wonderful event she hopes it will be, because "after all, Christmas is the one time of the year when all families try to get together. And it always reminds me in a sentimental way of my father, who loved those carols so much."

I share with her the fact that my favourite of all the Christmas songs she ever recorded was "In the Bleak Midwinter," and I hear a catch in her voice.

"I loved that one, too. So beautiful, but so sad."

I'm about to say goodbye, when she adds one final, wistful memory.

"You know, when I used to put an album together, I always chose the lyrics first."

I was fortunately out of town on assignment when *A Royal Christmas* played Toronto, but my colleagues assaulted it as an overstuffed exercise in rank commercialism, only redeemed by the elegant presence of Dame Julie. It was, however, a huge success at the box office — testimony to the ongoing power of the Andrews name.

She also made her directorial debut in the summer of 2003 with the revival of her first stage hit, *The Boy Friend*.

Sing-A-Long Sound of Music
Rene Johnston/Toronto Star

SING-A-LONG SOUND
OF MUSIC

The Thrills Are Alive

O n a frosty February evening in 2001, I found myself outside
an aging Toronto movie palace, surrounded by enough
overdressed Bavarian stereotypes to make me think I had stumbled
into the casting call for *Springtime for Hitler*.

That wasn't far from the truth.

It starts softly, like the cooing of a million microscopic pigeons, as
the camera swoops over the Salzburg countryside.

"juliejuliejuliejuliejulie . . . "

Now it grows in force, as we scan the horizon, looking for the
diminutive dot that will turn into our heroine.

"JulieJulieJulieJulieJulie!"

Finally a full-throated roar — not unlike being underneath a
747 at takeoff — as she finally comes into focus.

"JULIEJULIEJULIEJULIEJULIE!!!!!"

Julie Andrews throws out her arms in a gesture that embraces
the Alps and us at the same time as she sings:

"The hills are alive with the sound of music . . . "

Only she's not alone. . . . We're all singing with her.

Welcome to *Sing-A-Long Sound of Music*.

It's a cold winter night, but the street is buzzing. All the
Rodgers and Hammerstein-istas have answered the siren call of

their favourite musical and are flocking like postulant pilgrims toward an interactive shrine.

They're young and old, gay and straight, with all the permutations and combinations thereof. Watch them as they perform for the TV cameras and pose patiently for the still photographers. Is it their 15 minutes yet?

Here's the young married couple who've duplicated Maria and the Captain's wedding outfits to perfection. They spring into the aisles of the theatre to waltz at the slightest three-quarter provocation.

Then there are the more mature ladies who have gussied themselves up as the female Von Trapp children, led by a Liesl whose theme song might well be "I Am 60, Going On 70."

Don't forget the 40-ish divorcee who rips off her parka to reveal a makeshift pinafore, her son's striped hockey socks and two tortured pigtails. "What the hell," she says, hoisting a beer, "I'm here to have a blast." So are we all, and that's why we're singing along with Julie.

Not the preternaturally cool, half-to-yourself murmur you summon up to accompany Paul Simon when he breaks into your favourite tune in concert.

Not the what-the-hell, no-one-can-hear-me burble you churn out behind closed windows in your car as the morning drive show pumps forth the latest pop fave.

And not the get-off-my-case, the-girl-can't-help-it spontaneity that show queens flaunt at touring musicals, much to the chagrin of ushers and audiences alike.

No. This, my friends, is the real thing. Fully voiced, fully sanctioned, "Sing Out, Louise" belting, along with close to a thousand choristers united in glorious (depending on whom you're next to) harmony.

The hills (and the aisles) were alive Wednesday night for a special gala media opening of the phenomenon, which has made "raindrops on roses" and "whiskers on kittens" the pop Popsicle du jour.

It's *Survivor* for Show-Tune Queens, *Millionaire* for Middle-Aged Mommies, prominently profiled everywhere from the *New York Times* to *Entertainment Weekly*.

Cuddly and camp at the same time, it appeals to boomers as well as busters. With the possible exception of *The Wizard of Oz*, what other film can ring the bell with gays as well as grannies? (If you're a gay granny, you probably dig it twice as much.)

Where else can you costume yourself as a nun, a snowflake, or a "brown-paper package tied up with string" and not worry about whether you're going to end the evening lip-synching to "YMCA"?

It makes you wonder what kind of wild and crazy guy could have thought this whole thing up.

That's why it's a bit of a shock to meet the show's producer, Ben Freedman. He's a very pleasant, quiet-voiced, neat and trim family man. Although born in England, his Toronto connection comes from his parents: showbiz entrepreneur Bill Freedman and actress Toby Robins.

Ben runs the Prince Charles Cinema in the West End of London. He smiles a bit archly as he describes it: "We're an . . . um . . . unusual repertory theatre. We specialize in slightly subversive film experiences." Like what?

"Well, when we showed *From Russia with Love*, we had Cossack dancers and served vodka." Oh. What else? "We've had *The Rocky Horror Picture Show* on Friday nights for more than ten years, and when we revived (*The Adventures of*) *Priscilla: Queen of the Desert*, we brought in a complete drag show."

Freedman explains *Sing-A-Long*'s nativity: "It began at the Gay and Lesbian Film Festival in London, and initially we agreed to co-produce it for eight shows. We thought it might be fun, maybe we could get a few weeks out of it, but it became obvious very quickly that this was not some niche novelty but a mainstream entertainment.

"The average audience for this movie isn't gay, but it is overwhelmingly female. Roughly 70 to 80 per cent of our audience is made up of women. Once you talk to them, you discover that this is a completely seminal experience for them."

It's strange, but there's no trace of irony in the way he uses such words to describe the most totally sexless movie musical ever made.

In point of fact, Freedman is drifting into Mariaspeak, a clinical disorder that afflicts fans as they try to justify their profound adult attachment to a piece of fundamentally adolescent kitsch.

"It's a new version of the classic fairy-tale scenario, only this time around, the princess saves the prince. That's why little girls love it."

All this is part of the radical revisionist approach that seems to have taken over the project since it started becoming a viable commercial entity.

Initially *Sing-A-Long* was a lark (no, not the kind who is learning to pray), and as Freedman indicated, was meant to be a novelty of a few weeks' duration. Consequently, no official sanction was sought from the notoriously tough-minded Rodgers and Hammerstein Organization, which acts as guardian of the flame for all R&H works.

But with *The Sound of Music* turning into *The Sound of Money*, it was necessary to get them on side, and so Freedman and company invited them to see it in London.

"We all thought, what is this, *The Rocky Horror Picture Show?*" That was the initial reaction of Theodore S. Chapin, the organization's president. "But by intermission, I was screaming along with everybody else at the top of my lungs."

Not to take away from Mr. Chapin's joy, but it's likely that he was also screaming with delight at the thought of the additional dollars this riff on an old favourite could pour into the corporate coffers.

The film's initial gross of US$163 million was record-breaking at the time of its release in 1965 but has been surpassed many times over. But an easily portable version of this beloved property that can bring in big bucks (tickets are $25.50 a pop in Toronto) is always one of a producer's favourite things!

So the Rodgers and Hammerstein's gatekeepers said "yes" to the *Sing-A-Long* concept, and the show continued its run in London. It's still touring England and Ireland, playing in New York, and about to open in San Francisco at the Castro Theatre. (Picture the audience there!)

Let the spin-doctoring begin.

"Every time I see it," enthuses Freedman with the fervour of a born-again Von Trapp, "I keep telling myself how good the performances are, how well-written the script is, how beautifully it's shot, how carefully it's put together."

Let's pause a minute. Yes, *The Sound of Music* has always been very popular, but has anyone ever really thought it was any good?

When the stage version opened on Broadway in 1959, critic Walter Kerr led many of his colleagues in commenting that "it will be most admired by the people who have found Sir James Barrie pretty strong stuff. . . . The taste of vanilla overwhelms the solid chocolate. The people on stage have melted long before our hearts have."

And the film version may have earned five Oscars, but Judith Crist called it "icky-sticky," and Pauline Kael contented herself with "self-indulgent and cheap."

But the people who flock to *Sing-A-Long Sound of Music* are not devotees of Kerr or Crist or Kael. They've come for the songs, the scenery, the children, and their beloved Julie Andrews.

Oh, and don't forget the nuns. Nuns on one side, Nazis on the other. That's the ying and yang of this sentimental saga. And since it would be in decidedly poor taste to have a Nazi as a spokesperson, management has created a faux nun named Sister Beatrice to act as the evening's compère.

"God loves all of you, children," Sister Beatrice chirps from the stage, "no matter what you're wearing, He loves you!"

Indeed, the Almighty had many different varieties of His

creatures to love that night. Apart from the nattering novices, lederhosened lads, and dirndled damsels, there were several unique costumes.

One imaginative chap wore a price tag marked $150, which was slashed down to $125. "That's easy," he explained, "I'm a good buy." (As in: "So long, farewell, auf Wiedersehen, goodbye.")

A bright sextet of young guys and dolls garbed in bright red collars made a standout impression as "raindrops on roses," and another enterprising fellow came attired as the Lonely Goatherd with a basket that held everything from a "crisp apple strudel" to "schnitzel with noodles."

The same lad scored major points by bringing a bell, which he rang with perfect timing on every occasion a doorbell, church bell, or any other kind of tintinnabulating device was featured in the film.

Sister Beatrice carefully explained the tropes of audience participation to us. Some were obvious ("Hiss the Baroness, and bark every time you see Rolf because he's a dirty dog"), while others were more inventive and amusing ("Every time dear Julie has to think she puts her hand on her head. Well, you do the same thing, darlings"). It's amazing how many times Ms. Andrews indulges in that gesture once you're looking for it.

But after the film gets rolling, the major joy is not in the preplanned fun (you get a "party pak" with edelweiss, curtain swatches, etc.) or even in the singing along (most people drop out of the lesser-known numbers), but in the unscripted ad libs.

As Julie picked up her guitar for the first time, one demented fan yelled out "Play 'Stairway to Heaven.'"

When asked what was the important lesson she had learned in the convent, someone pre-empted Julie by screeching, "black is slimming."

And let's not forget the moment when Ms. Andrews emerges from a dunking in the lake looking like the winner of a wet T-shirt contest. That evoked the comment: "Her hills are alive!"

At such moments, *Sing-A-Long Sound of Music* is the kind of happy, joyous, undemanding fun that it intends to be. Don't make it any more than that. Just tie up your brown-paper packages with string, check your inhibitions at the door, and hope for some magic moments . . . like the one last Wednesday when many in the audience followed the lead of one brave soul and began waving a sea of Bic lighters during "Climb Ev'ry Mountain."

> *"Climb ev'ry mountain,*
> *Ford every stream.*
> *Follow ev'ry rainbow,*
> *Till you find your dream."*

At that point, the gap between Summer Stock and Woodstock was well and truly bridged.

This was just the beginning. In rapid succession we had *Sing-A-Long* versions of *Evita*, *Fiddler On the Roof*, and *West Side Story*, but none captured the — er — magic, of the original.

Sing-A-Long-Carrie? I'm still waiting.

Julianne Moore
AP/World Wide Photos

JULIANNE MOORE

Better Naked Than Dead

She's one of those actresses who sneak up on you. I can't recall the first time I saw Julianne Moore act (although it was probably in *The Hand That Rocks the Cradle*), but by *The Fugitive* I started definitely noticing this unique talent.

After *Boogie Nights*, *The End of the Affair*, *Magnolia*, and *Hannibal*, I was truly hooked.

During the 2002 Toronto International Film Festival, everyone wanted to talk to Moore about *Far From Heaven*, but she had very little free time. I lobbied shamelessly for one of the available slots, and I'm very glad that I did.

Julianne Moore loves to make men cry.

When I told her that one of her scenes in *Far From Heaven* had brought me to tears, she clapped her hands in glee and said, "Good! I'm glad to hear that."

Don't get me wrong. It's not that Moore has a penchant for sadism. It's just that she feels so strongly about writer-director Todd Haynes' movie that she lights up like a Roman candle whenever someone shares her enthusiasm.

Moore is a bit of a Roman candle herself, an elegant five-foot-five creature with shining auburn hair and sparkling green eyes that grab you instantly.

I'm supposed to be asking the questions, but Moore flips the roles around.

"Tell me about the movie. What part made you cry? I really want to know."

I described the scene to her.

In the movie, Moore plays Cathy Whittaker, an ever-optimistic beaming blonde in suburban Connecticut during the 1950s. She manages to ignore the fact that her spouse is drinking heavily to cover up the guilt of his latent homosexuality.

He finally crosses the line from latent to blatant and Cathy walks in on him in his office late one night. She drives into town to bring him dinner and finds him kissing another man. She runs for the elevator to flee, and once inside, the emotions playing across her face are so complex and deeply felt that I found my eyes welling up. That's what I tell Moore.

"Good!" she says, "that's one of the moments I'm proudest of. You know what it's like, there are some scenes in a movie when the camera or the music can do all the work for you, but that wasn't one of them. I was acting my socks off in that one, believe me."

Moore always acts her socks off, and often the rest of the wardrobe vanishes along with them. For an A-List star, she's certainly exposed a lot of her body on film in a series of highly graphic nude scenes, but to her, it's all part of acting.

"Look, sometimes the movies are crap, and then the nude scenes are crap as well. I made some movies early on in my career that I'm not proud of. I can say that now." (The film she trashes most often in interviews is that exercise in SM excess she did with Madonna called Body of Evidence.) But if you're dealing with people like Neil Jordan (The End of the Affair) or Robert Altman (Short Cuts), you know you're in good hands."

Once again, she shifts the roles around and becomes the interviewer. "You know, it's usually you male reporters that ask me about nude scenes. Any idea why?" As I fumble for an answer, she roars with laughter at my discomfort.

"Don't worry, I know what it is. You've seen all of me buck naked on a giant movie screen and now we're sitting two feet apart. That can be just a bit awkward. Look, if the positions were reversed, I'd be the one blushing, not you."

"Robert Altman asked me to appear naked from the waist down for him and I thought I'd better warn my mother. You know what she said? 'Dear, after some of those terrible thrillers you've been in, that will be a relief. It's better to see you naked than dead.'"

"Better naked than dead," she intones with mock solemnity. "You think that should be my motto?"

It's becoming obvious that this is not an ordinary interview, but then Moore is not your ordinary actress.

She was born Julie Anne Smith on December 30, 1960, at the Fort Bragg army base in Fayetteville, N.C., the daughter of a military judge and a Scottish social worker. ("That's the perfect right brain/left brain mixture for an actress, don't you think?")

She lived in more than two-dozen cities during the first 20 years of her life, but "please don't ask me to name them. Some of them I've forgotten, and I'm sure some of them have forgotten me."

She finally wound up at Boston University, where she earned a BFA in acting in 1983. After graduation she headed for New York, determined to start a career in the theatre, but despite some high-profile off-Broadway shows like Caryl Churchill's *Serious Money*, she soon succumbed to the siren call of daytime soaps.

She began on *The Edge of Night* and then landed on *As the World Turns*, where her inventive turn as half-sisters Franny and Sabrina earned her a Daytime Emmy Award.

"Every now and then," she admits, "someone comes up to me and tells me they've loved my work for a long time. I'd like to think they saw me play Ophelia at the Guthrie Theatre, but it usually meant they watched me on the soaps."

She was also married to actor John Gould Rubin in 1986, and they divorced in 1995, during the period when she had decided to shift her base of operations to the West Coast.

Gruesome screen entries like *Tales from the Darkside* and *The Hand That Rocks the Cradle* led to a small but memorable performance in 1993's *The Fugitive*, which caused Steven Spielberg to cast her in *Jurassic Park* without an audition.

Since then, she's been in nearly three-dozen movies, alternating commercial projects such as *The Lost World* and *Hannibal* with more avant-garde work for directors such as Robert Altman and Paul Thomas Anderson.

(When asked why so many A-List directors want to work with her, Moore blushes and says self-deprecatingly, "I don't know, maybe they like the way I cry.")

She's been nominated for two Oscars (*Boogie Nights* and *The End of the Affair*) and her salary for big-budget films runs well into seven figures.

When confronted with the full extent of her good fortune, she sheds about 35 years and seems to have sprouted pigtails.

"Wow!" she exclaims, "what dumb luck was that? I really feel incredibly fortunate. When I started out in this business, I was incredibly naïve. I never thought I'd get to be this successful. My idea of heaven was getting to work steadily. Period. I didn't think it would be like this.

"I know I've been lucky, but I've also been pretty determined. This is a tough racket, and you have to work hard and be hard to keep on top." Her eyes soften as she goes back in time. "When I was growing up as an army brat, I always used to worry if people liked me. Because we moved around so much, I was always searching for approval. Now I know that — first of all — I have to like me, and then the rest all falls into place. I'm pretty happy now."

A bonus is the bliss of her personal life. In 1997, while working on a film called *The Myth of Fingerprints*, she met and fell in love with the director Bart Freundlich. Their second child, daughter Liv, was born this year on April 11. (Their son, Cal, was born in 1997.)

A quick look at the math reveals that Moore was pregnant during the entire shoot of *Far From Heaven*. "It didn't cause any problems at all. Todd was great about it, though, and we just kept working.

They shot the bathing suit scenes first, and the ones where I could wear bulky winter coats later, but that was all part of the challenge."

While Moore doesn't think being pregnant changed her characterization, "the hormones and emotions that were whirling around sure made it easy to plug into the weepier scenes, and working on the movie helped the pregnancy pass quickly. It was also a great gift to be able to offer my daughter, that she was around all the time I was working on this wonderful film."

She pauses for a second, and then bursts into laughter. "I was carrying my son Cal during *The Big Lebowski* and that was a totally different kind of a gift," she says about the surreal Coen Bros. comedy.

But then, Moore's career has been a total study in contrasts, playing everything from 1970s porn queens to 1940s British adulteresses to her current 1950s housewife, but she claims it hasn't been a conscious choice. "I just read the scripts they send me, and pick the ones I want to do."

And the best part of acting?

"It's when the whole thing surprises you, the way life surprises you. When you just let the script happen to you, and something wonderful is created on that day, something that makes you laugh, or think . . . "

But she'll be happiest if it makes you cry.

In addition to the well-reviewed but commercially unsuccessful *Far From Heaven*, Moore made another vivid impression with her work in *The Hours*, holding down the screen against stiff competition from the likes of Meryl Streep and Nicole Kidman.

Oscar time loomed into view and Moore snagged two nominations: Best Actress for *Far From Heaven* and Best Supporting Actress for *The Hours*, but when the big night finally came, she walked away empty-handed.

Not to worry. She'll be around for a long time.

Drew Barrymore
AP/World Wide Photos

DREW BARRYMORE

Getting Zen with the Fish-Wrap

I went into this interview with decidedly mixed feelings. Although I had appreciated a lot of Drew Barrymore's work on screen, the image she seemed to project in most of her interviews was that of a Space Cadet Without Portfolio, saying and doing wacky things for the sake of headlines.

Maybe the press had been getting her all wrong, or maybe I caught her on a special day, but the woman I talked to in December 2002, was quiet, reflective, and amazingly self-aware, with just enough humour to keep things interesting.

So much for preconceptions.

"Love doesn't necessarily come in the package that you were hoping for," says Drew Barrymore, "it just shows up — like something from FedEx — and all you have to do is decide if you're going to sign for it."

A little over a year ago, she was in Montreal filming a wedding scene for George Clooney's *Confessions of a Dangerous Mind* while her marriage to gonzo comedian Tom Green crashed and burned. True, it had only lasted six months, but they'd been through a lot together, including Green's bout with testicular cancer and a fire that destroyed their US$3-million Los Angeles home.

After they separated, Barrymore submerged herself in work, completing three films, and this promotional trip for *Confessions* has been her first full-scale public appearance since then.

As we sit down together in her Manhattan hotel suite, I vow to myself that I'm not going to ask her about Green. Earlier in the day, I'd seen a pack of journalistic hyenas descend on her in a feeding frenzy at a roundtable interview, searching for choice pieces of flesh.

How did she feel about the divorce? Was she dating? When would she have a lasting relationship? Didn't she ever feel lonely? What did she eat for dinner last night? And — most importantly — what was the coolest outfit she gets to wear in *Charlie's Angels 2*?

Barrymore glided through the minefield, seeming to reply to every question, but actually giving them very little that they could use. "You were there this morning," she remembers, "but you didn't ask me anything." A chuckle. "I suppose I should thank you."

I compliment her on her technique with the media, but she shrugs it off.

"I learned years ago that if you don't give them an answer, they'll just make one up, so you better play along. If you want to be a celebrity, this is the polarity that comes with it.

"You've gotta get Zen with that shit. Sure, you can cry about it to a friend, but then you have to go live your life, because — no offence — it really is fish-wrap the next day."

If anyone would know about these things, it would be Barrymore, whose entire life has been lived in the public eye.

Born in Los Angeles in 1975, her grandfather was the legendary "great profile," John Barrymore, her grandmother was silent-screen seductress Dolores Costello and both her parents were actors as well.

She made her first professional appearance at 11 months in a TV commercial for Puppy Choice and had her film debut at 4 as William Hurt's daughter in *Altered States*.

But it was as the wide-eyed Gertie in *E.T.*, shot by her godfather Steven Spielberg when she was only 7, that Barrymore became a star. A solid dramatic turn two years later in *Irreconcilable*

Differences seemed to solidify that reputation, but then it all started to go wrong.

She got drunk for the first time at the age of 9 ("at Rob Lowe's birthday party, if you can believe it!"), began smoking pot at 10 ("because it helped me sleep at night after I was strung out from filming"), and was snorting cocaine by her 12th birthday ("It didn't make me look as bloated as the booze did").

A three-year roller-coaster ride in and out of rehab culminated in a suicide attempt when she was 15, but she pulled through and lived to write about it in her autobiography, *Little Girl Lost*.

But when she talks about those "bad old days" now, it's with the wit and wisdom of time. "Look, most teenagers go through an awkward phase," she jokes, "mine just lasted five years."

She raises her hand to stop my laughter, because she doesn't want to give the impression that she takes what happened to her lightly, so she continues in a different tone. "When you have things — a job, stability, friends — and they're taken away, it makes you appreciate them. So much of life can be humbling, but it only seems to benefit you in the long run."

The clean and sober Barrymore, however, still turned out to be one hell of a sex kitten: posing nude for *Playboy*, burning up the screen in films like *Poison Ivy*, and flashing her breasts to David Letterman on-air to wish him a happy birthday.

"I'm glad everything happened the way it did," is her straightforward comment about that period, "it was all part of me. But I'm happy I got to make the transition."

Barrymore still bears some traces of a beguiling youthfulness (she chews on strands of her hair non-stop throughout the interview), but her green eyes are serene.

The next phase of her career saw her reclaiming star status with a series of popular romantic comedies like *The Wedding Singer*, before she finally made the leap into independent production.

"That's the crazy thing about this business," muses Barrymore, "you can't do anything alone, but you still have to go out there and get things started for yourself."

So, along with her professional partner, Nancy Jevonen, Barrymore created Flower Films, launching things in 1999 with *Never Been Kissed*.

Her next major project, *Charlie's Angels*, would have tried the patience of a veteran producer. All during shooting, rumours kept leaking about constant cast bickering.

"That was so totally misrepresented in the press," explodes Barrymore in a rare display of anger. "We all got along just fine and couldn't wait to make the sequel. It was like a family reunion when we all got back together to shoot it."

But it's two other recent Barrymore films that prove interesting for what they reveal about her. *Riding in Cars with Boys* was based on the life of Beverly D'Onofrio, who gave up her dreams of being a writer when she became a single mom at the age of 15. The story of her marriage to a drug addict and her efforts to care for her son touched something deep in Barrymore.

"I'm usually this little ball of sunshine in my movies," she admits, "which is cool, because that's the way I feel most of the time in my life. But there's also darkness inside me and that movie let me go there and explore it."

It also caused her to reconcile with her mother (actress-author Ildiko Jaid) after a decade of silence following Barrymore's much-publicized legal independence from her parents at age 15.

"I suddenly understood what she'd been through." She looks out the window at Central Park, staring at the leafless trees, dusted with snow.

"Married to a drug addict, raising a kid by herself, putting her own life on hold. That was her story."

And, in that same way, *Confessions of a Dangerous Mind* was part of Barrymore's story.

She plays Penny, the free spirit who sticks with Chuck Barris through all the manic highs and rock-bottom lows of his career, and Barrymore admits that her feelings about the role bordered on the obsessive.

"When I read this script, I became almost animalistically possessive of it, because I knew that I could make her more than a doormat or someone who was terminally needy. I wanted her to be a life-grounding force, a reminder of what was real out there."

"She saw that Chuck was funny and playful, an idea man — and that's very sexy to women. Okay, he was weird, too, but that's part of the bargain. She just loves him. She loves him very much."

Her gaze has a sudden intensity and I start to realize why she identified so closely with Penny. It's the same reason that I'm going to be able to keep my promise to myself and not ask her about Tom Green. She's doing it herself, without ever mentioning his name.

"The heart chooses what the heart wants and sometimes we can't rationalize it. We don't always know what's going on when we're in the middle of something tumultuous."

She's curled up onto her chair in a little ball, and when she tilts her head to one side, it's like she's seven years old and back in *E.T.* again.

"Sure, you can sit down and question and try to figure out why, but sometimes it's just easier to love and be happy instead of letting yourself get all tortured about it."

She sighs. "But funny and playful gets tired pretty quick. You start to wonder if they're ever going to grow up."

Then the light behind her eyes goes out like someone had flipped a switch. "How do you make love stay? And what do you do when it goes?"

The silence hangs until she is asked how she did the most amazing scene in the movie.

While driving away from their wedding, Barris finally tells Penny that he's not just a wacky game show host but a CIA killer. She reacts in stunned silence and then breaks into hysterical laughter.

"After a few takes," Barrymore admits, "I just couldn't laugh naturally anymore, so I asked George to put a walkie-talkie in the car and say something that would make me laugh."

"So I get the news, I pause, and I'm waiting. Then I hear Clooney's voice say, 'Corn,' and you can see me on screen looking puzzled. He held it just long enough and then he finished: 'Corn in my doody this morning.' I let the cacophony come out full throttle."

She laughs for real and the "little ball of sunshine" is back again.

Barrymore continues on her amazing productive streak with six wildly differing movies scheduled to appear by the end of 2004.

They range from the purely commercial (*Charlie's Angels 2: Full Throttle*) to the decidedly artistic (a film version of John Kennedy Toole's black comedy *A Confederacy of Dunces*).

And while tabloid gossip still keeps linking her to Fabrizio Moretti (drummer for *The Strokes*), things seem to have remained a lot quieter on the personal front.

Jason Biggs
Peter Power/Toronto Star

JASON BIGGS

Bye, Bye, American Pie

When *American Pie* was released in 1999, the name of Jason Biggs became famous overnight.

Or maybe the word should be "infamous."

As the overeager virgin who plowed a piece of his mother's pastry after a friend told him having sex felt like "warm apple pie," Biggs instantly became a poster boy for erotic underachievers everywhere.

The movie grossed well over US$100 million, so of course they made a sequel, and this time Biggs got sexually entangled with a tube of Krazy Glue. (Don't ask; you had to be there.)

When the Broadway-bound tour of *The Graduate* decided to latch onto him as further box office insurance for a cast that already boasted Kathleen Turner, it seemed like a good idea to interview him, which I did — in Toronto, in January 2001.

Things are looking up for Jason Biggs.

He's gone from apple pie to Alicia Silverstone and from Krazy Glue to Kathleen Turner.

The super-hot star of *American Pie* (and its sequel) is playing Benjamin Braddock, the title role of *The Graduate* in the stage version of the famous 1967 film, now on its way to Broadway. It's the role that made Dustin Hoffman a star on screen and Biggs is exhilarated by the change it means for him.

"Look, I'm not putting down my ability to only get baked goods and never close the deal with young ladies, but this is exciting."

Biggs has a grin as wide as the hotel ballroom where we sit perched on two solitary chairs in the middle of an echoing cream-and-gold cavern.

He's like a kid in an X-rated candy store as he talks about his character having affairs with both the libidinous Mrs. Robinson and her dewy daughter, Elaine. "Jeez, this makes me look like a champ. I mean, is this lucky or what? Kathleen Turner and Alicia Silverstone, me in between them and them both wanting me. Does wonders for my ego."

You would think the ego doesn't need much stroking. At 23, Biggs has already had his name attached to the pair of mega-grossing *Pie* films as well as other high-profile teen epics such as *Saving Silverman* and *Loser*.

But the craggy-faced dude in shirt and jeans doesn't have a drop of Hollywood pretension about him. If anything, he's more engaging in real life than on screen — not at all the nerdy loser whose sexual proclivities lead him to do the most embarrassing things possible in search of release.

Biggs has done his homework when it comes to Benjamin and his fix on the character seems sure. "He's very complex, multilay-ered. He's at a time in his life when he's not quite sure what the next step is, so he's confused, alienated, ready to break free from the normal middle-class route you're supposed to go."

He speaks with such conviction, in fact, that I ask him how close he is to Benjamin Braddock.

There's a momentary hesitation, and a slight blush creeps up the back of his neck before he continues in a softer voice.

"Alienated? Yeah, that was me, absolutely. But you know why? Because I was a child actor, and that was certainly not the norm where I was growing up."

That would be Hasbrouck Heights, N.J., a suburban enclave about an hour west of New York City. Biggs was born there on

May 12, 1978, to Gary (a shipping company manager) and Angela (a nurse). There were Jason's two sisters as well and his mother thought work in TV ads might help pay for their educations.

"To tell you the truth, it all happened kind of quickly," Biggs admits. "One day I was modelling ski jackets for a Sears catalogue, and then — boom! — off to La, La Land."

Biggs succeeded to a greater degree than anyone had ever planned. By the time he was 13 in 1991, he and his mother moved out to Los Angeles where he landed a part in the short-lived Fox series, *Drexell's Class.*

After it was cancelled, he came back to the East Coast and soon found himself starring on Broadway opposite Judd Hirsch for a year's run in the hit play *Conversations with My Father.*

"I loved it. Until we got our first audience for *The Graduate* in Baltimore, I forgot how much I loved it. It's thrilling to work with a live audience and act a part straight through from point A to point B in an unedited performance."

A season on the soap opera *As the World Turns* followed, which landed him a Daytime Emmy nomination, but doors didn't start to fling open for Biggs. In fact, it wound up getting a lot tougher.

"When I graduated high school, things had dried up for me on the work front and so I thought going to college was the natural next step. Wasn't that what everybody was supposed to do? So I went to NYU."

He shakes his head as he remembers the pain of that not-so-distant time. "I've never been so confused in my life. No clue what to do. I switched to a smaller college near home, but that still didn't do any good."

He looks at you with a bunny-in-the-headlights expression on his face. "People wonder how I can play the kind of loser that I often do. Man, they should've seen me when I was trying to make it in college. I had nothing going for me."

"It's good to remember that, just in case I start thinking that a couple of movie roles makes you a bigger or better person. You are what you are, and you can't ever forget it."

But just when things seemed lowest for Biggs, he was offered a TV series called *Total Security*. Ironically, it folded after 13 weeks, but it served to get him into the L.A. casting loop and *American Pie* soon followed.

The rest was tenderflakey history.

Since so much of the buzz around *The Graduate* concerns Kathleen Turner's nude scene and the onstage sexual relationship she has with Biggs, it seemed inevitable to ask if he'd ever been drawn to an older woman.

"Oh sure, oh yeah! Still am, absolutely. Physical attraction, of course!" he affirms with his face lighting up. He changes tone as though an invisible chaperone might be listening. "Of course, I haven't acted upon that attraction with any Mrs. Robinsons of the world . . . " and then he smiles again. "But there's a lot of older women that I'm attracted to."

Post-*Graduate*, Biggs won't rule out *American Pie 3*. "I wouldn't be surprised if they made another one. After all, at the end of the day, it is a business.

"I'm relieved, though, that I'm starting to get sent lots of non-Pie kind of scripts as well. I want to make movies with amazing people and I want to keep coming back to the theatre as well. I wanna have my cake and eat it, too."

Not to mention, of course, his pie.

Biggs gave an amazingly good performance in *The Graduate* and escaped most of the poisonous press that greeted the show in New York.

He left the show after six months to continue his film career, and his 2003 releases include *Jersey Girl* (where he appeared with Ben Affleck and Jennifer Lopez) as well as the final film in the *Pie* trilogy, this one called *American Wedding*, where the hapless Biggs finally ties the matrimonial knot.

Alicia Silverstone
Peter Power/Toronto Star

ALICIA SILVERSTONE

The Bambi of Beverly Hills

As Hollywood starlets go, Alicia Silverstone was fairly refreshing.

When I sat down to interview her during a Toronto press blitz in January 2001, she instantly started chattering away about her jetlag ("I am so totally fried right now"), her chocolate addiction ("Sometimes I think I'd commit murder for a really great brownie"), and her looks ("Can you believe this stupid zit had to pop out on my forehead on a day when we're shooting all these photos?").

No hidden agenda, no "public persona." She was just what you would've expected from her on-screen appearances: nothing more, nothing less.

And in a world where pretense is as prevalent as Prada, I enjoyed her approach a great deal.

Just don't call her clueless.

Alicia Silverstone is playing her first major theatre role, Elaine Robinson, in the stage version of *The Graduate*, and she's taking it very seriously.

"She's got a really tough situation. The guy she's in love with had sex with her mother. It's very hard for me as an actress to get over that. During the whole scene where we're discussing the reasons why I won't marry him, I keep wanting to scream, 'And then there's the fact that you fucked my mom. Can we talk about that for a second?'"

Even though we're sitting knee to knee in one of those claustrophobic hotel meeting rooms, I still find myself gasping. The peach-faced star of *Clueless* isn't supposed to talk like that.

But look more closely. She's grown up. Silverstone is 25 now and it's been nearly seven years since she broke through to stardom as Cher, the perfectly accessorized, loveable Beverly Hills dingbat who asserted her virginity by saying, "You know how picky I am about my shoes, and they only go on my feet."

Since then, she's survived the relentless glare of the celebrity spotlight with only a few burns.

Sure, her career as an independent producer (and the film she created, *Excess Baggage*) was less than glorious, while gossips had a field day with the tensions that existed between her and director Joel Schumacher on the set of *Batman & Robin*. ("He can play Batgirl in the sequel," she once snapped to a reporter.)

Then there was the constant media monitoring of her weight as well as the guessing games about who was filling the gaps in her love life (Leonardo DiCaprio? Kenneth Branagh?).

It finally got to a point that her well-received performance in the successful 1999 film *Blast from the Past* was hailed as a "comeback."

"A comeback?" she asked at the time, "Where did I go?"

Okay. She may no longer be the concupiscent kewpie doll who fuelled adolescent fantasies, but she's grown into an extremely attractive woman. She's older, wiser, and although there's a hint of sadness around her Bambi eyes, she still radiates the glow that made her everybody's favourite space cadet.

I ask her about her interpretation of Elaine and her answer is straight from the hip. "I haven't in all honesty figured her out yet. I have seven-and-a-half months from here on to do that."

"There's one moment when I find out they've been sleeping together." She's talking about her mother (the infamous Mrs. Robinson, played by Kathleen Turner) and her lover (the feckless

Benjamin, played by Jason Biggs). "It's the first scene with all three of us together. It's so intense to grasp. I walk up the stairs and I go, 'Oh my God!' . . . I keep saying 'Oh my God!' about eight million times as I imagine them going at it."

She shudders slightly before continuing.

"Every night is different for me, depending on what comes up in the scene. Sometimes I wonder 'Have I lost my mom?' and sometimes it's 'Have I lost my boyfriend?'"

For an instant, she's back to her little-girl image. "I always feel a little juvenile at this moment in the play. I think these characters act younger because it's the sixties. She's supposed to be nineteen or twenty, but when I was fourteen, I was way ahead of her."

That's probably not a fair comparison, because Silverstone got very far, very fast in her career and had to grow up far more quickly than most other adolescent girls.

She was born on October 4, 1976, in San Francisco. Her parents were both British, with father Monty being a real estate investor and mother Didi a flight attendant he had met in Florida.

It all started with a proud papa snapping pics and passing them around, but instead of ending at the office water cooler, Monty's efforts launched Alicia on a modelling career by the time she was eight. She started dance and acting classes because she knew where her ambitions really were.

"I didn't get into film because I wanted to be a movie star," is her surprising assertion. "I just wanted to act, but I didn't have a very good understanding at the time of what it really meant. In many ways, it's still all the same to me, all the same possibility, all the same puzzle to figure out."

By the time Silverstone hit her teen years, everything began happening at once. A Domino's pizza commercial led to a spot on *The Wonder Years*, which got her the role as the cutest stalker of all time in the cult film, *The Crush*.

All well and good, but not superstar material. That came when she appeared in three Aerosmith videos, most notably "Cryin'." The buzz her appearances generated caught the attention of director Amy Heckerling, who was looking for an archetypal California girl with irresistible appeal to play the lead in her contemporary remake of Jane Austen's *Emma*, which she called *Clueless*.

The movie scored big with audiences and Silverstone shot to instant stardom, hailed widely for her deft comic creation. In reality, she now admits that she was more like the character than anyone suspected at the time. "You know when Cher was discussing the Haitians and she said 'The Hate-ians need to come to America,' well, I really thought they were called Hate-ians."

She does find some similarities between her star-making role and the part she's now playing in *The Graduate*. "They're both odd, rich, kind of princessy. But they also have a heart, a moral centre. They're both so optimistic, and I'm like that, too."

There is one aspect to being live onstage that she's found a little distracting. "There is this scene," she confides, "where I have to wear my little undies." She mock-gags in horror. "I'm totally not nude! But I'm still freaked out. This is Miss I'll-Never-Do-A-Nude-Scene-Silverstone talking. When I read the script, I thought 'Oh, we can just cut that part.' My brain read it the way it reads any film script. 'She takes her top off.' Yeah, whatever, I'm not going to do it. Okay, I take my dress off, but I have my bra and undies on, so I'm fine." A pause, and then she drops the pretense. "Oh God, no, I'm not fine!"

Her reluctance to go nude on stage and screen has more to do with her sense of propriety than with self-image. She defends her decision fiercely. "In a perfect world, I'd be naked all the time. I mean, you take me to Jamaica and put me on a beach with coconuts and I'd be naked all day long. But not for entertainment; that's just cheap to me."

"Will they still be talking about my body shape and size? Probably. Why wouldn't they? They always do. Who cares, I'm happy. There's so much beauty in the world that that stuff has always been boring to me and it always will be. Of course it's hurtful, but it's just . . . "

She leaves the sentence unfinished and as she leans back in her chair, I think of how she described Elaine. "She only knows how to deal with honesty. She doesn't know how to deal with anything else."

Funny, but that sounds a lot like Alicia Silverstone.

Poor Alicia.

She really wasn't very good in *The Graduate*, playing most of her big dramatic scenes as one long sustained scream. "She starts to share a problem with aging sopranos," I wrote in my review, "she can hit the note, she just can't leave it."

And I was one of the kind ones.

After keeping a low profile for a while, she began work on a pilot for a new TV series created by Darren (*Sex and the City*) Starr.

The show is to be called *Miss/Match* and she's slated to play "a New York lawyer who meddles in everyone else's love life because her own is so mixed up." It's on the NBC schedule for the fall of 2003.

Ralph Fiennes
Tannis Toohey/Toronto Star

RALPH FIENNES

The Spider and the Fly

"**I** love interviewing Ralph Fiennes," gushed one of my colleagues, "he's the only actor I know who talks in paragraphs."

She was right. After a frequent diet of monosyllables or terse phrases separated by "you know?" recaps, it's a relief to encounter a professional who is as eloquent as he is talented.

We met in Toronto in September 2002.

It's the eyes you notice first.

Cool, even, slate blue. Looking right through you with a calm, measured gaze.

Then the hand, reaching out to shake yours with a firm, uncomplicated grip.

Finally, the voice — low, soft, full of subtle shadings.

"How do you do? I'm Ralph Fiennes."

You put your mind on freeze-frame for a second and think of all the films you've seen him in: *Schindler's List, The English Patient, The End of the Affair.*

But all those images fade beside the most recent one: the hollow-eyed, nicotine-stained, stooped and shambling hero of David Cronenberg's latest film, *Spider.*

Fiennes tour-de-force performance as Dennis Clegg (nick-named "Spider" in his youth by his mother) was the talk of the 2002 Toronto International Film Festival.

An actor who had made his reputation for the skill with which he could portray characters of profound intellectual complexity dazzled everyone with his work as a virtually incoherent schizophrenic, living in a British halfway house.

Speaking barely a word, scribbling incomprehensible ciphers in a tattered notebook, he made a lasting impression with this character shattered by traumatic acts of violence from his childhood.

I met with Fiennes the day after the press screening of the film, and the hyperactive atmosphere of the Intercontinental Hotel in full festival frenzy seemed to fade away as he spoke of the attraction this strange role held for him.

"I responded to the character, his loneliness, his fears. I liked the privacy of it, the inner quality of the emotions." A tight smile. "He's certainly one of a kind. There's never been anyone quite like Spider, has there?"

When asked about how different this silent man was from most of the highly verbal roles in his career, he interrupts with, "But that's what I loved about it. It was a wonderful challenge. The thrill for me was to be able to portray him without language, using purely the physical. An actor should be able to say nothing and be understood."

This minimalist approach embraced by Fiennes was just what Cronenberg had in mind. "You see, there's so little in the movie, you have to get it just right, but David is someone with a great eye for detail."

His eyes light up as he remembers how elements of the character came together. "It was David who came up with the idea of my feet shuffling. He would focus in on tiny things, watching the way I sat on the bed, letting me know when I got it just right."

The suggestion that such micro-management might prove stifling brings an emphatic denial. "I loved it. I love being guided. I never felt imposed on with David, because I completely trusted his vision, not just his intellectual vision, but his literal, photographic vision that enriched the work enormously."

But none of this implies that it was an easy film to make. "It was physically a very oppressive role. We shot in the summer. I was wearing layer upon layer of shirts, and an overcoat. The makeup made my skin look so dirty, and my hands."

Fiennes stretches out his tapering fingers that are now clean and trim, but were covered during *Spider* with disfiguring layers of nicotine from the character's chain-smoking.

"Ah, the nicotine stains," he remembers with a shudder. "It took us a long time to get them appropriately old and green and yellow and decrepit."

He shakes his shoulders as if removing a burden. "After spending fourteen hours a day with Spider, I had to jump in the shower, wash my hair, scrub all the makeup off and breathe as myself again. It was a great relief. I'm not the kind of actor who wants to keep it going."

A bit of a sigh. "And then the next day, the ritual begins again. Putting on the makeup, the shirts, reapplying those nicotine stains on the fingers. Gathering Spider up again."

But to Fiennes the physical involvement is secondary to the level of commitment he feels obliged to provide mentally.

"I look on acting as manipulating yourself imaginatively to be someone else. You want audiences to believe you, so the stakes are high. It demands such focus, such concentration. You have to keep yourself perpetually ready for those little short takes."

I ask Fiennes about the strange cryptographic symbols that Spider keeps filling his notebooks with during the film

"I created a series of hieroglyphics. I have to confess that it wasn't a coherent code, but I did know what I was writing at the time." He grins sheepishly.

"If I looked at them now, I couldn't tell you what they said. What ultimately began to fascinate me was the very look of them, their shape on the page, how I would arrange them."

For an instant, he almost goes off into the strange mental twilight he shared with Spider and I bring him back by asking if the film is simply a case study of one schizophrenic, or if it has more universal applications.

"I share David's feelings on this. He was interested in the mythic, in the bits of Spider that are in everyone. The confusion about our sexuality and our identity that we hide inside ourselves. I think if we get locked into medical accuracy, we get lost."

His focus grows more intense. "The humanity of these people is what's important. We're too easily suspicious of other languages or other cultures. We have to realize they might have a more direct conduit to the truth than we do. We just have to learn to understand them.

"We just have to learn to understand each other."

Trying to ease the atmosphere after his intense discussion of the role, I conclude by asking Fiennes what it was like to shift from a film like Spider to a piece of fluff like *Maid in Manhattan*.

"Oh, you mean my Hugh Grant movie?"

He gets a mischievous sparkle in his eyes. "You figure it out. There I was, covered in nicotine, scribbling in a notebook, talking to no one, and along comes this offer. Would I like to go to New York, wear nice suits, and play love scenes opposite Jennifer Lopez?"

He grins, "I think that is what's known in this business as a no-brainer."

After a year that featured *Spider*, *Maid in Manhattan*, and the grisly thriller *Red Dragon* ("In that one, I had to eat Philip Seymour Hoffman's face, which was rather a hearty meal"), Fiennes returned to his real love, the stage.

As a tribute to the Royal Shakespeare Company's departing artistic director, Adrian Noble, Fiennes spent 2003 with the company, most notably in the title role of Henrik Ibsen's *Brand*.

Julia Stiles
Peter Power/Toronto Star

JULIA STILES

She's Working Her Way Through College

I n the 18 months prior to this interview, I had seen Julia Stiles in five totally different movies, playing an assortment of characters that would have challenged many actresses twice her age.

This wasn't just another perky teen starlet with attitude for days and Styrofoam between the ears. From the evidence on screen, she was the real thing. Now, I wanted to find out a bit about what she was like in real life.

When she came to the Toronto International Film Festival in September 2001, I made sure I got to talk to her.

She didn't disappoint me.

She drove Ethan Hawke crazy, nearly wrecked Alec Baldwin's career, and now she's messing with Stockard Channing's head.

Sounds like Julia Stiles could be a scary young woman.

It's hard to know what to expect from the 20-year-old actress whose credits in the last two years include O, *State and Main*, *Save the Last Dance*, *Hamlet*, *10 Things I Hate About You*, and now *The Business of Strangers*.

Who's going to be waiting inside the hotel room? Will it be the viper, the victim, the vixen — or all three?

On meeting her, the answer is immediately clear.

None of the above.

The straight-ahead blonde with the purple T-shirt and the

level gaze has a cut-to-the-chase immediacy matched with an arm's-length warmth that engages yet distances. And she's smart.

"I'm very careful about the choices I make. It's very important to me that I don't just become another show-business personality. Why? Because it's awfully hard to be an actor when you're a personality. Besides, I get bored so quickly that I love to go out and explore a new type of character that I've never explored before."

That's a good description of the role she plays in *The Business of Strangers*: Paula, the tattooed cyberbrat whose late arrival at a business presentation makes the high-powered exec played by Stockard Channing go ballistic. Then, after airline troubles trap the two for the night in a hotel, they embark on a strange journey of mutual discovery.

"Life imitated art on the shoot," she says smiling. "Stockard and I didn't know anything about each other personally at the start. There was a little bit of mystery, and then we opened up to each other more. Trust. That's what it's all about."

They had only 23 days to shoot writer-director Patrick Stettner's gripping black comedy in which Stiles leads Channing into a booze-and-pill-fuelled night that could teach Darth Vader a thing or two about the dark side.

Stiles insists the character of Paula "was my imagination. Sure, there was a lot of myself I could bring to her. She's bratty, which I can be," she says with a laugh.

"But all the real scary stuff was like playing dress-up. I based it on girls who fascinate me, girls who like to manipulate people, be the centre of attention; whereas I always try to shy away from that. I like to make people feel comfortable."

Stettner claims Stiles used elements of her own "highly charged" relationship with her mother to enrich her scenes with Channing, and when asked whether it's true that her mother once called her "a triple type-A personality," she finishes the quote with you and then says: "No." Pause. "Yes." Pause. Grin. "Okay, I have that in me, but I try to keep it in perspective."

The New York–born-and-raised child of a teacher and a ceramics artist (she described them once as "loudmouth liberals"), Stiles wrote a letter to a stage director that landed her first job at age 11. She's never looked back.

An Apple Jacks commercial brought her to the attention of casting people and soon she was starring on tween shows like *Ghostwriter*. For a job or two, she was credited as the more youthful "Julie Stiles," but that soon changed.

"I wanted to be serious about my career, and that meant every aspect of it. I don't do dumb PR or photo shoots, and, yes, I even decided I should be billed as Julia, not Julie."

TV work in series like *Chicago Hope* and *Promised Land* followed, as did a featured part opposite Brad Pitt and Harrison Ford in *The Devil's Own*.

She showed her evil side in 1998's *Wicked* ("I enjoyed that!") and was one of the endless leads lost in the sudsy miniseries *The 60s* ("Forget that one, please!").

Then came her starring role in the teen hit *10 Things I Hate About You*, a modern remake of *The Taming of the Shrew* that revealed Stiles' flair for deadpan comedy and allowed her to strike some romantic sparks with Aussie heartthrob, Heath Ledger.

"I knew I was clicking on that film," Stiles recalls, smiling. "You walk onto the set and you can tell from the way everybody is looking at you that it's all working just the way it's supposed to. That kind of positive energy inspires you to do better."

But what if it goes the other way? "That's happened to me too, and I'm NOT going to tell you what movie that was. But believe me, it is so disheartening to go out there every day and know that what you're doing just isn't any good."

Things started moving a little fast for her in the next few years, with intense material and high-powered stars surrounding a girl not even out of her teens.

"There were times when what I was portraying on screen was years ahead of my own life experience, but I tried not to let that worry me. That's why it's called 'acting,' right?" A grown-up smile — tart and tight.

"Sure, it was tough to keep my head screwed on straight," she says with her disarmingly straight-ahead candour, "but I just worked on it. I knew that Hollywood was full of girls like me who had big chances, but didn't know how to deal with them and I didn't want to join that club, no thanks."

In addition to a film career that would be enough to fatigue most people, she's just begun her second year of full-time studies at Columbia University, living in a dorm and trying to have an ordinary life.

"People don't hassle me. I would hate to get to that point where I walked into a room and wondered if everyone was looking at me. Because sometimes they're not looking at you, and guess what? You're not the centre of the universe."

Stiles admits her peers sometime react differently to her, depending on the last role they've seen her play. She roars with laughter at the prospective fallout from *The Business of Strangers*, where she's anything but your average cuddly co-ed.

"Wait for the dates to evaporate after this one hits the screen! Talk about your feminazi!"

And now it's back to her second year at college. But no sophomore slump for Julia Stiles.

Now or ever.

True to her word, Stiles continued juggling her studies at Columbia with her career. A 2002 N.Y. Shakespeare Festival engagement in Central Park as Viola in *Twelfth Night* drew merely polite notices, but on screen, her stock continued to go up with entries like *The Bourne Identity*.

And for the romantic comedy *A Guy Thing*, released in January 2003, her salary was a reported $4,000,000, which certainly pays a lot of tuition.

Kevin Spacey (with Sam Mendes)
Steve Russell/Toronto Star

KEVIN SPACEY

The Unusual Suspect

The following encounter seems to begin on a somewhat tentative note, and with good reason.

A few hours before our scheduled interview in February 2003, I had been present at a roundtable session where one reporter continued to annoy Spacey with questions about his personal life, even when the actor had indicated he'd rather stick to professional inquiries.

Spacey was polite, then firm, then angry, and finally ended the trivial line of examination.

I almost wondered if he was going to cancel the rest of the day's interviews, but he was a professional, and was waiting in his room for me a few hours later.

We were both somewhat apprehensive at first, but — fortunately — we got past it.

Standing outside a suite at the Regency Hotel to interview Kevin Spacey feels a bit like walking barefoot over broken glass while carrying a tray of nitroglycerine cocktails.

One false move and the whole thing could blow up in my face.

The 43-year-old actor has been known to have a notoriously short fuse with journalists who want to pry into his sex life or wallow in showbiz trivia. And the dark-suited, dark-eyed individual who greets me is definitely on his guard: tight, wary, controlled.

So I try to warm things up by reminding him we've met once before: when John Neville introduced us backstage after a 1982 Broadway performance of Ibsen's *Ghosts* in which they both appeared opposite Liv Ullmann.

The thaw is instant, the smile warm and inviting. "God, I was young then! I'd just turned twenty-three. How was I in the part? Wait a minute, I remember. Let's not talk about it."

He laughs and we sit down to discuss the real passion in Spacey's life: the art of acting.

I ask what drew him to this current project, *The Life of David Gale*, a political thriller about an opponent of capital punishment who finds himself on death row for a murder he insists he didn't commit.

"I thought it was the most remarkable script. It puzzled me, it disturbed me, it fired my imagination. And with Alan Parker on board to direct, man, it was a slam-dunk. He's such a skilled director that I knew he wouldn't turn this into some speech-making, banner-waving kind of movie.

"It's a thriller and not a social polemic. Look, if you want to listen to someone give a speech, then find a politician, but let's not have the issues outweigh the entertainment value of the movie."

He also makes it clear that his personal beliefs on the death penalty are not the reason he's on board. "I have no dog in this fight. I'm grappling with the issue, as most people are."

Like many of the characters in Spacey's films (including his Oscar-winning performances as Verbal Kint in *The Usual Suspects* and Lester Burnham in *American Beauty*), David Gale is a complex individual, not necessarily easy to like.

Spacey took the challenge. "You have to enjoy playing a character. If you don't enjoy it, then you can't embrace it, which is what you have to do if you're going to commit yourself to every one of those things that might cause an audience to say, 'Wait a minute, why are you making me feel this?'

"Look, I never pass judgment on my roles. I have to play them for all their flaws and contradictions and blemishes and let the chips fall where they may."

When I point out to Spacey that a similar ambiguity seems to surround most of his work on stage and screen, he throws up his hands helplessly.

"Sure, I'm drawn to those projects, but I don't seek them out. I just read 'em and respond. After you make the movies you can look for patterns, but that's just how it evolves."

Spacey has often said that he hates being a celebrity, but loves being an actor, and once he's realized our conversation is going to stick to a discussion of his craft, he becomes visibly more relaxed as he warms to the topic.

"You can't decide to play a good guy or a bad guy. If you've done your homework, then all you can do is show up every day like a big palette of various colours for the director to pick and choose from in any particular scene. Ultimately, he's the one who's going to take those colours and make a painting. I'm not. . . . That's why I try to give him lots of choices. I'll attack a scene seven different ways in a single day and then leave the decision in his hands."

He isn't concerned with controlling his performance. "I don't go to the dailies. I don't fall in love with moments. I have no idea what they're going to use until I see the picture. The only thing I care about is if it works."

That concern with acting has fuelled Spacey for most of his life. Growing up in California, he always was "a born performer," but it never found a focus until his teenage years.

By his own admission, he was "a bit of a hell-raiser" as a kid, with a string of disciplinary problems that finally led his guidance counsellor to suggest he might put that energy into something constructive. "I chose drama," he remembers, "and that's when it all started."

Chatsworth High School has a Web page that immortalizes

the work Spacey (class of 1977) did there, including his starring role as Captain Von Trapp in *The Sound of Music* opposite Mare Winningham. ("No, I won't sing 'Edelweiss' for you," he grins.)

After that, he began studies at Juilliard, only to grow impatient and drop out after two years, drifting through the regional theatre circuit, working as a stand-up comic and becoming "a very dark young man. I drank too much and was going nowhere fast."

The event that turned his life around was a 1986 Broadway production of *Long Day's Journey into Night* where he starred opposite Jack Lemmon. "He was a great man who taught me a lot about how to live my life in an atmosphere of professionalism and generosity. To this day, I sometimes stop and ask myself what Jack would have done in the same situation."

And just like Lemmon did, Spacey continues to divide his time between the stage and the screen. He's recently been announced as the new artistic director of London's Old Vic Theatre, he frequently drops by our Stratford Festival to check things out, and if you ask him to name one of the most rewarding experiences of his career, he has no hesitation in pointing to his stage performance as Hickey in *The Iceman Cometh*, both in London and New York.

"I originally agreed to do the play because of (director) Howard Davies. Back in 1987, he closed his Broadway production of *Les Liaisons Dangereuses* when the producers wouldn't approve me as Alan Rickman's replacement, because I wasn't a big enough star. I never forgot that and, eleven years later, when the Almeida Theatre asked me to star in *Iceman* with Howard Davies directing, I didn't have to think twice.

"Then came the joy of working on a play like that with a wonderful director and a cast beyond belief. Every day it just got better and better, more exploratory, more fascinating . . . "

He's got a smile that reaches from ear to ear as he stretches out his arms. "Hey, I guess that's why I'm in this business."

Spacey's love for the theatre also includes his plans for the Old Vic, where his first season as artistic director of the once-famed British theatre will begin in the fall of 2004.

"I plan to consult with a variety of directors and pick a season of plays. Then I'll put a company of actors together to appear in them."

It's been no secret that Spacey has taken a keen interest in our own Stratford Festival over the past two seasons and he admits that when he went there this past fall, "I already had the Vic in mind and I was looking at the work of specific directors and actors I might use."

As for doing this in England rather than his native America, Spacey is quick to point out, "In no way should this decision be viewed as an abandonment of my own country. I want this to break down walls about where actors can work."

One of those vinegary Spacey grins twists across his mouth.

"That's what I'd like it to read on my tombstone: 'Here lies Kevin Spacey, Working Actor.'"

The Life of David Gale didn't create much excitement at the box office, but Spacey kept moving ahead, preparing his first season as the artistic director of the Old Vic and — with the kind of contrast that he seems to thrive on — playing singer Bobby Darin in a film biography entitled *Beyond the Sea*.

Maggie Smith
Ian West/PA Photos

MAGGIE SMITH

The Crème de la Crème

This is the encounter that probably took the longest to arrange, because of Dame Maggie's well-known aversion to interviews. And, to be fair, she was also involved in shooting a series of films around the world during the time I was pursuing her.

The first request went out in June 2000, and by August 2001 we were no closer to a final commitment. A mutual friend, director Robin Phillips, finally interceded, and things started to move a bit faster.

At last, the word arrived that we could get together in London in October 2001. The events of 9/11 and the subsequent international tensions made travel difficult, but I wasn't going to give this one up easily.

The expression "it's not over 'til it's over" came back to haunt me, however, as I waited outside my hotel for her limousine to arrive . . .

Dame Maggie Smith can still stop traffic.

It's the day after the bombing of Afghanistan has begun and the streets around this Grosvenor Square hotel are sealed off with police barricades. The U.S. Embassy is just around the corner, and no one's taking any chances.

Not the most relaxed of circumstances in which to conduct an interview that has taken 18 months to organize.

Smith hardly ever agrees to talk to the media ("They always want to aaaaaask me things," she wails with apparent surprise), not even to promote her appearance as Professor Minerva McGonagall, deputy headmistress of Hogwarts, in the film version of J.K. Rowling's *Harry Potter and the Philosopher's Stone.*

While standing outside, waiting for this rare encounter to come to fruition, I notice a cluster of people gathered around a black sedan. Several police officers clear a path for the vehicle, which finally pulls to a stop directly in front of me.

The red hair springs into view first, and then comes the sound of that often-imitated but never-duplicated voice. "I'm sorry to have you caused you soooooo much inconvenience," she assures the officer who helps her from the car.

"No trouble at all, Dame Maggie," he says, all but clicking his heels. "Our pleasure. We're all waiting to see you in the movie."

As Smith moves away from the car, the police officer quietly tells me what the holdup was all about: "A man kept shouting 'It's McGonagall. It's Minerva McGonagall!' and a crowd started gathering."

We cross the lobby to the elevator and Smith steps inside, relieved to be alone. "It's like nothing else I've ever experienced. Potter madness. Pottermania." She likes the sound of that phrase and repeats it as the doors slide shut. "Pottermaaaaaania!"

It may seem strange, but in all Smith's illustrious 50-year stage-and-screen career she's never been involved with anything destined to garner quite as much media attention as her presence in the first of the Harry Potter films.

London is plastered with Potter posters, the shops are full of Potter paraphernalia, and the day before we met, the venerable *Times* had even included a lengthy Harry Potter supplement in its Sunday edition.

So it's not surprising that people stop the award-winning Dame on the street and that kind of attention tends to rattle her.

"It's been a busy time for me. I've finished three movies in the past year, which is quite a lot at my age, thaaaaaank you very much." (Besides *Harry Potter*, she worked on *Gosford Park* and *Divine Secrets of the Ya-Ya Sisterhood*.) "I don't know what that last one is going to be like, but I adoooooore saying the title. Ya-Yaaaaaa!"

"And then," she confides, sounding like any mother, "my son Toby (Stephens) got married (to actress Anna-Louise Plowman) and I had to deal with the whole matrimonial phantasma-goooooooria . . . which is something else I adoooooore saying."

She finally settles down with a cup of coffee in the tranquillity of a hotel suite, relaxes, then smiles, and the effect is dazzling.

The 66-year-old actress avoids the heavy makeup and fashion getups that cause some of her contemporaries to resemble exhibits at Madame Tussaud's. Smith's gingerbread hair is stylishly coiffed, her black cashmere sweater coat is elegance itself, and around her neck she wears a solitary jewel.

"The Bedford diamond," she explains, holding it up proudly. "(Actor) Brian (Bedford) gave it to me when we finished our years at Stratford together."

The years Smith spent at the Stratford Festival, from 1976 to 1980, under the direction of Robin Phillips, are "some of the happiest memories of my career," she says.

But before we journey there, I ask her more about Harry Potter. "Well," she says lowering her voice conspiratorially, "I knew the books were popular, but I never thought the film would become so immense. It's absolutely bizaaaaaare.

"There was a veil of secrecy surrounding everything we did at first — the script, the locations — and then we realized it had to do with keeping all those people who were obsessed with Harry Potter from baaaaaarging in and disturbing our work."

Smith did have one advantage over her celebrated co-stars such as Richard Harris and Robbie Coltrane: she had actually worked before with her leading man, Daniel Radcliffe, the 12-year-old Harry Potter himself. They appeared together in the 1999 made-for-TV version of *David Copperfield*, directed by Simon Curtis, with Radcliffe as young David and Smith as Aunt Betsey Trotwood.

"I think it was the very first thing Daniel had done, and his parents were concerned because he was such a shy boy." A knowing smile twists her upper lip. "They needn't have worried. By the end of the shoot, he knew all there was to know about sound, lighting — everything."

I share with her the story Richard Harris (playing Dumbledore in the film) told me about how director Chris Columbus got Harris together with Radcliffe to read a few scenes and "put Daniel more at ease." After they were finished, Radcliffe looked seriously at Harris and said, "You know, I think you're going to be very good in the part." Smith hoots with glee. "Oh, that sounds like our Daniel! Exactly, exaaaaaactly like him."

It's fascinating to hear Smith in a one-on-one situation. Many of her well-known vocal trademarks (the elongated vowels, the repeated words) occur in normal conversation, but in a much more low-key manner. It's almost as though the public Smith is simply the private Smith, played at a higher volume.

She was born Margaret Natalie Smith in North London on December 28, 1934, left school at 16 to go to work for the Oxford Playhouse, and was well embarked on her acting career by the time Bedford first met her in 1954.

"I remember," recalled Bedford between performances at Stratford, "that Maggie was doing a play with Kate Reid, and afterwards we went back to Kate's house in Chelsea, sat on the floor, and talked about Maggie's virginity. When we finally worked together more than twenty years later, we were considerably different," he said grinning, "she'd lost her virginity by then and I hadn't."

A brief detour to America found Smith starring in the revue *New Faces of 1956*, wearing little more than a bunch of oranges. She fled back to England, and after a stint at the Old Vic, achieved West End stardom in Jean Kerr's comedy *Mary, Mary*.

Sir Laurence Olivier tapped her to join the first company at the National Theatre in 1963. "One of the first things I played was Desdemona to Larry's Othello. What was it like? It was friiii-iightening! You know how intense he could be. He'd put his hands around my neck and I was sure he was going to straaaaaan-gle me."

She remained at the National until 1971. While there, she married fellow actor Robert Stephens and gave birth to two sons, Chris and Toby.

She also found time to work on her film career and won her first Oscar for her legendary 1969 performance in *The Prime of Miss Jean Brodie*. (Her second Oscar was for a supporting role in *California Suite*.)

"It was just amaaaaaazing what that film did for me, but I surely paid for it. To this day, people come up to me in airports and feel obliged to imitate me, saying 'My girls are the *crème de la crème*" in Scottish accents that are absolutely appaaaaaalling!"

However, by the mid-seventies, things were on a downward spiral. Her marriage to Stephens was on the skids, film roles were evaporating, and critics were accusing her of becoming a slave to her comic mannerisms.

Enter her saviour, in the person of newly appointed artistic director of the Stratford Festival, Robin Phillips.

"I was in Toronto," Smith recalls, "doing *Private Lives* in — what was it called, 'The Alex'? — and Robin invited me to go for a weekend to Grand Bend, in the absolute middle of winter with all this snoooooow." Phillips asked her to join the company for the next season, playing — among other things — Cleopatra.

Smith's eyes still grow wide as she recalls the moment. "That really threw me for a loop because I don't believe anybody else in the world would have thought of me for that. I just assumed he was maaaaaad."

But she came, and she stayed for five seasons, "It was a changing point in my life. And it was like starting not just with a clean page, but with a whole new notebook. It was a wonderful new beginning and a very liberating time."

You start to notice that as the conversation becomes truly serious, the vocal mannerisms vanish, and realize that they're as much a function of nerves as anything else. As Robin Phillips warned, "Maggie is really a very shy creature."

Her gallery of performances during that period — Rosalind in *As You Like It*, Masha in *The Three Sisters*, Beatrice in *Much Ado About Nothing* — rank high in the history of Stratford. Smith gives most of the credit to Phillips.

"I will be forever grateful for what he did for me. It's difficult to explain, but Robin gave one courage in a very sort of subtle way. He used to say a wonderful thing: 'It's never how do I do this? It's why do I do this?' It's something I still think about to this very day."

I ask her what else she still thinks about when Stratford is mentioned, and her voice grows very gentle. "When my boys were very young there, they used to go 'round the car parks and see how many different licence plates they could find. Then they'd run to my dressing room and say, 'They're from Florida, they're from Maryland, they're from everywhere!' And I'd think how terrific it was that people were driving from all over to come to Stratford.

"It's a marvellous place. I just hope that it goes on and on and on and on and on!"

Much like the Harry Potter films — the first on the eve of its release, the second about to start filming, and the third in pre-production — with Smith and her co-stars committed to star in all of them.

"You see me here before you," she intones with mock drama, "the former Maggie Smith, but now the once and future Minerva McGonagall."

And then she laughs. Wickedly.

Of course, the first Harry Potter film was a huge success, as was the second, and the third is in production as this book goes to press, although Smith and the company suffered the loss of the original Dumbledore, Richard Harris, who died in 2002 after completing the second movie.

Smith also scored heavily in *Gosford Park*, winding up with another Oscar nomination (her sixth) for Best Supporting Actress.

The greatest triumph Dame Maggie has enjoyed since our interview, however, occurred on the stage, when she starred with Dame Judi Dench in David Hare's *Breath of Life*. After a sellout London run in 2002, she's scheduled to take it to Broadway, as early as the fall of 2003 — Master Potter willing.

Richard Harris
Peter Power/Toronto Star

RICHARD HARRIS

The Once and Future King

This is one that I owed Richard Harris. When we met at the Toronto Film Festival in September 2001, I felt as if I had spent a privileged patch of time with a unique man.

As you'll read below, he opened his heart and soul to me about a great many things.

Unfortunately, most of it never got into the *Star*. When I returned from our time together, my editors told me to "play up the Harry Potter angle and forget about the rest," just as Harris had suspected they would.

The next day, when the truncated interview appeared, Harris was rightly furious and vented about it to one of my colleagues, *Star* film critic Peter Howell: "I trusted that bastard, and told him a lot of important things, but what does he print? Nothing but goddam Harry Potter."

That day, by the way, was September 11, and everything soon acquired a different perspective.

I never saw Harris again, and I thought of trying to write to him, but time slipped through my fingers.

Harris died on October 25, 2002, of Hodgkin's Disease. And when, shortly after his passing, I found out that this book was to be published, I made myself a promise. I vowed to dig out my notes from that afternoon we spent together and print the interview that Richard Harris had entrusted me to deliver.

Here it is.

"Don't ask me about that damned stupid Harry Potter movie. That's not why I'm here."

Richard Harris, as always, isn't afraid to speak his mind, even to the point of denigrating his work as Aldus Dumbledore in the upcoming *Harry Potter and the Sorcerer's Stone*.

He's at the Toronto International Film Festival to help drum up support for something that he *does* believe in: *My Kingdom*, the film by Don Boyd that sets Shakespeare's *King Lear* in contemporary Liverpool.

Harris, who turns 71 on October 1, plays a British crime lord named Sandeman whose wife's murder causes him to divide his "kingdom" among his three daughters.

"I like this movie because it's not afraid to embrace the darkness. Most films run around lighting tiny candles and think they make a damn bit of difference. Don Boyd has a pretty good idea of how black the universe can be and so do I."

His rheumy eyes search me out. "I know what it's like to scrape the bottom of the barrel of despair and stir the shavings into your Guinness. That's a cup we've drained to the dregs many times, both me and Lear."

The parallels with Shakespeare's tragedy are skillfully worked out by director Boyd, and Harris does some of his richest work, made even more effective because it's so understated. "At first they wanted me to rant and rave, but I told them no. People will see it and say, 'Look, it's Richard Harris going over the top again,' and I won't do it."

He sees me smiling and pokes my arm roughly. "All right now, tell the truth, what was the worst bit of overacting you ever saw me do . . . out with it!"

I volunteer that it was probably in 1977's *Orca* and Harris laughs until he's stopped by a fit of coughing, something that happens several times during our 90 minutes together.

"Oh, that fucking killer whale! What a piece of shite that was. No wonder I was hitting the blow so heavy in those days." His gaze is suddenly level. "You know cocaine nearly killed me?" I nod feebly in agreement, having heard the gossipy reports over the years. "My heart stopped, and they had to bring me back to life again — 1978, I think that was."

He sips at his coffee. "I'd like to say I changed my life overnight, but that wouldn't be the case. I tried though, and I got better . . . even if my acting didn't."

I ask him why he seems so eager to put himself down.

"Because I had a gift of gold once, and I threw it all away for a handful of silver. I took the talent God gave me and pissed it into a river called Hollywood."

He was one of nine children born to an Irish farmer named Ivan Harris in Limerick on October 1, 1930. "All nine of us were looking for a way out, and I thought mine was going to be rugger, but the TB ended all that.

"So I decided to become an actor instead, Why? I had the gift of the gab and I could charm the knickers off any girl that drew breath. I was a handsome bugger then. No, not handsome, beautiful."

Harris sees me staring askance at his vainglorious boast and chafes. "Well, I *was* beautiful, dammit, and I'm such an ugly old beast now that I can take some pride in the joys of my youth."

He made a huge stage success in Brendan Behan's *The Quare Fellow*, and a spate of British films followed, culminating in his performance as Frank Machin in Lindsay Anderson's 1964 *This Sporting Life*.

"They cast me as a rugger player who was a bastard. That didn't take much acting from me. No wonder it made me a star." And brought him his first Oscar nomination for Best Actor.

After a detour to Italy to star in Michelangelo Antonioni's *Red Desert*, Harris went to Hollywood, making a decorative hole on the screen in films like *Hawaii* and *Caprice*.

Then, in 1967, came *Camelot*.

"Don't ask me why I still love that bloody story so much. But I can't look at the movie anymore. I was too gorgeous then. It makes me weep to see what a rag-and-bone man I've turned into."

A young waiter retrieves Harris's coffee cup, giving his disreputable looks a wide berth. "Can I smoke here?" Harris shouts after him. Getting no answer, he shrugs and lights up a cigarette. "I'll just do it till they order me to stop, which is what I've done all my life."

Camelot made him a superstar, and then he hopped to the top of the recording charts as well, with his unexpected rendition of Jimmy Webb's "Macarthur Park." I tell Harris how much I used to enjoy hearing him sing it.

"Sentimental bollocks," is his initial reply, but then he softens. "I still remember some of it, especially when I'm in my cups." And then, magically, he rasps out a few lines:

> *"I will drink the wine while it is warm*
> *And never let you catch me looking at the sun . . . "*

We look at each other for a moment, and then he breaks the spell. "That's not bad, but don't ask me why they left that fucking cake out in the rain . . . "

And again he laughs, until a bout of coughing stops him. "I'm not well, not at all well, but after all I've done to my body in my lifetime, that shouldn't surprise me."

Harris had one last film hurrah with the surprise success of *A Man Called Horse* in 1970, but for the rest of the decade, the work got worse and worse, while the antics got wilder and wilder.

In the 1980s, the excesses of his early days gave way to relative sobriety, while years of touring as King Arthur in the stage version of *Camelot* rebuilt his finances, and allowed him the luxury of choice.

"When you're poor and raising a family, you take what comes along. Now I can commit to the work I do. I cannot put it on at eight in the morning and take it off at six in the evening. When the picture is rolling I give it my all, and then when it's over, I disappear. I tell the rest of the cast, 'You'll never hear from me again.'"

Quality films like 1990's *The Field*, which earned him his second Oscar nomination, were the result of his new work habits, as are pictures like *My Kingdom*, which he's eager to start discussing again after our journey through his past.

"I like the way they've worked out my motivation. You see, the beginning is the tricky part. You always wonder why Lear gives his kingdom away, but now that they've added the murder of my wife, I have a reason."

He smiles wickedly. "It reminds me of the day years ago when John Major put his leadership of (Britain's) Tory party up for grabs. I ran into Brian Mulroney in an elevator at the Savoy Hotel, and asked him what he thought of Major's move. Mulroney shook his head and said to me, 'I don't understand it. You never give up power.'"

Another thing Harris likes is the fact that this Lear has no Fool, but spends his time instead with his grandson, and Harris is well known for his devotion to his grandchildren.

In fact, were it not for one of them, he would not have agreed to take part in the Harry Potter films.

"Look, I had never even read the books," admits Harris. "All I knew was that they kept offering me the job and raising the salary every time they called me. And I turned them down for a very good reason."

"You see, anyone who signs up for the Potter films has to agree to be in the sequels, all of them! I didn't know if that's how I wanted to spend the last years of my life, and so I said no."

He chuckles as he recalls the flurry surrounding his reluctance. "Newspapers, radio, television all had a go at me. The world wanted into this film and this cantankerous fucker called Richard Harris said no.

"But then my granddaughter Ella, who is eleven and whom I worship with my life, came to me one day and said, 'Papa, I hear you're not going to be in the Harry Potter movie.' I told her that was indeed the case, and then she looked me right in the eye and said, 'If you don't play Dumbledore, then I will never speak with you again.'"

Harris holds out his hands to show how helpless he felt. "What could I do? I didn't dare have that hanging over my head, and so I said yes.

"It actually turned out to be a pleasant experience. I worked two days one week, then two weeks off, then a few more days' work. Maybe three weeks in all spread out over months. Very nice at my age — that's the way to do it."

He's also fond of his leading man, 12-year-old Daniel Radcliffe, who plays Potter. "Well, a bit before shooting started, Chris Columbus asked if I'd mind spending some time with the kids so they'd get used to me, and I said 'Sure.' So we all got together one evening, and I sat there showing them card tricks while they sat around discussing show business.

"Finally, Chris got us to read some of our scenes together, and when I finished, young Daniel said to me, 'That was quite a good reading. I think you'll be good in the part.' Lord, to have that much confidence at his age. I don't have that much confidence now."

Although he hadn't read the books before accepting the role, Harris has come to have great respect for author Rowling. "I'd like to crawl inside her mind and her bank account. Her command of language is extraordinary. My name, Albus Dumbledore, means 'a white Dorset bumblebee,' and that's certainly what I look like nowadays."

Harris, suddenly tired, looked at me. "There, I gave you the stuff about Harry Potter. That's what the papers want. But try to use the rest of what I said as well."

"Because, you see, I don't just want to be remembered for

being in those bloody films, and I'm afraid that's what going to happen to me."

As he stood up, we shook hands, and he held mine for a long time. "To tell you the truth, lad, I've done damn little that I'd like to be remembered for — except my sons."

My *Kingdom* has never been released in North America, except for a one-week "memorial" showing in Los Angeles in December 2002, after Harris's death.

It deserves a wider audience for many reasons, but most of all, to see this great actor looking unafraid at the shadow of mortality as it moved inexorably toward him.